Reasoning and Writing

Level D
Textbook

Siegfried Engelmann

Jerry Silbert

A Division of The McGraw-Hill Companies

Columbus, Ohio

Cover Credits

(t) Artville, (bl) PhotoDisc.

SRA/McGraw-Hill

2008 Imprint

Send all inquiries to:
SRA/McGraw-Hill
4400 Easton Commons
Columbus, OH 43219

Printed in the United States of America.

ISBN 0-02-684781-7

14 15 16 17 18 QWT 10 09

Lesson 1

Part A

Level D of ***Reasoning and Writing*** will teach you a lot about writing. It will help you think like a writer. That's tricky because writing is like speaking in some ways, but it's different in some ways.

- When you speak, you don't always have to use complete sentences. When you write, you should use complete sentences.
- When you speak, you don't always have to use words that are clear. When you write, you should use words that are clear.
- When you speak, you don't have to think about punctuating what you say. When you write, you have to punctuate sentences correctly.
- You have to be more careful when you write than when you speak. The reason is that when you speak, people can ask you questions. When you write, all the questions must be answered by what you write.
- You're going to learn how to write so the questions are answered.

Part B

Write a regular-order sentence for each picture.

Part C Write a paragraph that tells about what Mrs. Brown must have done in the missing picture.

Check 1: Is each sentence punctuated correctly?

Check 2: Does each sentence tell what Mrs. Brown did?

Check 3: Did you tell about the important things she must have done?

Part D Read each fact. Write the letter of each statement that is consistent with your impression.

Fact 1: Mary is better at arithmetic than any other student in the first grade.

a. Mary is 19 years old.

b. Mary knows all her multiplication and division facts.

c. Mary almost never makes mistakes on problems her teacher gives the class.

d. Mary cannot count to ten.

Fact 2: Rex is a dog that does tricks in a circus.

a. Rex comes when his master calls.

b. Rex has read more than 20 books on flowers.

c. Rex runs away when his master says "wait."

d. Rex can walk on a tightrope.

Part E

You're going to write descriptions of figures. When you write descriptions, you must use clear wording.

- This is the **left end** of the line: 
- This is the **left side** of the line: 
- This is the **middle** of the line: 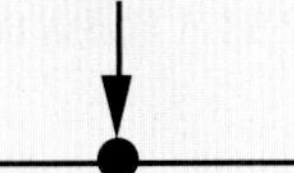
- This is the **right end** of the line: 
- This **B** is **on** the left end of the line: B
- This **B** is **just above** the left end of the line: B
- This **B** is **just below** the left end of the line: B
- This **B** is **an inch below** the left end of the line: B

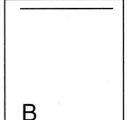

Write clear sentences to describe where each dot is.

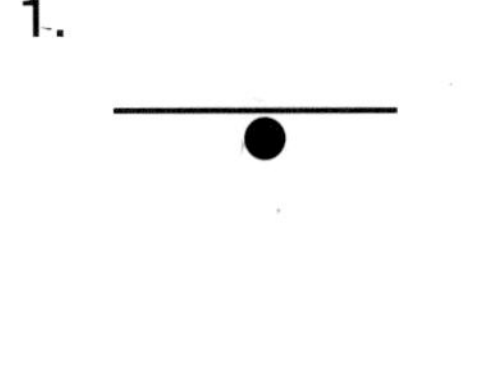

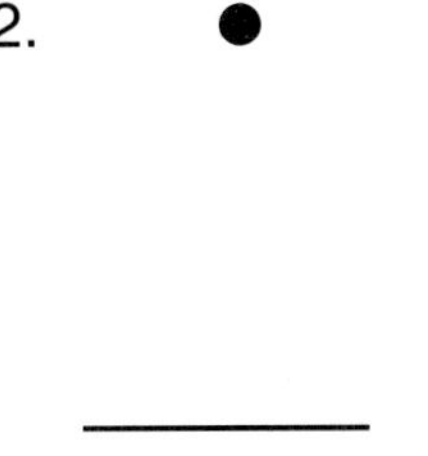

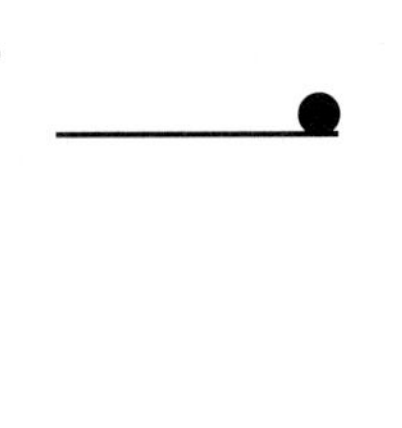

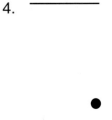

4.

Part F

- Sentences have two parts—the **subject** and the **predicate.**

  The **subject** names somebody or something.

  The **predicate** tells more about the subject. It tells what the subject did, was or had.

  In regular-order sentences, **the subject comes first.** You usually don't need any punctuation in these sentences, except the period at the end.

- Here's a sentence:

  The girl was tired.

  The sentence names **the girl.** So the subject is **the girl.**

- Here's a different sentence:

  The girl in the red bathing suit was tired.

  The sentence names **the girl in the red bathing suit.** So the subject is **the girl in the red bathing suit.**

- Remember, the part that names is the subject.

Write the subject of each sentence.

1. The man was standing next to a tree.
2. The man wearing a white shirt was standing next to the tree.
3. The man and his two sisters were standing next to the tree.
4. The top of the anthill was covered with sand.
5. The package in the truck was going to Nebraska.
6. The car with the best mileage was a Bumpo.

Lesson 2

Part A Write the subject of each sentence.

1. The woman wearing a yellow dress was in the elevator.
2. A girl and her mother went into the elevator.
3. We went into the barn.
4. Three cows and a horse were standing near the fence.
5. The girl in a red jacket stood on the bridge.
6. All the cars stopped on the bridge.
7. Everybody stopped what they were doing.
8. Nobody wanted to eat that pie.

Part B Write three regular-order sentences for the picture.

Part C Read the fact. Write the number of each statement that is consistent with your impression.

Fact: Mr. Davis has a large house and three new cars.

1. Mr. Davis has lots of nice furniture.
2. Mr. Davis doesn't have enough money for groceries.
3. Mr. Davis has only one pair of shoes.
4. Mr. Davis earns a lot of money.
5. Mr. Davis is very poor.

Part D Write clear sentences to describe where each square is.

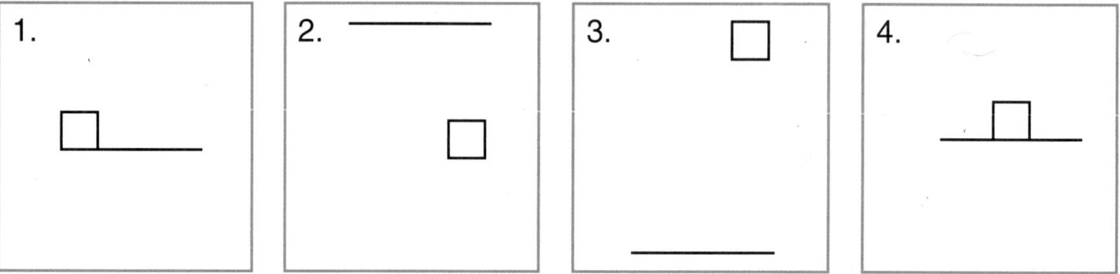

Part E Write a paragraph that tells about what Mr. Jones or Ann must have done in the missing picture.

Ann

Mr. Jones

Check 1: Is each sentence punctuated correctly?

Check 2: Does each sentence tell one thing a character did?

Check 3: Did you tell about the important things someone must have done?

Lesson 3

Part A Write the subject of each sentence.

1. They wanted to buy the bike.
2. The new cars cost a lot more than the older ones.
3. A man carrying a large bag came up the road.
4. The most widely used toothpaste is Gleamo.
5. The most popular actor was Blade Glade.
6. Almost everybody was hungry.

Part B Write two regular-order sentences for each picture.

1.

2.

Part C Read each fact. Write the number of each statement that is consistent with your impression.

Fact: Mrs. Castro spent a lot of time watering her grass during the summer.

1. Her grass turned brown and died.
2. She used up more water than some of her neighbors did.
3. Her grass grew fast during the summer.
4. Mrs. Castro didn't care about the appearance of her yard.
5. Her grass stayed green all summer.

Part D Write clear sentences to describe where each square is.

1. 2. 3. 4.

Part E Write a paragraph that tells about what a character must have done in the missing picture.

Check 1: Is each sentence punctuated correctly?

Check 2: Does each sentence tell one thing a character did?

Check 3: Did you tell about the important things someone must have done?

Lesson 4

Part A

1. Most of the girls on the beach were sunburned.
2. Lots of people wore sunglasses.
3. Three of the sailors were singing.
4. A few of the rabbits were sick.
5. Some people in our class came from New York.

Part B

For each sentence, write the regular-order sentence. Then circle the subject and underline the predicate.

1. For three hours, they stood on the porch.
2. When the sun went down, they were still on the porch.
3. Yesterday morning, four birds and six worms were in the yard.
4. After he finished his speech, people started talking.

Part C

Rewrite each sentence so it reads well.

1. The square is in the middle of the line just under the line.
2. The square is at the left end on the line.
3. The square is at the right end of the line just under the line.
4. The square is at the left end of the line an inch below the line.

Part D

You can figure out what impressions an advertisement gives by answering questions about things that are not told in the ad.

Here's an ad:

EZ Step shoes give the look and feel of leather.

Imagine, EZ Step even guarantees shoelaces for one year.

People with very small feet or very large feet will find an EZ Step shoe that fits them perfectly.

From that ad, you would get a lot of impressions about EZ Step shoes.

Questions

1. What material do you think EZ Step shoes are made of?
2. Do you think the top part of an EZ Step shoe is guaranteed for one year?
3. Do you think the heels of EZ Step shoes are guaranteed for one year?
4. Do you think a person with very narrow feet would find an EZ Step shoe that fits well?
5. Do you think a person with average size feet would find an EZ Step shoe that fits well?

Part E

Write a paragraph that tells about what a character must have done in the missing picture.

Check 1: Is each sentence punctuated correctly?

Check 2: Does each sentence tell one thing a character did?

Check 3: Did you tell about the important things someone must have done?

Part F

Facts about EZ Step Shoes

Material	Sizes available	Parts guaranteed
imitation leather	only extra small and extra large	only the shoelaces

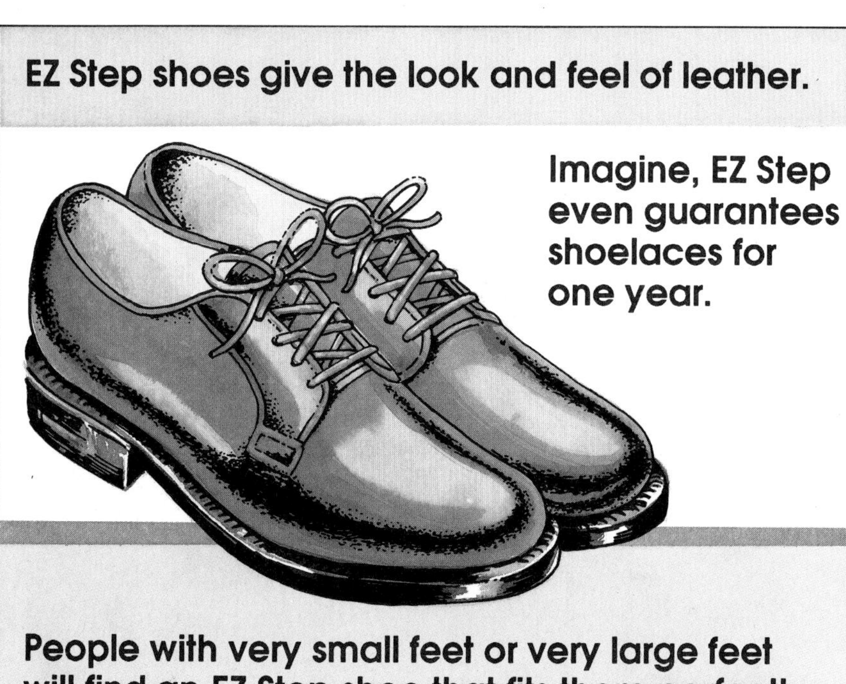

EZ Step shoes give the look and feel of leather.
Imagine, EZ Step even guarantees shoelaces for one year.
People with very small feet or very large feet will find an EZ Step shoe that fits them perfectly.

Lesson 5

Part A

1. The first article in the paper told about a plane crash.
2. The house next to the corner had a new roof.
3. They went swimming.
4. Most of the men on the train wore heavy jackets.
5. Some of them were smiling.

Part B

1. (They) were tired, but (they) kept working.
2. Mr. Jones was skinny, but he was very strong.
3. The house was new, but the garage was very old.
4. They ate and ate, but Mary was still hungry.

Part C

Speech

I'll tell you why James T. Bond would make a good mayor of Richland. James has had experience making decisions that involve a lot of money. James worked for the state for eight years. And talk about being honest! James is well known for the way he keeps his word.

Questions

1. Do you think James made good decisions involving money?
2. Do you think James had an important job working for the state?
3. Do you think James is honest?

Part D

Rewrite each sentence so it reads well.

1. The dot is on the line at the middle of the line.
2. The dot is on the end of the line at the left end.
3. The dot is at the right end of the line and just above it.

Part E

For each sentence, write the regular-order sentence. Then circle the subject and underline the predicate.

1. By the end of the game, she was tired.
2. Yesterday, nobody in our class was absent.
3. During the night, we could hear strange sounds.

Part F

Write a paragraph that tells about what happened in the missing picture.

Check 1: Is each sentence punctuated correctly?

Check 2: Does each sentence tell one thing a character did?

Check 3: Did you tell about the important things that must have happened?

Part G

Facts about James T. Bond

Decisions involving money.	In 1985, James decided to steal $100,000 from two banks.
How James worked for the state.	He made license plates at the state prison for 8 years.
Why James is well known for the way he keeps his word.	He is considered the most dishonest person in the city.

Speech

I'll tell you why James T. Bond would make a good mayor of Richland. James has had experience making decisions that involve a lot of money. James worked for the state for eight years. And talk about being honest! James is well known for the way he keeps his word.

Lesson 6

Part A

Some graphs show two different sets of numbers. One set is up and down. The other set is across the bottom.

Look at the graph below. The up-and-down numbers along the left side of the graph show **Years.**

The letter **D** is on the graph. To find the year for letter **D,** go to the left from **D** and read the year.

The letter **R** is on the graph. To find the year for letter **R,** go to the left from **R** and read the year.

The numbers across the bottom of the graph show the **Number of Ducks on Fern Lake.**

To find the number of ducks for letter **D,** go down from **D** and read the number.

To find the number of ducks for letter **R,** go down from **R** and read the number.

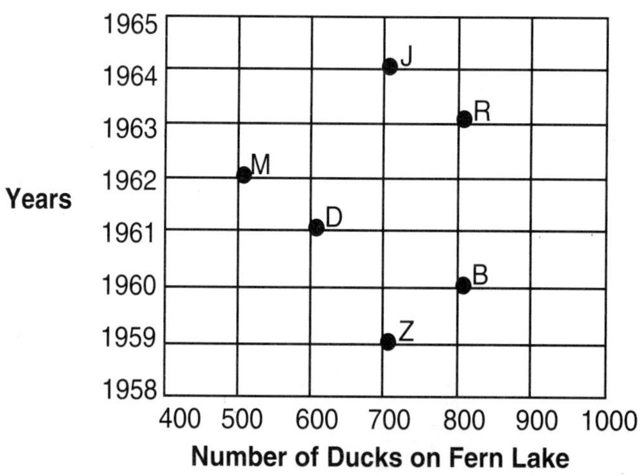

1. Write the year for **J**. Write the number of ducks for **J**.
2. Write the year for **B**. Write the number of ducks for **B**.
3. Write the year for **M**. Write the number of ducks for **M**.
4. Write the year for **Z**. Write the number of ducks for **Z**.

Part B For each sentence, write the regular-order sentence. Then circle the subject and underline the predicate.

1. After Mona sat down, the play started.
2. While the sun came up, more than a dozen birds landed.
3. Yesterday evening, Edna and her children went jogging.
4. In the future, she will be very careful.

Part C Write the number of the figures that are consistent with the directions.

One inch line: ______

Directions: Make a horizontal line that is about one inch long.
Make a triangle above the right end of the line.
Make a **C** below the left end of the line.

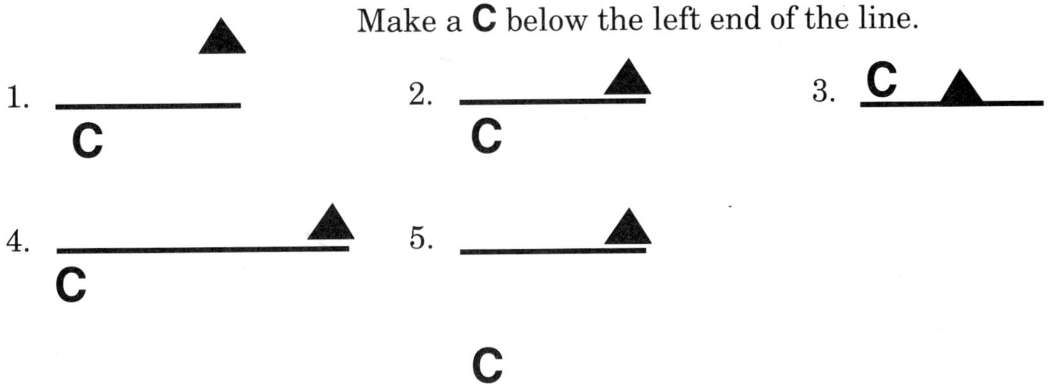

1. ▲ ______ C
2. ______▲ C
3. C ▲______
4. ______▲ C
5. ______▲ C

Part D Some statements are not clear because they have more than one meaning.

- Here's an item: **The hat had a feather. It was large.**

  The word **it** is not clear. The second sentence could mean that **the hat** was large or that **the feather** was large.

- Here's an item: **The children caught flies. They were nasty little things.**

  The second sentence is not clear. **They** could mean the **flies** were nasty little things. **They** could also mean the **children** were nasty little things.

Part E

1. The chickens laid eggs. <u>They</u> were brown.
2. Mary put her gum next to her radio. <u>It</u> was gone the next day.
3. Irma made two mistakes on math problems. <u>They</u> were terrible.
4. They discussed a plan for the library. <u>It</u> was new.
5. Bill claimed that Greg was injured. <u>He</u> made a mistake.

Part F

Sentences can be hooked together or combined. The most common words that are used for combining sentences are **but, or,** or **and.**

- Here are two sentences:

  She worked very hard. She didn't have any money.

  Each sentence has a subject and a predicate.

  Here are the same two sentences combined with the word **but:**

  She worked very hard, but she didn't have any money.

  There's a comma at the end of the first sentence—just before the word **but.**

- Here are two new sentences:

  The boys painted the fence. They raked the front yard.

  Here are the same two sentences combined with the word **and:**

  The boys painted the fence, and they raked the front yard.

  There's a comma at the end of the first sentence.

1. She was tired, and her hands were sore.
2. That car is old, but it is in very good shape.
3. They will go on a boat, or they will take a train.

Part G Write a paragraph that tells about what the character must have done in the missing picture.

Check 1: Is each sentence punctuated correctly?

Check 2: Does each sentence tell one thing a character did?

Check 3: Did you tell about the important things someone must have done?

Lesson 7

Part A Write the subject of each sentence.

1. Six of the men had never worked here before.
2. She didn't like any of his arguments.
3. Nobody in our class reads that paper.
4. The last article on the page was very funny.

Part B

1. He put his backpack near the flower. It smelled terrible.
2. An advertisement was in the newspaper. It was full of lies.
3. Her car has a new battery. It will last for years.

Part C

- Some sentences are unusual because they do not have a subject. All they have is a predicate. These sentences tell somebody what to do. You use this type of sentence when you write directions.
- Here are some of those sentences:

  Stop bothering me.
  Make a line under the T.
  Pick up your tray.
  Don't erase your mistakes.

- All these sentences start with a capital letter and end with a period.

make a vertical line
Write 7 on top of the line
write the letter R just below the line

Part D

Directions

Make a square about one inch high.

Write the letter **M** [in the center of the square].

Write the letter **A** [under the letter M].

Part E

Write the correct sentence for each item.

1. Sam is not as strong as Bill.
2. Sam is not as tall as Bill.
3. Sam does not sleep as long as Bill sleeps.
4. Sam does not run as far as Bill runs.

Part F

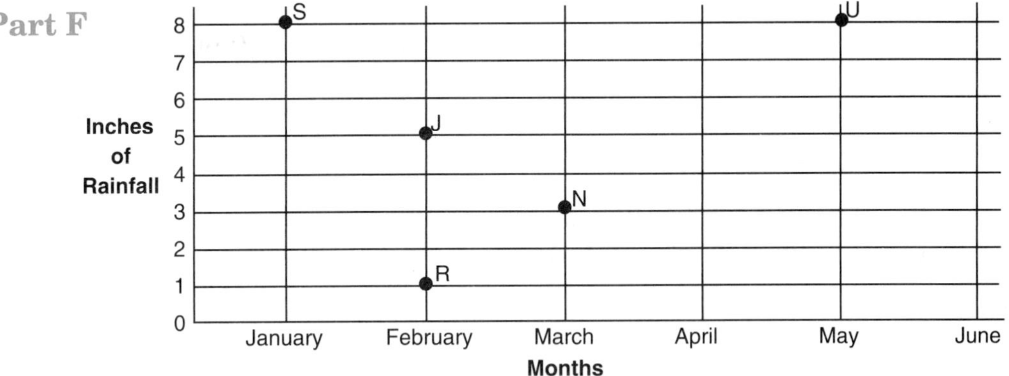

1. How many inches of rainfall does **J** show? What month does **J** show?
2. How many inches of rainfall does **R** show? What month does **R** show?
3. How many inches of rainfall does **S** show? What month does **S** show?
4. How many inches of rainfall does **U** show? What month does **U** show?

Part G

Fact: James is the friendliest person in our class.

1. James doesn't smile very much.
2. James almost never talks.
3. A lot of people like James.
4. James likes to be with people.
5. James has many fights.

Lesson 8

Part A

1. Alice played checkers with Sarah. She won five games.
2. The cow walked into the truck. It weighed over one ton.

Part B

Fact: The day was very hot.

1. My brother wore his winter coat.
2. Everybody went swimming.
3. We could see snow near the road.
4. We stayed at the beach all day.
5. Nobody wore shorts.

Part C

- You can rewrite most sentences that have a part that tells when.

  You start the sentence with the part that tells when.

  You make a comma after the part that tells when.

  You write the subject after the comma.

  Then you write the rest of the predicate.

- Here's a sentence:

  (She) ran inside after the bell rang.

  The subject is **she.** The predicate is **ran inside after the bell rang.** The part that tells when is **after the bell rang.**

- Here's the sentence rewritten:

  After the bell rang, (she) ran inside.

  That sentence uses all the words that are in the regular-order sentence.

Part D Rewrite each sentence so it begins with the part that tells when.

1. They slept soundly during the storm.
2. Nobody listened to him after he told those lies.
3. My sister woke up when the car stopped.
4. They ordered new machines last month.

Part E Write the correct sentence for each item.

1. Fran does not run as fast as Jill runs.
2. Fran does not drink as much water as Jill drinks.
3. Fran does not earn as much money as Jill earns.
4. Fran is shorter than Jill.

Part F

Here's a figure we want somebody to make:

________________A

Here are the directions:

Make a horizontal line about two inches long.
Write the letter A on the line.

The first sentence in the directions is clear. The rest of the directions are not clear because somebody could follow the directions and make a figure that **doesn't look** like the figure we want the person to make.

Here are two figures that are made by following the directions:

________A________ A________________

Lesson 9

Part A

1. Four teachers watched the children. They had a good time.
2. A red light was on top of the bus. Mrs. Smith couldn't fix it.

Part B

Write two combined sentences about Alice. Combine one sentence with the word **and.** Combine one sentence with the word **but.**

Fact: Alice loved animals.

1. She spent hours at the zoo.
2. She didn't want to own a dog.
3. She was afraid of cats.
4. She wanted to be an animal doctor.

Part C

Here's the figure we want somebody to make:

A
B

Here are the directions:

Make a horizontal line about one inch long.
Write the letter A just over the line.
Write the letter B under the line.

Here's how to test whether those directions are clear: Follow the directions and see if you can make a figure that does **not** look like the figure.

Part D

1. Nobody made a sound during his speech.
2. Most of the people will leave before the meeting ends.
3. They ate popcorn last night.

Part E Write the accurate sentence for each false statement.

1. The cat ate less than the dog ate.	cat	✔ dog
2. The truck used less fuel than the tractor used.	✔ truck	tractor
3. Creamo paint lasts longer than Smootho paint.	Creamo	✔ Smootho
4. G computer has fewer parts than D computer.	G computer	✔ D computer
5. April has fewer cloudy days than May.	✔ April	May
6. G computer weighs less than D computer.	G computer	✔ D computer
7. Sparko batteries last longer than Dino batteries.	Sparko	✔ Dino
8. Jean is younger than Sam.	Jean	✔ Sam
9. Sam weighs more than Jean.	✔ Sam	Jean

Part F Rewrite the underlined sentences so they are clear.

<u>They arrived there by lunch time.</u> They rested and then walked around. Tom said, "This is a beautiful campground." Kelly agreed.

<u>Finally, Tom and Kelly went to it.</u> They went inside and made a fire in the fireplace.

Kelly said, "There's dust in our cabin."

Tom said, "That's true, but I don't feel like sweeping up."

Kelly said, "Me neither."

Lesson 10

Rewrite the underlined sentences so they are clear.

They found it near the stream. Bill heard it first. "What's that sound?" he asked.

Fran said, "That sounds like a baby bird."

Fran and Bill followed the sound and found a baby bird a few feet from the stream. Then they heard the mother bird scolding them and telling them not to bother her baby.

She spotted it in a tree. "There's where that bird came from," Fran said. She pointed to a nest that was about ten feet above the ground.

Bill asked, "Should we try to put that baby bird back in the nest?"

"I think we should," Fran said. "That bird will get in trouble on the ground."

Fran climbed the tree. Bill stayed below. She kept screeching at her all the time. At last, Fran reached the nest. She said, "That mother bird is really mad at us."

Fran took off her sweater, held one sleeve and lowered the sweater until Bill could grab the other sleeve. Then Bill took it off and put the bird in it. Then he tied his shoe to the sweater.

Slowly, Fran pulled up the sweater. The baby bird kept swinging back and forth in Bill's shoe. The mother bird kept screeching.

Finally, Fran was able to grab Bill's shoe. She took the baby bird from the shoe and put it in the nest. Then she climbed back down the tree.

The mother bird was still screeching. Fran looked at her and said, "You're welcome."

Test 1

Part A Write the subject of each sentence.

1. Everybody in our family loves to swim.
2. Three of the fish were blue.
3. Nobody went home early.
4. The first boy in line was named James.

Part B For each item, write two sentences to show the two possible meanings of the second sentence.

1. The house was near a hill. It was covered with trees and bushes.
2. My uncle picked up baby Robert. He was crying and kicking.

Part C Write two combined sentences about Bill. Combine one sentence with the word **and.** Combine one sentence with the word **but.**

Fact: Bill knew all the multiplication facts.

1. He did poorly on the math test.
2. He knew all the division facts.
3. He could do any kind of multiplication problem.
4. He didn't know any subtraction facts.

Part D For each item, write a sentence that tells about the dot. Each sentence will begin with the words: **The dot is.**

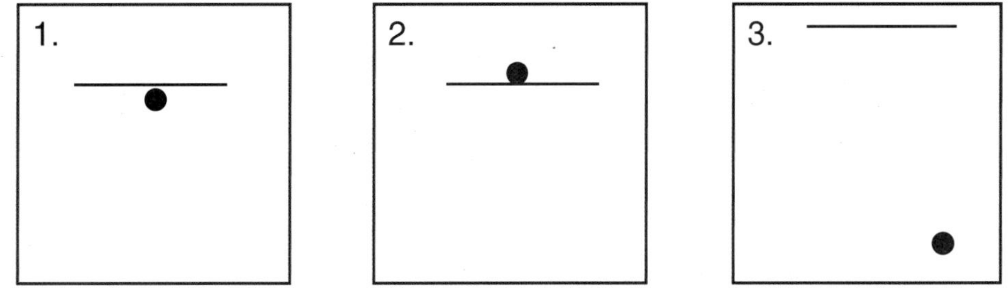

Lesson 11

Part A Rewrite all the regular-order sentences.

1. They finished their lunch before Fran joined them.
2. When the rain ended, we went outside.
3. The company purchased nine items during the last month.
4. That salesperson argued with her for three hours.
5. At the end of the day, everybody in our class cheered.
6. When I talked to her, she said some silly things.

Part B This is one inch: ______

Directions	Figure
Make a horizontal line three inches long. Write the letter **B** on the line. Draw a small square over the line.	□ ______B______

Part C Write sentences that tell what each person said.

1.
The water is cold.
Donna
2.
I am tired. I am going home.
Billy
3.
This word is hard.
Jane
4.
Is she going to quit?
Fran

Part D
Write the accurate sentence for each false statement.

1. The Ritz Hotel is not as far from the beach as the Polo Hotel.	✔ Ritz	Polo
2. Ticko watches have fewer moving parts than X-Brand watches.	Ticko	✔ X-Brand
3. H-Mart stores are open longer hours than T-Mart stores.	H-Mart	✔ T-Mart
4. Creamo paint covers as much bare wood as Splatto paint covers.	✔ Creamo	✔ Splatto
5. T-Mart televisions have a smaller screen than H-Mart televisions.	T-Mart	✔ H-Mart
6. Zermos cost less than Bumpos.	✔ Zermos	Bumpos
7. B-Brand batteries do not last as long as Sparko batteries.	B-Brand	✔ Sparko

Part E
Rewrite the underlined sentences so they are clear.

<u>She went inside it.</u> She sniffed around and wandered down the long tunnels. After wandering around for almost an hour, she was lost inside that giant cave.

Bill went searching for her. Bill called from the mouth of the cave, "Here, Spot! Come here, Spot."

Spot ran toward the voice. <u>On her way, she found it.</u> She picked it up and carried it in her mouth. When she came out of the cave, she wagged her tail and dropped the wallet in front of Bill.

Bill said, "That looks like an old wallet." It was. Bill picked it up and looked inside. It had more than 100 dollars in it.

Part A For each sentence, write the part that tells when.

1. We went to the mountains last year.
2. Before class began, Ginger left the room.
3. Rabbits went through our garden all morning long.
4. During the night, a tree branch broke off.
5. When the sun was going down, Uncle Al drove up.

Part B Write sentences that tell what each person said.

1.

Who is that?

Dan

2.

I'm hungry.
Let's eat.

Alice

Part C Write the correct sentence for each item. Start with the name that has the bigger number.

Sentence	Fact
1. Fran is not as tall as Bill.	How tall each person is: Fran – 60 inches Bill – 58 inches
2. Dimmo batteries do not last as long as Sparko batteries last.	How long each battery lasts: Sparko – 3 months Dimmo – 4 months
3. A Bumpo car costs less than a Dort car.	How much each car costs: Bumpo – $39,000 Dort – $35,000
4. Jason is older than Tom.	How old each person is: Jason – 9 years Tom – 12 years

Part D Rewrite all the regular-order sentences.

1. Our teacher graded papers for hours.
2. One month ago, she got sick.
3. The lawyer made a mistake yesterday.
4. After the workers left, the desks were covered with dust.
5. When I tried to find their house, I got lost.
6. We had a fire alarm during lunch period.

Part E

Write clear sentences for each item.

1. It is on the corner.
2. It has two of them.
3. It is the biggest one.

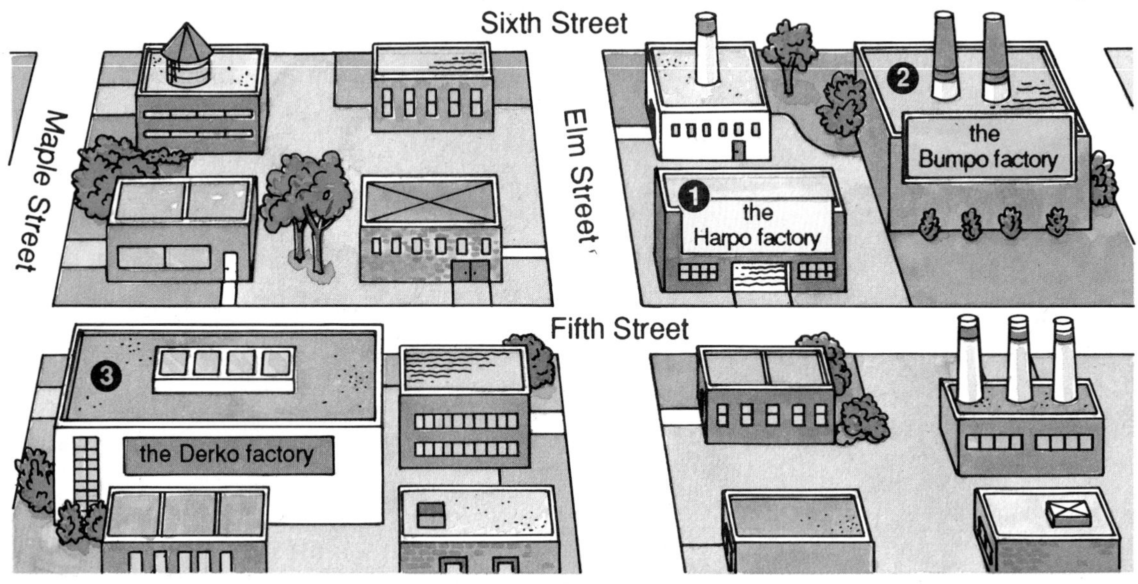

Part F

Write a paragraph that tells about what the characters must have done in the missing picture.

Check 1: Is each sentence punctuated correctly?

Check 2: Does each sentence tell one thing the characters did?

Check 3: Did you tell all the important things they must have done?

Lesson 13

Part A Rewrite each sentence so it begins with the part that tells when.

1. Dr. James worked on three cavities during my last visit.
2. Her brother waited for twenty minutes.
3. The argument sounded better after Sally told the facts.

Part B

You're going to work with statements that are too general. Statements are too general if they don't give you a clear picture.

- Here's a horizontal line: __________
- Here's a statement:

A letter is on the middle of a horizontal line.

The underlined part of the sentence is too general. We don't know what letter is on the middle of the line.

- Here's another statement that is too general:

A capital letter is on the middle of a horizontal line.

We still don't know what letter it is.

- Here's a specific sentence:

A capital F is on the middle of a horizontal line.

Now we have enough information to get a clear picture:

_____F_____

Part C

For each statement, write **specific** or **general.**

Statements	Figure
1. A dot is on the line.	
2. A letter is on the line.	
3. A dot is on the end of the line.	B
4. A 7 is just below the left end of the line.	7
5. The **B** is on the end of the horizontal line.	
6. The dot is on the left end of the horizontal line.	

Part D

Write the correct sentence for each item. Start with the name that has the bigger number.

1. How hot the days were:
   Monday – 96 degrees
   Tuesday – 98 degrees

2. How heavy the ships were:
   Red ship – 146 tons
   White ship – 100 tons

3. How fast they went:
   The wagon – 13 miles per hour
   The bike – 17 miles per hour

4. How far they went:
   The plane – 90 miles
   The train – 20 miles

Part E

Write two combined sentences about the skunk. One sentence will have the word **and.** One sentence will have the word **but.**

Fact: The skunk made a terrible stink.

1. The dog wanted to play with the skunk.
2. The children held their nose.
3. Sam just stood there and smiled.
4. We ran away.

Part F

Directions	Figure
Make a horizontal line about two inches long. Draw a small square under the line. Write the letter **R** on the line.	R ________ ☐

Part G

Write two paragraphs. The first paragraph should tell the important things that must have happened in the missing picture. The second paragraph will tell what happened in the last picture.

Check 1: Is each sentence punctuated correctly?

Check 2: Does each sentence tell one thing a character did?

Check 3: Did you tell about all the important things someone must have done?

Lesson 14

Part A

- Punctuation sometimes shows where a word is missing.
- Here is a sentence that needs no punctuation:

They had cats and dogs and goats.

- If one of the **and**s is removed, a comma must be put in its place:

They had cats, dogs and goats.

1. Mary and Tom and Linda went with us.
2. They rode their bikes and played tag and ate dinner.

Part B

This is an ad for Creamo paint.

- Creamo paint lasts longer.
- One coat of Creamo covers completely.
- Creamo will not fade for years and years.
- Creamo never chips or flakes.
- No other brand costs less than CREAMO.

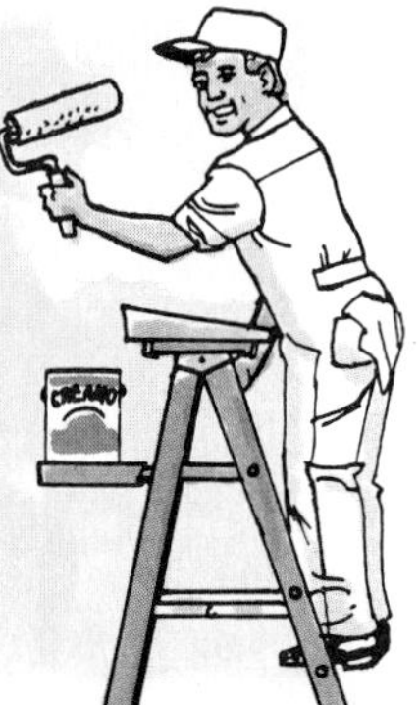

If we want to write about what the ad says, we can do it two different ways. We can write the **exact words** and use quote marks:

The ad claims, "Creamo never chips or flakes."

Or we can use the word **that:**

The ad claims *that* Creamo never chips or flakes.

For a lot of work you'll do, you'll write about claims that people and ads make. You'll write sentences with the word **that.** Those sentences don't have quote marks. Remember, start with the words: **The ad claims that . . .** Then tell the claim.

Part C

- These are vertical lines.

- This is the top end of the vertical line.

- This is the bottom end of the vertical line.

- This square is just to the left of the vertical line.

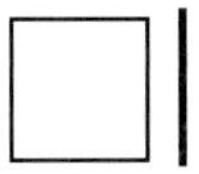

- This square is on top of the vertical line.

- This square is not on top of the vertical line. It is above the vertical line.

1. 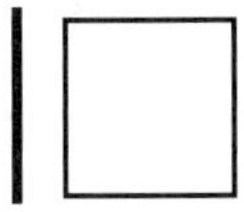

2. 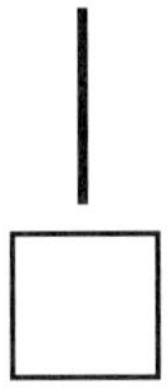

3. 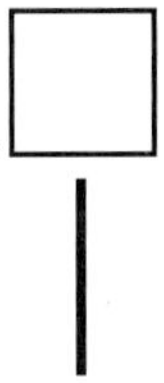

Part D

Statements	Figure
1. The letter **B** is just below the left end of the horizontal line. 2. The letter **J** is just above the left end of the horizontal line. 3. A number is on the right end of the horizontal line. 4. The letter **J** is just above the right end of the horizontal line. 5. A number is on the middle of the horizontal line. 6. The **3** is on the horizontal line.	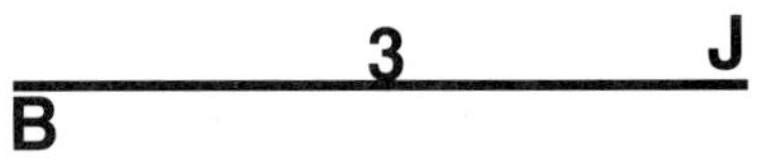

Part E

Write sentences that compare. Start with the name that has the bigger number.

1. How much each item costs:
   Jumpo skateboard – $40
   TR skateboard – $30
2. How far each person jumps:
   Fran – 2 yards
   Obo – 3 yards
3. How fast each vehicle goes:
   Car – 64 miles per hour
   Truck – 65 miles per hour

Part F

You'll be doing a lot of work with **deductions.** A deduction presents two pieces of **evidence.** From the pieces of evidence, you can draw a **conclusion.**

Here's a deduction that draws a conclusion about what you should do:

You should do everything you can to be attractive.
Wearing Ginko shoes makes you attractive.
So you should wear Ginko shoes.

There really aren't any Ginko shoes. But if you believed the first two sentences, you would have to believe the conclusion.

The first two sentences are the **evidence:**

You should do everything you can to be attractive.
Wearing Ginko shoes makes you attractive.

The last sentence is the **conclusion:**

So you should wear Ginko shoes.

Here's the evidence for a different deduction:

People who want to get ahead should wear a Flambo hat.
You're a person who wants to get ahead.
So ________________________ .

Part G Write the conclusion for each deduction, starting with the word **So.**

Deduction 1: You shouldn't wear colors that clash.
Green and red are colors that clash.
So ______________________.

Deduction 2: You should obey all traffic signs.
Stop signs are traffic signs.
So ______________________.

Deduction 3: You shouldn't be cruel to animals.
Ants are animals.
So ______________________.

Part H Rewrite the underlined sentences so they are clear.

He finally decided to get it fixed. He took it there. Bill asked the mechanic, "How much will it cost to get it fixed?"

The mechanic at Al's Garage looked at it for a long time. Finally, the mechanic said, "I'll have to charge over $500 to fix up this old car. I'm not sure it's worth fixing."

Bill loved his old car, but getting it fixed would cost too much money. Bill drove his old car away from Al's Garage.

Part A

The new Bumpos are more comfortable than ever.

More people than ever are switching to Bumpo.

Bumpo performs better than other cars of its kind.

The ad claims that ______________________________ .

Part B

Write **general** or **specific** for each set of directions.

Directions	Figure
1. Make a vertical line about one inch long. Write a **B** on top of the line. Write a **J** just below the bottom of the line.	B J
2. Make a vertical line about one inch long. Write a **B** above the line. Write a **J** to the left of the line.	B J
3. Make a horizontal line that is about two inches long. Make a **B** to the left of the line and a **D** above the **B.**	D B

Part C Follow the X-box rules and write a sentence that tells the problem with each direction.

Direction __ states that you should ____________ ____________________________,	but you should ________ __________________________ __________________________.

Direction	Figure
1. Make a horizontal line two inches long.	
2. Make a line two inches long.	
3. Make a vertical line.	

Part D Write the conclusion for each deduction.

Deduction 1: Children shouldn't play near dangerous places.
Rivers are dangerous places.
So ____________________.

Deduction 2: People shouldn't buy products that are overpriced.
Dinko hot dogs are overpriced.
So ____________________.

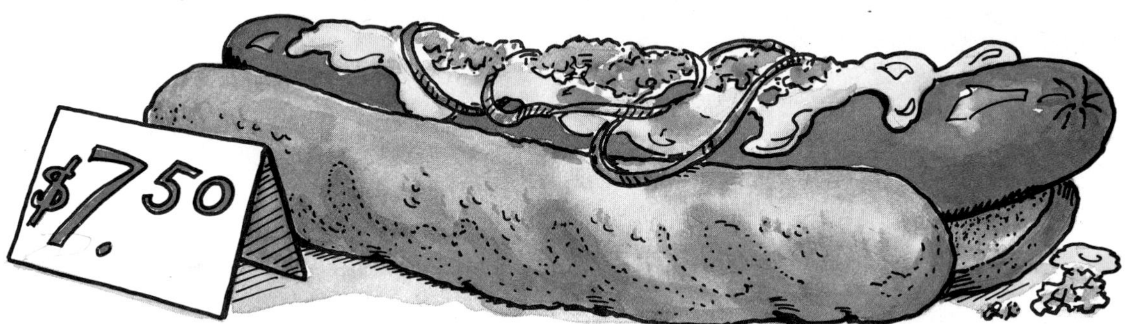

Part E

You've learned that some names are capitalized. If a name tells about one thing, it is capitalized.

Your name tells about one person. All the parts of your name begin with a capital.

The names of states, cities and countries tell about one thing. They are capitalized. All parts of the name **River City, Idaho,** are capitalized. All parts of the name **Los Angeles, California,** are capitalized.

The names of companies and products are also capitalized. They are treated just like the names of people. Both parts of the name **Bumpo Special** are capitalized. Both parts of the name **Creamo Supreme** are capitalized. All parts of the name **Zee Boo Toy Company** are capitalized.

Remember, if the name tells about one product or one business, the name is treated like any other name. It is capitalized.

1. They went to the zoo.
2. They went to the ballard zoo.
3. My mother shopped at the corner store.
4. We prefer shopping at h-mart.
5. The painters used five gallons of blue paint.
6. We called ace plumbing company.
7. They own a new van.

Part F

For each item, write the two possible meanings of the second sentence.

1. The movie was about a city. It was old and boring.
2. Three cats chased butterflies. They were very playful.

Lesson 16

Part A

- You cannot capitalize accurately unless you know the complete name of the place or thing.
- Here's a sentence:

They painted their house with **Creamo** paint.

The name **Creamo** is capitalized. The word **paint** is probably not part of the name. The word **paint** is not capitalized. A lot of companies make paint.

Not Correct	*Correct*
They bought a bumpo car.	They bought a Bumpo car.
Two tillman factories are near my house.	Two Tillman factories are near my house.
Products are sold at r-mart stores.	Products are sold at R-Mart stores.

1. They are building 13 brand-new stores.
2. The sales of new zermo cars and trucks are very good.
3. Those cars have miller engines.
4. The workers had a lot of heavy equipment.
5. That island was just off the coast.

Part B

Write the conclusion for each deduction.

Deduction 1: Children shouldn't do things that are unhealthy.
Staying up late is unhealthy.
So ______.

Deduction 2: You should try to do well in all school subjects.
Math is a school subject.
So ______.

Deduction 3: You shouldn't eat food that contains a lot of fat.
Crumpo candy contains a lot of fat.
So ______.

Part C

For each item, write the word that goes in the blank.

speed	distance	direction	age	height	weight	length

1. Tim went north. Tina went north. So Tim and Tina went in the same ____.
2. Tim went five miles. Tina went five miles. So Tim and Tina went the same ____.
3. Tim went ten miles an hour. Tina went ten miles an hour. So Tim and Tina went the same ____.
4. Tim is five feet tall. Tina is five feet tall. So Tim and Tina are the same ____.
5. Tim is twelve years old. Tina is twelve years old. So Tim and Tina are the same ____.

Part D

Write **general** if the directions tell about more than one figure.
Write **specific** if the directions tell about only one figure.

M———P   P———M   M | P

1. Make a line that is an inch long.
   Write the letter **M** at one end of the line and make the letter **P** at the other end of the line.
2. Make a horizontal line that is an inch long.
   Write the letter **M** next to the right end of the line and the letter **P** next to the other end of the line.
3. Make a vertical line that is an inch long.
   Write the letter **M** just over the line.
   Write the letter **P** just under the line.
4. Make a line that is an inch long.
   Write a letter at the left end of the line.
   Write a different letter at the other end of the line.

Part E Follow the X-box rules and write a sentence that tells the problem with each direction.

Direction __ states that you should ______________ ,	but you should ______________ .

	Direction	Figure
1 inch	1. Make a vertical line.	
	2. Make a vertical line one inch long.	
	3. Make a **C** two inches high.	C

Part F Make each figure on your lined paper.

1. Make a capital **L** that has both lines about one inch long.
2. Make a capital **L** that has a vertical line one inch long and a horizontal line two inches long.
3. Make a backward **L** that has a horizontal line one inch long and a vertical line two inches long.
4. Make a backward **L** that has a horizontal line one-half inch long and a vertical line one inch long.
5. Make a capital **L** that has a horizontal line two inches long and a vertical line one-half inch long.

Part G Rewrite each sentence so it begins with the part that tells when.

1. Our car broke down after we left town.
2. I met them when I was in California.
3. That cat has been making noise for three hours.

Part A

1. They paid rent to the bank.
2. They wanted to go to the country.
3. They sold six bumpo cars.
4. They went to colorado.
5. They bought four fletcher tires.

Part B

Step __ doesn't tell that ______________________________.

Directions	Figure
A. 1. Make a horizontal line. 2. Make a **4** on the middle of the line.	____4____
B. 1. Make a line one inch long. 2. Make a **7** just to the left of the line.	7______
C. 1. Make a horizontal line two inches long. 2. Make the letter **M** on the end of the line.	__________M

Part C

Write the conclusion for each deduction.

Deduction 1: Birds have feathers.
Hawks are birds.
Therefore, ______________________.

Deduction 2: Mammals do not have feathers.
Bears are mammals.
Therefore, ______________________.

Deduction 3: You should eat all foods that are low in fat.
Yogurt is low in fat.
Therefore, ______________________.

Part D

Follow the X-box rules and write a sentence that tells the problem with each direction.

Direction __ states that you should ________________ ,	X	but you should ________________ .

1 inch

Direction	Figure
1. Make a **T** that is two inches high.	
2. Make a **T** that is one inch high.	

Part E

Make each figure on your lined paper.

This is 1 inch: ————

1. Make a capital **T** that has a horizontal line about two inches long and a vertical line that is about one inch long.
2. Make a capital **L** that has a horizontal line about half an inch long and a vertical line about one inch long.
3. Make an upside-down **T** with a horizontal line that is about one inch long and a vertical line that is about one inch long.
4. Make a capital **T** that has both lines about two inches long. Make a small dot on the right end of the horizontal line.
5. Make a backward **L** that has both lines about two inches long. Make a small dot on the bottom end of the vertical line.

Part F

Write the word or words that complete each item.

direction	age	distance	number	weight	speed	height

1. Don is 12 years old.
   Dan is 12 years old.
   So Don and Dan are the same ____.

2. Bumpo cars hold six people.
   Zermo cars hold six people.
   So Bumpo cars and Zermo cars hold the same ____.

3. Bill sold six tickets.
   Ann sold six tickets.
   So Bill and Ann sold the same ____.

4. April had nine rainy days.
   May had nine rainy days.
   So April and May had the same ____.

5. Rita weighs 105 pounds.
   Her mother weighs 105 pounds.
   So Rita and her mother are the same ____.

Part G

Rewrite each sentence so it begins with the part that tells when.

1. She was sick yesterday.
2. We left before the game ended.
3. My sister laughed when I slipped on the rug.

Lesson 18

Part A For each item, follow the directions and draw the figure.

1
inch
long

1. • Make a backward **L** that has a vertical line about one inch long and a horizontal line about two inches long.
   • Make a dot in the middle of each line.
   • Draw a slanted line that goes straight from one dot to the other dot.

2. • Make a capital **L** with a vertical line about two inches long and a horizontal line about one inch long.
   • Make a dot in the middle of the horizontal line.
   • Make another dot on the top end of the vertical line.
   • Draw a slanted line that goes straight from one dot to the other dot.

3. • Make a capital **L** that has a vertical line about one inch long and a horizontal line about two inches long.
   • Make a dot in the middle of the vertical line.
   • Make another dot about one inch below the middle of the horizontal line.
   • Draw a slanted line that goes straight from one dot to the other dot.

Part B

1. She was very smart. She didn't do well in school.
2. She loved animals. She was always bringing home stray cats.
3. The sun came out. The ice did not melt.

Part C

speed	color	distance	direction	age	height	number

1. The oak tree was 30 feet tall.
   The maple tree was 30 feet tall.
   The oak tree and the maple tree were the same ____.

2. The worm went 3 feet per minute.
   The snail went 3 feet per minute.
   The worm and the snail went the same ____.

3. The leaf was green
   The grass was green.
   The leaf and the grass were the same ____.

4. The wind blew from the north.
   The clouds blew from the north.
   The wind and the clouds blew from the same ____.

5. The turtle had four legs.
   The alligator had four legs.
   The turtle and the alligator had the same ____.

Part D

Step __ doesn't tell that ______________________________.

Directions	Figure
A. 1. Make a horizontal line that is about two inches long. 2. Write the letter on the middle of the line.	
B. 1. Make a horizontal line one inch long. 2. Make a □ just under the left end of the line. 3. Make the letter **T** just over the line.	

Part E

Directions	Figure
• Make an **L** so both lines are about one inch long. • Make a **T** just under the horizontal line.	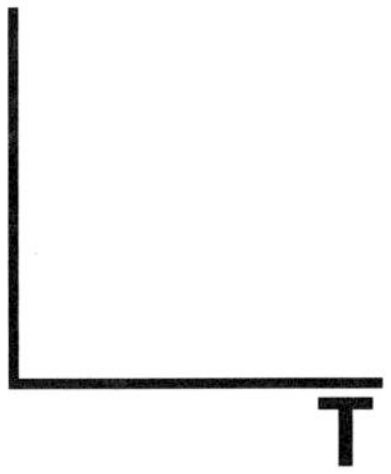

Part F

Write a paragraph that tells about what the characters must have done in the missing picture.

Check 1: Is each sentence punctuated correctly?

Check 2: Does each sentence tell one thing the characters did?

Check 3: Did you tell all the important things the characters must have done?

Part G

Rewrite each sentence so it begins with the part that tells when.

1. I had a wonderful dream last night.
2. Fran kept talking during the movie.
3. We have to clean our room before we can go out.

Lesson 19

Part A

When you write, you must make sure that the words in the predicate agree with the words in the subject. If the subject tells about more than one, the predicate must tell about more than one.

John is fast.

John and Alice are fast.

In the first sentence, there is one person in the subject. The underlined word in the predicate tells about one.

The subject of the second sentence names more than one. The underlined word in the predicate tells about more than one.

1. Last year's Bumpo cars were expensive.
2. Creamo paint are on sale.
3. Mary's house is next to the corner.
4. Their car were not running.
5. Her eyes was beautiful.
6. Z-Mart stores stay open until 10 p.m.

Part B

1.

Sentence	Facts
Sales increased.	They increased by 600.
	They were sales of Bumpo cars.

[Which] **sales increased** [how much] .

2.

Sentence	Facts
They built it.	They were three women.
	They built a huge kite.

[Who] **built** [what] .

3.

Sentence	Facts
Sales increased.	They were sales of Creamo paint.
	They increased in 1992.

[Which] **sales increased** [when] .

Part C

Write the word or words that complete each item.

1. The turtle was 76 years old.
   The man was 76 years old.
   The turtle and the man were the same ____.

2. The car went 60 miles per hour.
   The truck went 60 miles per hour.
   The car and truck went the same ____.

3. Juan read 12 books.
   Kevin read 12 books.
   Juan and Kevin read the same ____.

4. The train arrived at 2 p.m.
   The bus arrived at 2 p.m.
   The bus and train arrived at the same ____.

Part D

Rules:

1. Write one paragraph for each picture.
2. For the first picture, tell who had the problem and what the problem was.
3. For the missing picture, write a paragraph that tells all the things that Lisa must have done to solve her problem.
4. For the last picture, tell how the story ended. Tell what the last picture shows. Write a sentence that tells the exact words Lisa said.

Lesson 20

Part A Write the conclusion for each deduction.

Deduction 1: People shouldn't do things that shorten their life.
Smoking cigarettes shortens their life.
Therefore, ______________________.

Deduction 2: Every bone needs calcium.
The skull is a bone.
Therefore, ______________________.

Deduction 3: You should do all the things that prevent cavities.
Brushing your teeth with a Flexi toothbrush prevents cavities.
Therefore, ______________________.

Part B Write the combined sentence for each item.

1. The alarm clock rang. James got out of bed.
2. Everybody likes that singer. Nobody buys her records.

Part C For each item, follow the direction and draw the figure.

1 inch

1. • Make a capital **T** that has a vertical line about one inch long and a horizontal line about two inches long.
   • Make a dot in the middle of the vertical line.
   • Draw a slanted line from the left end of the horizontal line to the bottom of the vertical line.

2. • Make a capital **T** that has a vertical line about two inches long and a horizontal line about half an inch long.
   • Make a dot just above the middle of the horizontal line.
   • Make a dot just below the bottom of the vertical line.

Test 2

Part A

1. They smiled when she came into the room.
2. He cleaned his room before he went out to play.

Part B

1. She climbed a tall mountain.
2. He lives in new york.
3. We bought two bumpo cars.
4. I like shino toothpaste.
5. I bought two plastic toothbrushes.
6. We bought four fletcher tires.

Part C

The direction states that you should ______________,	but you should ______________ ______________.

Direction	Figure
Make a horizontal line.	———

Part D

distance	speed	direction	length	age	number

1. The car went 55 miles per hour.
   The truck went 55 miles per hour.
   The car and truck went the same ____.

2. Janice sold 40 raffle tickets.
   Robert sold 40 raffle tickets.
   Janice and Robert sold the same ____.

3. Bill ran 17 miles.
   Tanya ran 17 miles.
   Bill and Tanya ran the same ____.

Lesson 21

Part A

- The claim that is shown is false:

Claim	Facts
Room A has fewer students than Room B has.	Number of students: Room A – 28 Room B – 28

- To write a sentence that tells about the students in the rooms, start by naming both rooms:

  Room A and Room B

- Then complete the sentence by telling how the rooms are the same:

  Room A and Room B have the same number of students.

Claim	Facts
1. The car went faster than the truck.	Speed of each vehicle: car – 65 miles per hour truck – 65 miles per hour
2. Tim was older than Rita.	Age of each person: Tim – 10 years old Rita – 10 years old
3. The horse went faster than the dog.	Speed of horse – 20 miles per hour Speed of dog – 20 miles per hour
4. Fran arrived later than Tina.	Time of arrival: Fran – 10 a.m. Tina – 10 a.m.
5. The horse was heavier than the bull.	Weight of horse – 1800 pounds Weight of bull – 1800 pounds

Part B
Write a sentence that is specific for each item.

1.

Sentence	Facts
She improved at it.	She was Fran Davis.
	Her improvement was in writing clear sentences.

[Who] **improved at** [what] .

2.

Sentence	Facts
She was proud of her achievements.	Ginger's mother was the person who was proud.
	The achievements were Ginger's achievements.

[Who] **was proud of** [what] .

3.

Sentence	Facts
It frightened them.	It frightened the Johnson family.
	What frightened them was the experience on a narrow mountain road.

[What] **frightened** [whom] .

Part C Write the correct first word of the predicate.

1. A new Bumpo goes farther on a tank of gas.
2. They goes with us.
3. H-Mart stores stays open longer.
4. My friends are going with us.
5. My sister have a new bike.
6. His horses were black.
7. Her dogs was following us.

Part D Follow the X-box rules and write a sentence that tells the problem with each direction.

This is 1 inch: ▬▬▬▬

Direction __ states that you should ____________________,	X	but you should ____________ ____________________________.

Direction	Figure
1. Make a backward **C** that is two inches high.	
2. Make an upside-down **C** that is one inch high.	
3. Make a slanted line that is one inch long.	

Part E For each picture, write a sentence that tells what Liz might be saying. Start with the words: **Another possibility.**

1.
The man was walking through the alley. So that man must be a thief.
Another possibility is that ______ ______.
Lefty
Liz
2.
Fran missed a lot of school this year. She must really hate school.
Another possibility is that ______ ______.
3.
Linda has never called me on the phone. So she doesn't have a phone at home.
Another possibility is that ______ ______.

Part F For each item, follow the directions and draw the figure.

1. • Make an **H** with vertical lines about one inch long and a horizontal line about one inch long.
   • Make a dot on the top of each vertical line.
   • Draw a straight line from one dot to the other dot.
2. • Make an **H** with vertical lines that are about one inch long and a horizontal line that is about three inches long.
   • Make a dot on the top end of the left vertical line.
   • Make a dot on the bottom end of the right vertical line.
   • Draw a straight line from one dot to the other dot.

Lesson 22

Part A Write the conclusion for each deduction.

Deduction 1: Insects do not have bones.
Beetles are insects.
_______________________________________.

Deduction 2: You should be on time for important events.
School is an important event.
_______________________________________.

Deduction 3: All closed figures have at least three sides.
Polygons are closed figures.
_______________________________________.

Part B Write the correct first word of the predicate.

1. Creamo paint dry faster.
2. The Bumpo car hold more people.
3. Our dogs bark when we leave.
4. Zee Boo toy cars is the best you can buy.
5. Jill and Jan runs faster than ever.

Part C For each item, follow the directions and draw the figure.

1. • Make an **H** with all lines about two inches long.
   • Make a dot on each end of the horizontal line.
   • Make a dot on the bottom end of each vertical line.
   • Connect all four dots with an **X.**

2. • Make an **H** with all lines about two inches long.
   • Make a dot on each end of both vertical lines.
   • Connect all four dots with an **X.**

Part D

You're going to write **general** directions and **specific** directions. General directions tell about more things than specific directions do.

When you write general directions, you tell only about the things that are the **same** in **all** the figures.

B_______ C　　　_______B C　　　_B_ C

General directions: Make a horizontal line.
Make a **B** on top of the line.
Make a **C** just below the line.

Part E

For each item, write **general** directions for making the figures.

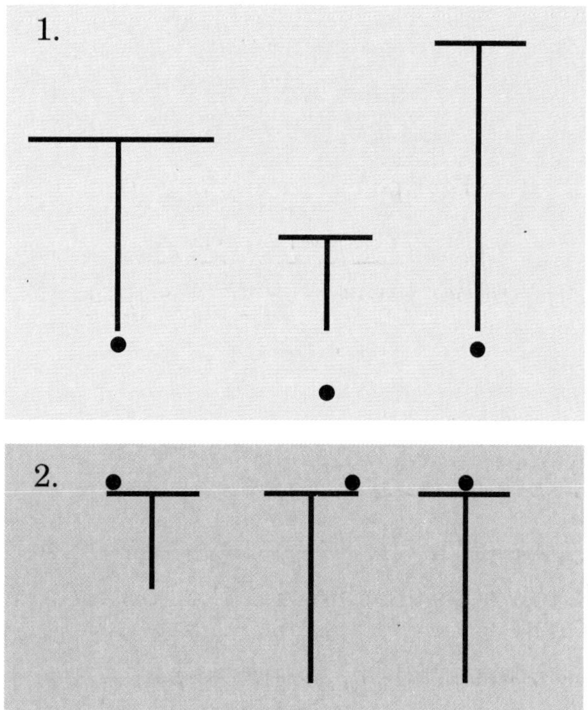

Part F For each item, write the sentence that tells how the things are the same.

Claim	Facts
1. Bumpo cars get better gas mileage than Zermo cars.	Gas mileage each car gets: Bumpo – 32 miles per gallon Zermo – 32 miles per gallon
2. Jill earned more money than Anna.	Amount each person earned: Jill – $18 Anna – $18
3. Donna and the dog were facing different directions.	Donna – north The dog – north
4. Dan ran slower than Greg.	Dan – 6 miles per hour Greg – 6 miles per hour
5. Fran was heavier than Ginger.	Fran – 67 pounds Ginger – 67 pounds

Part G Follow the X-box rules and write a sentence that tells the problem with each direction.

Direction __ states that you should ____________________,	X	but you should ____________ ______________________________.

Direction	Figure
1. Make a **B** on top of an **L.**	
2. Make an upside-down **L** on top of an **A.**	

Part H For each picture, write a sentence that tells what Liz might be saying. Start with the words: **Another possibility.**

1.
The only thing you can do when it rains is sit and look out the window.
Another possibility is that ______ ______.
Lefty
Liz
2.
The only thing we can do at the river is go fishing.
Another possibility is ______ ______.
3.
The only reason Bonnie has so many friends is that she is rich.
Another possibility is ______ ______.

Part I Write the combined sentence for each item, using **but** or **and.**

1. The sun went down. Everything turned dark.
2. My grandfather is very old. He can walk quickly.
3. She was tired. She couldn't sleep.

Part A

a. Milly had a poodle.

b. Ms. Brown had a dog.

1 Milly Jones 2 Milly Brown 3 Ann Brown

2 black poodle 1 white poodle 3 beagle

Part B

1.

M M M

2.

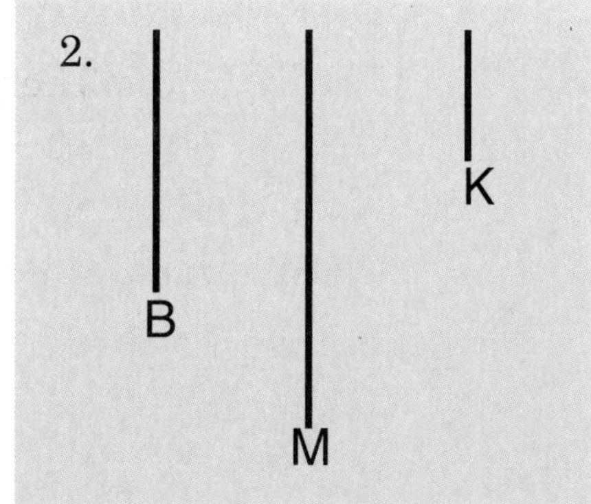

Part C

A lot of arguments tell you what you **should do** or what you **should buy.** Many of these arguments are **deductions.** But they often leave out a piece of evidence.

If the **conclusion** tells you something you should do, the evidence **must** have a rule that tells something you should do. That rule can be the first piece of evidence or the second piece of evidence.

Here's a deduction with a missing piece of evidence:

Tinko is the toothpaste that fights cavities best.

Therefore, you should use Tinko toothpaste.

Here's the whole deduction:

You should use the toothpaste that fights cavities best.

Tinko is the toothpaste that fights cavities best.

Therefore, you should use Tinko toothpaste.

Part D

Deduction 1:

Flammo makes the best tires.

Therefore, you should buy Flammo tires.

Deduction 2:

Your neighbors are people who care about you.

Therefore, you should help your neighbors.

Deduction 3:

Charles Smith is an honest man.

Therefore, you should respect Charles Smith.

Part E

Rules:

1. Write one paragraph for each picture.
2. For the first picture, tell who had the problem and what the problem was.
3. For the missing picture, write a paragraph that tells all the things that Luisa must have done to solve her problem.
4. For the last picture, tell how the story ended. Tell what the last picture shows. Write a sentence that tells the exact words Luisa said.

Part F

Write sentences that compare Jan and Henry. Each sentence should have the word **same** and a word from the vocabulary box.

direction	age	distance	speed	width	height

Claim	Facts
1. Jan goes slower than Henry goes.	Jan goes 13 miles per hour. Henry goes 13 miles per hour.
2. Henry throws a ball farther than Jan does.	Jan throws a ball 200 feet. Henry throws a ball 200 feet.
3. Henry is shorter than Jan.	Jan is 5 feet 1 inch tall. Henry is 5 feet 1 inch tall.

Lesson 24

Part A

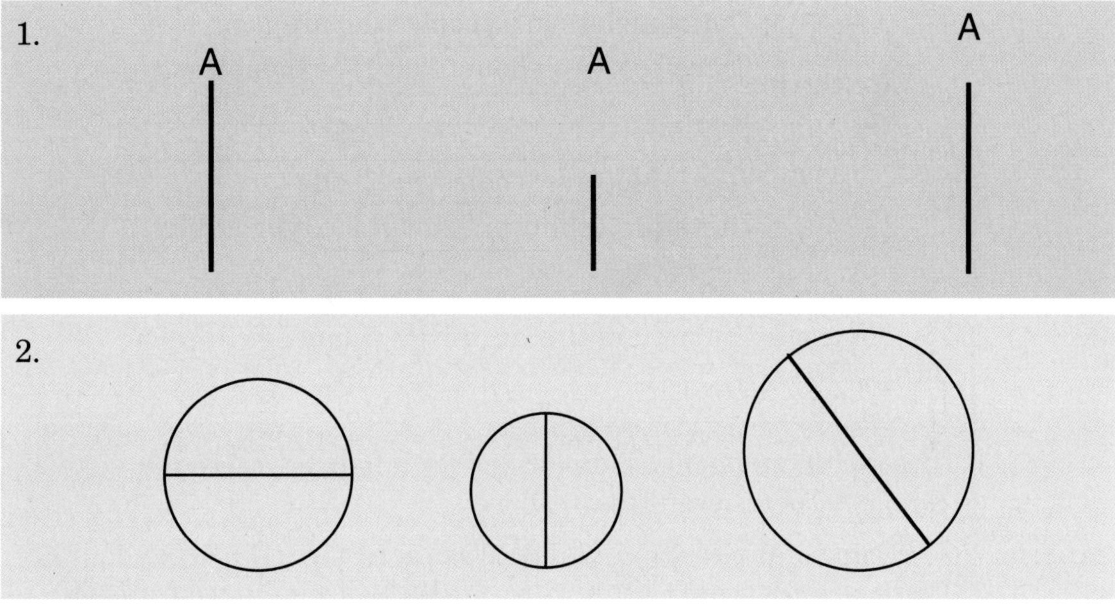

Part B

a. Mr. Smith drove a vehicle.

b. Larry drove a motorcycle.

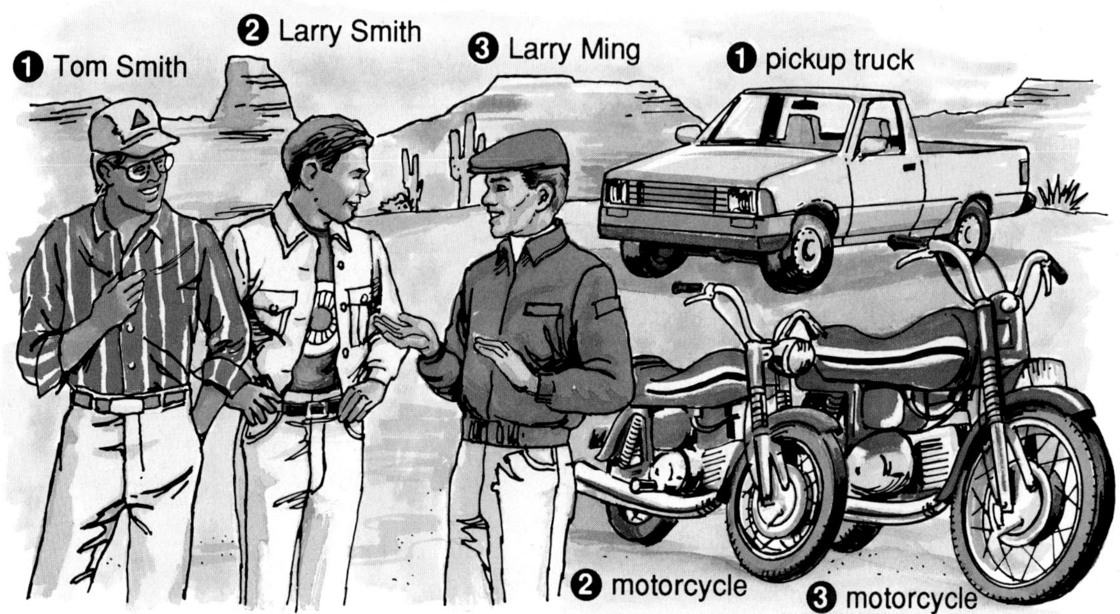

Part C

Write the missing evidence in each deduction.

Deduction 1: ______________________
The homeless are people who are poor.
Therefore, we should help the homeless.

Deduction 2: ______________________
Vegetables are wholesome foods.
Therefore, children should eat vegetables.

Part D

Some statements are **too general.** Some are false or **inaccurate.**

If a statement is **too general,** it is true, but it's not specific. If you followed general directions for a figure, you could make a whole lot of different figures.

Some statements are false or **inaccurate.** If a statement is false or inaccurate, it is wrong. If you followed inaccurate directions for making a figure, you would always make the wrong figure.

Sample

Statement	Figure
1. The horizontal line is four inches long. 2. The line is two inches long. 3. The vertical line is one inch long.	

Part E

Write **inaccurate** or **too general** for each item.

Statement	Figure
1. A horizontal line is two inches long. 2. A line is one inch long. 3. A line is vertical. 4. A vertical line is four inches long.	

Part F

Write **inaccurate** or **too general** for each item.

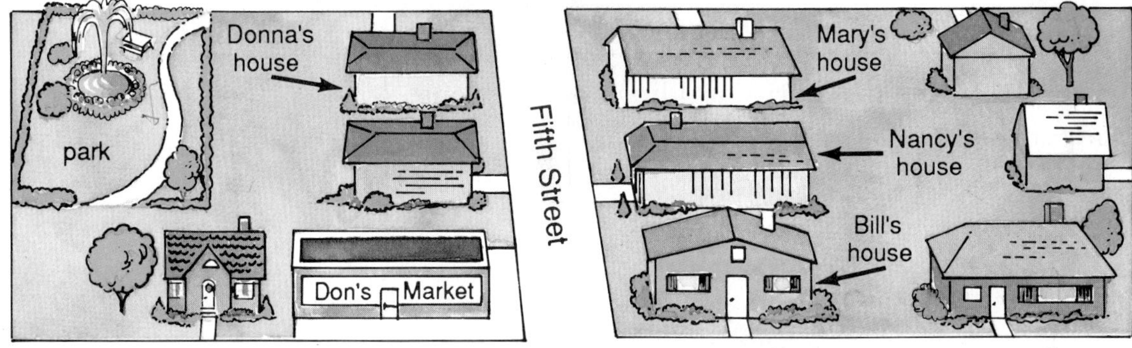

1. Bill's house is on the corner.
2. Jill's house is between two large houses.
3. Don's Market is on the corner of Fifth Street and Broadway.
4. Nancy's house is on Fifth Street.

Part G

For each picture, write a sentence that tells what Liz might be saying.

1.
Those people are riding the bus. They must be too poor to own cars.
Another possibility is ____________ ____________.
Lefty
Liz

2.
John was absent from school all last week. He must hate school.
Another possibility is ____________ ____________.

Part H Follow the X-box rules and tell whether each direction is **too general** or **inaccurate.** Then tell what kind of figure you should make.

Direction __ states that you should ________________,	but that direction is ______. You should make ________.

Direction	Figure
1. Make a horizontal line one inch long.	
2. Make a circle.	

Part I Write sentences that compare Anna and Lisa. Each sentence should have the word **same** and a word from the vocabulary box.

amount	direction	number	speed	distance	age

Claim	Facts
1. Lisa read more books than Anna.	Lisa read 10 books. Anna read 10 books.
2. Anna is younger than Lisa.	Anna is 14 years old. Lisa is 14 years old.
3. Anna has more money than Lisa.	Anna has $8. Lisa has $8.

Lesson 25

Part A

Some ads make claims that give the wrong impression.

The sentences in these ads are true, but they often leave out important numbers.

The sentences are designed to trick you.

They aren't lies, but they will probably give you the wrong impression.

Sentence	Fact
Dentists recommend Tino's toothpaste.	**Two** dentists recommend it.

With that fact, we can fix up the original sentence so it is not misleading. We just put the number in the sentence.

Here's the original sentence:

Dentists recommend Tino's toothpaste.

Here's the sentence that does not give the wrong impression:

Two dentists recommend Tino's toothpaste.

Part B Rewrite each sentence so it is not misleading.

Sentence	Facts
1. New Bumpo cars cost less than last year's cars.	How much less new Bumpo cars cost – $1
2. Bumpo cars come in attractive colors.	Number of attractive colors – two
3. Metro Zoo has more monkeys than it had last year.	Number of monkeys last year – 200 Number of monkeys this year – 202

Part C

Write a specific sentence for each item.

1.

Sentence	Facts
She looked at it.	She was Dr. Sue Morris.
	It was a white flower.

[Who] **looked at** [what] .

2.

Sentence	Facts
They requested information.	They were students in Mrs. Taylor's fifth-grade class.
	The information was about the cost of gold and silver.

[Who] **requested information about** [what] .

Part D

For each picture, write a sentence that tells what Liz might be saying.

1.
Everybody I know uses Shiny toothpaste. Shiny toothpaste must be the best.
Another possibility is ________________ ________________.
Lefty
Liz

2.
Those people are carrying books. They must be going to the library.
Another possibility is ________________ ________________.

Part E

Rewrite each sentence so it is accurate.

Claim	Facts
1. Fremont Farms planted more fruit trees in 1990 than in 1991.	1990 – 200 trees planted 1991 – 200 trees planted
2. Bumpo cars cost less in 1988 than they did in 1987.	1987 Bumpos – \$15,000 1988 Bumpos – \$15,000
3. The oven had a higher temperature on Monday than it had on Tuesday.	Monday – 350 degrees Tuesday – 350 degrees
4. H-Mart stores sold more shoes in February than in March.	February – 400 shoes sold March – 400 shoes sold

Part F

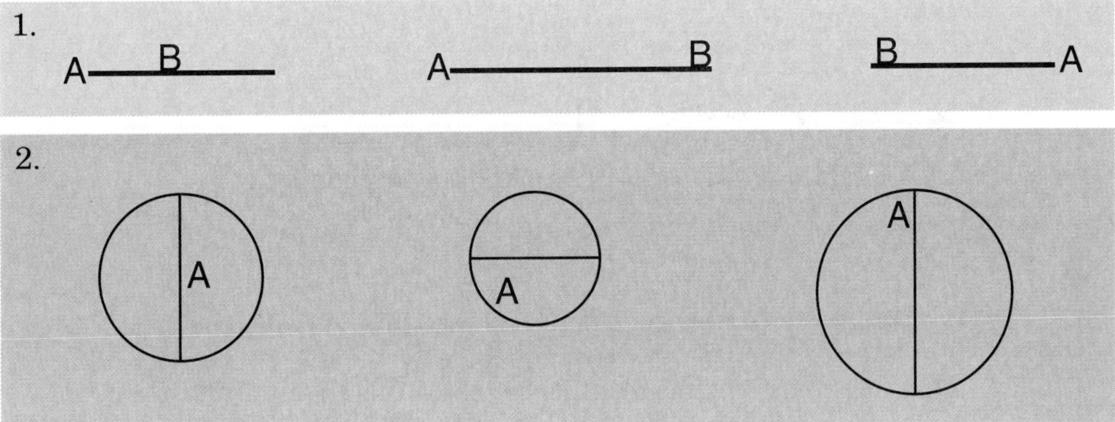

Part G Follow the X-box rules and tell whether each direction is **too general** or **inaccurate.** Then tell what kind of figure you should make.

1 inch

Direction __ states that you should ______________,	X	but that direction is ______.
		You should make __________.

Direction	Figure
1. Make a backward **C** one inch high.	
2. Make a **B.**	B

Part H For each item, follow the directions and draw the figure.

1. • Make an **H** with all lines about one inch long.
   • Make a dot at the top and at the bottom of the left vertical line.
   • Make a **C** that connects the two dots.

2. • Make an **H** that is on its side. Make all the lines about one inch long.
   • Make a dot on the right end of each horizontal line.
   • Make a backward **C** that connects the two dots.

Lesson 26

Part A Write a specific sentence for each item.

	Sentence	Facts
1.	It pleased them.	They were the owners of Downtown Motors.
		It was the trend in sales.

[What] **pleased** [who] .

	Sentence	Facts
2.	They increased after it came in.	The number of traffic accidents increased.
		The thing that came in was a dense fog.

[What] **increased after** [when] .

	Sentence	Facts
3.	She requested it.	It was information about the fire on Fifth Street.
		She was our teacher.

[Who] **requested** [what] .

Part B Rewrite each sentence so it is not misleading.

Sentence	Facts
1. Z bikes weigh less than Swifto bikes.	Weight of bikes: Swiftos – 28 pounds 10 ounces Z bikes – 28 pounds 6 ounces
2. New Bumpo cars go faster than last year's Bumpos.	Speed of cars: New Bumpos – 83 miles per hour Old Bumpos – 80 miles per hour
3. More people buy Blow Big gum than Big Dent gum.	Number of people who buy: Blow Big gum – 2950 people Big Dent gum – 2940 people

Part C Write the missing rule in each deduction.

Deduction 1: ______________________________

Bees are stinging insects.

Therefore, (children shouldn't tease) bees.

Deduction 2: ______________________________

Gruppo candy is a food that contains too much sugar.

Therefore, (you shouldn't eat) Gruppo candy.

Part D Follow the X-box rules and tell whether each direction is **too general** or **inaccurate.** Then tell what kind of figure you should make.

Direction __ states that you should ______________,	but that direction is _______. You should make __________.

Direction	Figure
1. Make a line one inch long.	
2. Make an upside-down **T** one inch high.	
3. Make a horizontal line one inch long.	

Part E Write **general** directions for the set of figures.
Then write **specific** directions for making the first figure.

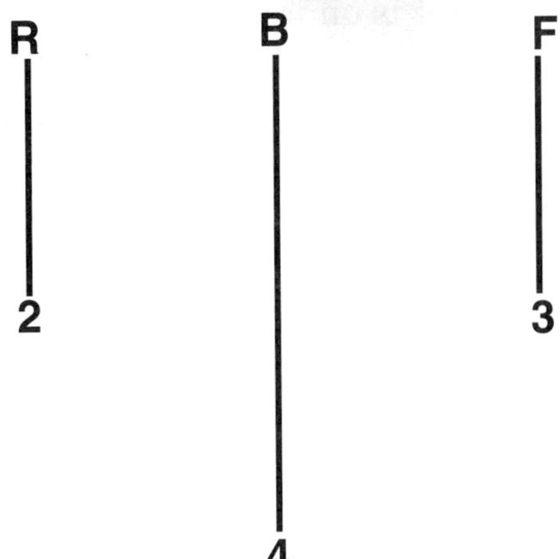

Part F For each picture, write a sentence that tells what Liz might be saying. Start with the words: **Another possibility.**

Part G For each item, follow the directions and draw the figure.

1. • Make an **H** that is on its side. Make all the lines about one inch long.
   • Make a dot on the bottom of the vertical line.
   • Draw a straight line from the dot to the right end of the top horizontal line.

2. • Make an **H.** Make all the lines about two inches long.
   • Make a dot on the bottom of each vertical line.
   • Draw a straight line from one dot to the other dot.

Part H For each item, write two sentences that are very specific.

1. Mary wore a jacket.
2. Ms. Brown wore a jacket.

Lesson 27

Part A Write sentences that are clear.

a. She (1) was proud of her (2) achievements.

b. She (2) was proud of her (2) achievements.

c. She (2) was proud of her (1) achievements.

Part B Write the missing rule for each deduction.

Deduction 1: ______________________

Very old stamps are things that may become valuable.

Therefore, (people should save) very old stamps.

Deduction 2: ______________________

Bumpo is the car that performs best.

Therefore, (wise shoppers should select) a Bumpo car.

Part C

For each item, follow the directions and draw the figure.

1.
   - Make a **D** that is about one inch high.
   - Make a dot in the middle of the vertical line.
   - Make a dot in the middle of the curved line.
   - Draw a straight line to connect the dots.

2.
   - Make a backward **D** that is about one inch high.
   - Make a dot on each end of the vertical line.
   - Make a dot in the middle of the curved line.
   - Connect the three dots so that you have a triangle.

Part D

Write a story about the first picture, the missing picture and the last picture.

Rules:
1. Write one paragraph for each picture.
2. For the first picture, tell who had the problem and what the problem was.
3. For the missing picture, write a paragraph that tells all the things that Ted and Sally must have done to solve their problem.
4. For the last picture, tell how the story ended. Tell what the last picture shows. Write a sentence that tells the exact words Sally said.

Lesson 28

Part A

- Some deductions are faulty because the conclusion presents only one possibility. Although the conclusion makes it seem that there's only one possibility, there are other possibilities. Here's a faulty deduction:

  You should use a toothpaste that contains fluoride.
  Shino toothpaste contains fluoride.
  Therefore, you should use Shino toothpaste.

- Here are some different toothpastes that contain fluoride:

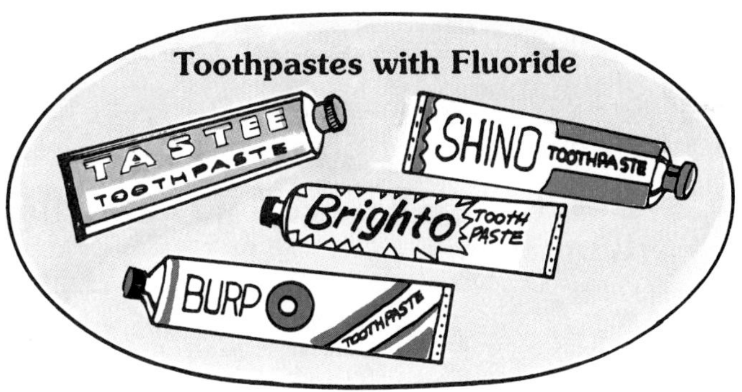

Part B

Argument 1:

You should play a sport.
Baseball is a sport.
Therefore, you should play baseball.

Argument 2:

You should get a pet.
A cat is a pet.
Therefore, you should get a cat.

Part C

Claim	Facts
1. Splatto paint dries faster than before.	Drying time before – 695 minutes Drying time now – 692 minutes
2. You can save by buying a Bumpo car instead of an Easing car.	Cost of a Bumpo – \$9000 Cost of an Easing – \$9013
3. Prices are now lower on all Dingo shoes.	Dingo shoes before the sale – \$37.50 Dingo shoes now – \$37.10

Part D

Write the missing rule in each deduction.

Deduction 1: ______________________________

Computers are complex electronic machines.

Therefore, children shouldn't try to fix computers.

Deduction 2: ______________________________

Bumpo car salespeople are people who make misleading statements.

Therefore, you shouldn't believe Bumpo car salespeople.

Part E

To tell about some problems, you have to figure out the right number.

- Here's a claim:

  New Bumpo cars cost no more than last year's Bumpo cars.

Table – Cost of Bumpos	
This year $87,000	Last year $86,000

The claim is inaccurate.

- Here are two different sentences that tell about the claim:

  New Bumpo cars cost more than last year's Bumpo cars.
  New Bumpo cars cost $1000 more than last year's Bumpo cars.

The last sentence is better because it is more specific.

- Here are sentences that do not tell that the claim is inaccurate:

  New Bumpo cars cost $87,000.
  New Bumpo cars cost a lot of money.

- Remember, the claim says that new Bumpo cars **do not** cost more. A sentence that tells why that claim is inaccurate has to tell that new Bumpo cars **do** cost more.

Part F

Item 1

Claim	Facts	Sentences
New Bumpo cars are faster than last year's Bumpos.	Speed of Bumpos: New Bumpos – 97 miles per hour Last year's Bumpos – 98 miles per hour	New Bumpo cars go 97 miles per hour. New Bumpo cars are 1 mile per hour slower than last year's Bumpos. New Bumpo cars are slower than last year's Bumpos.

Item 2

Claim	Facts	Sentences
H-Mart prices have been lowered on all shoes.	Shoes with higher prices – 3 kinds Shoes with lower prices – 34 kinds Shoes with the same prices – 11 kinds	H-Mart prices have not been lowered on 14 kinds of shoes. H-Mart prices have not been lowered on all shoes. H-Mart prices are the same on 11 kinds of shoes.

Item 3

Claim	Facts	Sentences
Burno batteries cost less than Sparko batteries.	Cost of batteries: Burno – 89 cents each Sparko – 89 cents each	Burno batteries cost 89 cents each. Burno batteries do not cost less than Sparkos. Burno batteries and Sparko batteries cost the same amount.

Part G Write sentences that are clear.

1 Greg
2 Robert
TICKETS

a. He (1) bought his (1) ticket.

b. He (1) bought his (2) ticket.

c. He (2) bought his (2) ticket.

Part H

Direction __ states that you should ___________,	but that direction is ______. You should make ______.

Direction	Figure
1. Make a horizontal line one inch long.	
2. Make a horizontal line.	

Part I Write sentences that compare the people or things. Each sentence should have the word **same.**

Claim	Facts
1. The jar holds more apples than the can holds.	Apples in jar – 12 apples Apples in can – 12 apples
2. It takes more time to mow the front lawn than it takes to mow the back lawn.	Time required: back lawn – 37 minutes front lawn – 37 minutes
3. Bill's weight was less in 1988 than in 1991.	Bill's weight in 1991 – 130 pounds Bill's weight in 1988 – 130 pounds

Lesson 29

Part A Rewrite each sentence so it is not misleading.

Sentence	Fact
1. H-Mart stores are giving away free court shoes.	These H-Mart stores are in Alaska.
2. You can feed many animals at Metro Zoo.	These animals are dogs and cats.
3. You can rent movies for half price.	These movies are very old.

Part B Write sentences that are clear.

(1) (2)
a. They reported on their experiences.

(1) (1)
b. They reported on their experiences.

(2) (1)
c. They reported on their experiences.

Part C For each item, write the sentence that does the best job of showing why the claim is inaccurate.

Item 1

Claim	Facts	Sentences
See-More TVs cost no more than Ace TVs.	Cost of TVs: See-More – $500 Ace – $499	Ace TVs cost $499. See-More TVs cost $1 more than Ace TVs. See-More TVs cost more than Ace TVs.

Item 2

Claim	Facts	Sentences
New Bumpo cars cost a lot, lot less than last year's Bumpos.	Cost of cars: This year's – $45,800 Last year's – $45,810	New Bumpo cars cost $45,800. Last year's Bumpo cars cost $45,810. New Bumpo cars cost only $10 less than last year's Bumpos.

Item 3

Claim	Facts	Sentences
Speedoo bikes cost the same as Safetee bikes.	Cost of bikes: Speedoo – $99 Safetee – $98	Speedoo bikes cost more than Safetee bikes. Speedoo bikes cost $1 more than Safetee bikes. Speedoo bikes cost $99.

Part D

If an argument starts with a rule that tells about all the things in the class, the argument can draw a conclusion about any of the things that are in the class.

Here's an argument that is okay:

You should eat all types of fruit that have vitamin C.
Oranges have vitamin C.
Therefore, you should eat oranges.

If an argument starts with a rule that tells about some things in the class, the argument cannot draw a conclusion about just one thing in the class.

Here's an argument that has a faulty conclusion:

You should eat some fruit that has vitamin C.
Oranges have vitamin C.
Therefore, you should eat oranges.

That argument does not start out by telling about **all** the things in the class. It tells about some. So the conclusion is faulty.

Other conclusions are possible because oranges are not the only fruit that has vitamin C.

Part E

Write **faulty** or **okay** for each argument.

Argument 1: You should do exercises that strengthen your legs.
Jumping up and down on your bed is an exercise that strengthens your legs.
Therefore, you should jump up and down on your bed.

Argument 2: You should be kind to all pets.
Goldfish are pets.
Therefore, you should be kind to goldfish.

Argument 3: You should wear warm clothes during cold weather.
Zemor mummy suits are warm clothes.
Therefore, you should wear Zemor mummy suits.

Part F Write **misleading** or **inaccurate** for each claim.

Claim	Facts
1. There are more than a thousand animals at Metro Zoo.	997 mice 95 wild animals
2. Metro Zoo stays open until 9 o'clock at night.	Closing time of Metro Zoo: 7 p.m.
3. A family can spend a day at Metro Zoo for only $5.	Cost to enter Metro Zoo: $3 for each person
4. You can spend hours watching the animals at Metro Zoo.	Hours Metro Zoo is open: 5 p.m. to 7 p.m.

Part G For each item, write the two possible meanings of the second sentence.

1. He put cheese on the table. It was green.
2. The music was coming from that car. It sounded terrible.

Part H For each item, follow the directions and draw the figure.

1. • Make a **D** that is about two inches high.
   • Make a dot in the middle of the curved line.
   • Make a dot on each end of the vertical line.
   • Make a sideways **V** that connects all three dots.

2. • Make an **X** that is about one inch high.
   • Make a dot on the left end of each line.
   • Connect the dots with a **C**.

Lesson 30

Part A

Claim	Facts
1. Bumpo cars cost much less than Cleo cars. 2. Bumpos cost much less than Dorfs. 3. Bumpos cost less than Dorfs. 4. Bumpos cost no more than Zurpos.	Cost of each car: Bumpo---$38,200 Cleo-------$90,000 Dorf-------$38,202 Zurpo-----$38,200

Part B

Write sentences that are clear.

a. He (1) had an accident in his (2) car.

b. He (2) had an accident in his (1) car.

c. He (1) had an accident in his (1) car.

Test 3

Part A

Deduction 1: ______________________

Matches are dangerous things.

Therefore, (children shouldn't play with) matches.

Deduction 2: ______________________

Sundays are weekend days.

Therefore, (you should relax on) Sundays.

Part B

Sentence	Facts
1. Bumpo cars cost less than Dento cars.	Cost of cars: Bumpo – $9540 Dento – $9542
2. Bumpo cars go faster than Dento cars.	Speed of cars: Bumpo – 95 miles per hour Dento – 94 miles per hour

Part C

distance	speed	number	direction	height

Sentence	Facts
1. Carlos ate more apples than Kevin ate.	Carlos ate 14 apples. Kevin ate 14 apples.
2. Carlos ran faster than Kevin.	Carlos ran 9 miles per hour. Kevin ran 9 miles per hour.

Part D

The direction states that you should ________________, but that direction is ______. You should make ________.

Direction	Figure
Make a vertical line.	

Lesson 31

Part A

Claims	Facts
1. Creamo paint lasts longer than Drippi paint.	How long each paint lasts:
2. Creamo paint lasts as long as Cover All.	Creamo------52 months
3. Creamo paint lasts much longer than Gleamo.	Gleamo------51 months
4. Creamo paint lasts as long as Finno.	Cover All----52 months
	Finno---------53 months
	Drippi--------51 months

Part B

2 Donna

a. She (2) tried to improve her (2) situation.

b. She (1) tried to improve her (2) situation.

c. She (1) tried to improve her (1) situation.

Part C

For each item, follow the directions and draw the figure.

1.
- Make a **C** about one inch high.
- Make a dot on the middle of the **C.**
- Make a dot on each end of the **C.**
- Make a vertical line to connect two of the dots.
- Make a horizontal line that connects the dot on the middle of the **C** with the middle of the vertical line.

2.
- Make a backward **C** that is about one inch high.
- Make a dot on the middle of the **C.**
- Make a dot on each end of the **C.**
- Make a sideways **V** that connects all three dots.

Part D For each item, write the sentence that does the best job of showing why the claim is inaccurate.

Item 1

Claim	Facts
Speedoo bikes cost much, much less than Whirlwind bikes.	Cost of bikes: Speedoo – $96 Whirlwind – $98

Sentences: Speedoo bikes cost 2 dollars less than Whirlwind bikes.
Speedoo bikes cost only 96 dollars.
Speedoo bikes cost less than Whirlwind bikes.

Item 2

Claim	Facts
Burno batteries last months longer than Sparko batteries.	Life of batteries: Burno – 6 months Sparko – 5 months

Sentences: Burno batteries last longer than Sparko batteries.
Burno batteries last only 1 month longer than Sparko batteries.
Burno batteries last 6 months.

Item 3

Claim	Facts
All the toys are on sale at H-Mart.	Number of toys: in store – 256 on sale – 250

Sentences: 250 toys are on sale at H-Mart.
Not all of the toys are on sale at H-Mart.
Six toys are not on sale at H-Mart.

Part E Write **faulty** or **okay** for each argument.

Argument 1:

You should buy a bike that has an adjustable seat.
Speedoo has an adjustable seat.
Therefore, you should buy a Speedoo.

Argument 2:

Drivers should obey all traffic signs.
Stop signs are traffic signs.
Therefore, drivers should obey stop signs.

Argument 3:

You should use a toothbrush that reaches your back teeth.
A Reacho toothbrush reaches your back teeth.
Therefore, you should use a Reacho toothbrush.

Argument 4:

You should complete your homework assignments in all subjects.
Math is a subject.
Therefore, you should complete your homework assignments in math.

Part F Follow the X-box rules and tell whether the direction is **too general** or **inaccurate.** Then tell what kind of figure you should make.

The direction states that you should ________________,	but ________________.
	You should make ________.

Direction	Figure
Make an upside-down letter one inch high.	

Lesson 32

Part A Write sentences to show why each claim is inaccurate.

Claims

1. Bumpo cars cost less than Macko cars.
2. Bumpo cars cost much less than Dort cars.
3. Bumpo cars cost less than Zoro cars.

Table – Cost of Cars

Bumpo	Macko	Dort	Zoro
$6000	$6000	$6003	$5999

Part B Write an argument that starts out the same way as the argument below but draws a different conclusion.

Argument:

People should buy things that cost less than $10.
Slopless hamburger turners are things that cost less than $10.
Therefore, people should buy Slopless hamburger turners.

Part C

You've learned about X boxes. If you see this symbol, you know that you will tell why you do not agree with a statement.

Here is a new symbol:

Any box that has this shape is a **summary box.** It tells you to summarize. You summarize when you don't want to repeat the same thing over and over and over and over.

You can summarize what people said or did.

Here's an item:

Before Billy went to school, he put on his socks.
Before Billy went to school, he put on his shirt.
Before Billy went to school, he put on his pants.
Before Billy went to school, he put on his shoes.

Each sentence has the same part. That part goes in the summary.

Before Billy went to school, he put on his . . .

You write a class name to tell about the things Billy put on:

Before Billy went to school,
he put on his **clothes**.

That's a summary of what Billy did.

1. MB Market has the best bananas in town.
MB Market has the best apples in town.
MB Market has the best grapes in town.
MB Market has the best oranges in town.

2. JM Products makes superior tables.
JM Products makes superior beds.
JM Products makes superior chairs.
JM Products makes superior couches.

3. Mr. Durkin hauls pigs in his truck.
Mr. Durkin hauls sheep in his truck.
Mr. Durkin hauls cows and horses in his truck.

Part D Write **inaccurate** or **misleading** to tell about each claim.

Claims from an ad for Z-Mart store:

Claim 1: Prices have been lowered on everything.

Claim 2: You'll save money when you buy JJ shoes.

Claim 3: TT tapes cost less.

	Old price	New price
JJ shoes	$20.00	$19.99
BB baseballs	$8.00	$9.00
TT tapes	$3.00	$2.95

Part E For each item, follow the directions. Draw the figure about one inch high.

1.
   - Make a sideways **D** so the horizontal line is on the bottom.
   - Make a dot in the middle of the curved line.
   - Make a small square just above the dot.
2.
   - Make a sideways **D** so the horizontal line is on the bottom.
   - Make a dot on each end of the horizontal line.
   - Connect the dots with a **V.**

Part F Rewrite each sentence so it is not too general.

Sentence	Fact
1. Now Strong Bod is offering free memberships to men.	These men are over 70 years old.
2. Women prefer Streako running shoes.	These women live in Alaska.
3. Parents depend on Safe-T car seats.	These parents have very young children.

Lesson 33

Part A Write each sentence so it is more specific.

Sentence	Fact
1. Dino shoes cost one dollar.	These shoes are made of cardboard.
2. Children love Fricko cereal.	These children are very hungry.
3. Used Bumpo cars may be worth $200,000.	These cars were built in 1921.

Part B Write **inaccurate** or **misleading** to tell about each claim.

Claim 1: Speedoo bikes cost less than Ace bikes.

Claim 2: The new Speedoo bike is longer than the Ace bike.

Claim 3: Speedoo bikes weigh less than Ace bikes.

	Weight	Length	Price
Speedoo bikes	95 pounds	6 feet	$148
Ace bikes	96 pounds	6 feet	$150

Part C Write sentences to tell why each claim is inaccurate.

Claims

1. Speedoo bikes cost much less than Whiz bikes.
2. Speedoo bikes cost less than Dino bikes.
3. Speedoo bikes cost less than Gulley bikes.

Table – Cost of Bikes

Speedoo	Whiz	Dino	Gulley
$148	$150	$148	$141

Part D Write a story about the first picture, the missing picture and the last picture.

Rules:
1. Write one paragraph for each picture.
2. For the first picture, tell who had the problem and what the problem was.
3. For the missing picture, write a paragraph that tells all the things that Mr. Brown must have done to solve his problem.
4. For the last picture, tell how the story ended. Tell what the last picture shows. Write a sentence that tells the exact words Mr. Brown thought.

Mr. Brown
It's not very pretty, but it works.

Part E For each item, follow the directions and draw the figure.

1. • Make an **N.** Make each line about one inch long.
   • Make a dot on the bottom end of the left vertical line.
   • Make a dot on the top end of the right vertical line.
   • Connect the dots with a straight line.

2. • Make an **N.** Make each line about two inches long.
   • Make a dot on each end of the left vertical line.
   • Make a dot on each end of the right vertical line.
   • Draw two horizontal lines to connect the dots.

Lesson 34

Part A

Follow the rules for the X box. Tell whether each claim is **misleading** or **inaccurate.** Then write a sentence that tells why.

Claim __ states that ______ ____________________________,	but that claim is __________. [Tell why.]

Claim	Facts
1. Speedoo bikes weigh less than Dino bikes.	Weight of bikes: Speedoo – 34 pounds Dino – 30 pounds
2. H-Mart tires cost less than Z-Mart tires.	Cost of tires: H-Mart tires – \$49.99 Z-Mart tires – \$50.00

Part B

Write an argument that starts out the same way as the argument below but draws a different conclusion.

Argument: You should eat a green vegetable every day.
Spinach is a green vegetable.
Therefore, you should eat spinach every day.

Part C

Write **inaccurate** or **misleading** to tell about each claim.

Claims from an ad for Dino tractors:

Claim 1: Dino tractors cost less than Bleepo tractors.

Claim 2: Dino tractors are longer than Bleepo tractors.

Claim 3: Dino tractors weigh much more than Bleepo tractors.

Type of garden tractor	Cost	Length	Weight
Dino	\$9000	20 feet 5 inches	604 pounds
Bleepo	\$9001	20 feet 3 inches	600 pounds

Part D

Write each sentence so it is more specific.

Sentence	Fact
1. Roses are huge.	These roses are grown in special soil.
2. Boys prefer Run-More shoes.	These boys are under six years old.
3. H-Mart customers save $150.	These customers spend at least $800.

Part E

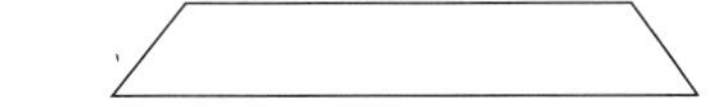

1. Here's something that Mrs. Crocker said:

   I bought a hammer at the hardware store.
   I bought a saw at the hardware store.
   I bought a screwdriver at the hardware store.
   I bought a wrench at the hardware store.

2. Here's something that Mr. Williams said:

   Bumpos will be available in a new red next year.
   Bumpos will be available in a new yellow next year.
   Bumpos will be available in a new blue next year.
   Bumpos will be available in a new brown next year.

3. Here's something that a TV commercial said:

   Skiing is great during January.
   Skiing is great during February.
   Skiing is great during March.

Part F

Directions 1

Step a. Make a horizontal line that is two inches long just above a horizontal line that is one inch long.

Step b. Make a dot on the right end of the horizontal line that is two inches long.

Directions 2

Step a. Make a horizontal line that is two inches long.

Step b. Make a dot on the right end of the horizontal line that is two inches long.

Part G For each item, write a sentence that is clear.

	Sentence	Facts
1.	**They built it.**	The thing they built was a huge birdhouse.
		They were the students in Ms. Anderson's classroom.

[Who] **built** [what] .

	Sentence	Facts
2.	**He was late meeting him.**	Jim Green was the person who was late.
		His brother had to wait.

[Who] **was late meeting** [which person] .

	Sentence	Facts
3.	**They went there.**	The place was a large tree stump.
		The things were four red ants.

[What] **went** [where] .

Lesson 35

Part A

You can summarize what people or articles say by using class names. You can make the summary more accurate by putting a number in front of the class name.

Here's an item:

These are things that Don said:

I met my friend Ron yesterday.
I met my friend Al yesterday.
I met my friend Rita yesterday.

Here's a summary that does not have a number:

Don said that he met friends yesterday.

Here are two summaries with a number:

Don said that he met three friends yesterday.
Don said that he met three of his friends yesterday.

These sentences give a good summary of what Don said.

1. These are things that Bonnie said:

   I got gifts from my mother.
   I got gifts from my uncle Al.
   I got gifts from my cousin Lilly.
   I got gifts from my sister Doris.

2. These are things that the president of Bumpo Company said:

   Bumpo's guarantee covers the steering wheel.
   Bumpo's guarantee covers the back bumper.
   Bumpo's guarantee covers the radiator.
   Bumpo's guarantee covers the battery.

Part B

Write an argument that starts out the same way as each argument below but draws a different conclusion.

Argument 1: You should eat fruit with every meal.
Pineapple is a fruit.
Therefore, you should eat pineapple with every meal.

Argument 2: You should do your homework in a quiet place.
A cave is a quiet place.
Therefore, you should do your homework in a cave.

Part C

Make the figure for each set of directions. Then rewrite the second step so it does not have unnecessary words.

Directions 1

a. Make a vertical line that is one inch long just above the middle of a horizontal line that is one inch long.
b. Make a dot in the middle of the vertical line that is one inch long.

Directions 2

a. Make a vertical line that is one inch long just above a vertical line that is one half inch long.
b. Make a dot in the middle of the vertical line that is one inch long.

Directions 3

a. Make a vertical line that is one inch long.
b. Make a dot in the middle of the vertical line that is one inch long.

Part D

Follow the rules for the X box. Tell whether each claim is **misleading** or **inaccurate.** Then write a sentence that tells why.

Claim __ states that ______ ________________________,	X	but that claim is __________. [Tell why.]

Claim	Facts
1. New Bumpo cars go farther on a tank of gas.	Distance Bumpo cars go on a tank of gas: New Bumpo – 234 miles Last year's Bumpo – 233 miles
2. New Bumpo cars cost no more than last year's Bumpo cars.	Cost of Bumpo cars: New Bumpo – $9006 Last year's Bumpo – $9000
3. The price of Speedoo bikes has been reduced.	Price of Speedoo bikes: Reduced price – $185 Regular price – $187

Part E For each item, write a specific sentence.

	Sentence	Facts
1.	**After school, they went there.**	They are the girls in our class.
		They went to the new video game arcade.

After school, [who] **went** [where] .

	Sentence	Facts
2.	**It made them laugh.**	Everybody in our class laughed.
		It was the joke that our teacher told.

[What] **made** [who] **laugh**.

	Sentence	Facts
3.	**It had one.**	It was the new car.
		What it had was a powerful engine.

[What] **had** [what] .

Lesson 36

Part A Follow the rules for the X box. Tell whether each claim is **misleading** or **inaccurate.** Then write a sentence that tells why.

Claim __ states that ______ ________________________,	but that claim is __________. [Tell why.]

Claim	Facts
1. New Bumpos cost less than last year's Bumpos.	New Bumpos – $12,000 Last year's Bumpos – $12,000
2. Speedoo bikes go much faster than Thrill bikes. 3. Thrill bikes go slower than Speedoo bikes.	Speedoo – 41 miles per hour Thrill – 40 miles per hour

Part B Write a summary sentence for each item.

Sample Item: Billy said, "I worked late on Monday, Thursday and Sunday."

1. Anna said, "I saw a robin, a pigeon, a bluebird, a sparrow and a crow."
2. Donna said, "My mother collected leaves from an oak, from a maple, from a redwood and from a fir."
3. Fran said, "My brother picked a rose, a lily and a tulip."

Part C

Sample Argument: You should eat fruit every day.
Watermelon is a fruit.
Therefore, you should eat watermelon every day.

Other conclusions are possible because watermelon is not the only fruit.

Argument 1: You should visit a city.
Dallas is a city.
Therefore, you should visit Dallas.

Other conclusions are possible because ____________.

Argument 2: You should learn a foreign language.
Chinese is a foreign language.
Therefore, you should learn Chinese.

Other conclusions are possible because ____________.

Argument 3: Everybody should have a pet.
Turtles are pets.
Therefore, everybody should have a turtle.

Other conclusions ____________________.

Part D

Write sentences that give a specific number for the claims.

Claim	Fact
Sample: Dino skates cost less than \$30.	Cost of Dino skates: \$29.99
1. Creamo paints dry in less than 12 hours.	Time it takes Creamo paints to dry: 11 hours and 50 minutes
2. Speedoo bikes weigh less than 40 pounds.	Weight of Speedoo bikes: $39\frac{1}{2}$ pounds
3. You can buy new hit tapes for less than \$25.	Cost of new hit tapes: \$24.99

Part E

Rewrite each step b so it does not have unnecessary words.

Directions 1

Step a. Make a letter **H** so that all the lines are one inch long.
Step b. Make a dot in the middle of the horizontal line that is one inch long.

Directions 2

Step a. Make a horizontal line that is one inch long.
Step b. Make a dot in the middle of the horizontal line that is one inch long.

Directions 3

Step a. Make a horizontal line one inch long just to the right of a horizontal line one half inch long.
Step b. Make a dot in the middle of the horizontal line that is one inch long.

Part F

Write an argument that starts out the same way as the argument below but draws a different conclusion.

Argument: You should use a toothpaste that fights cavities.
Sparko toothpaste fights cavities.
Therefore, you should use Sparko toothpaste.

Lesson 37

Part A Write sentences with the word **only** to tell why each claim is misleading.

Claim	Fact	Sentence
1. H-Mart stores give away free shoes.	These stores are in Alaska.	The only H-Mart stores that give away free shoes . . .
2. You can rent movies for half price.	These movies are more than 20 years old.	The only movies that you can rent for half price . . .
3. You can feed animals at Metro Zoo.	These animals are skunks.	The only animals that you can feed at Metro Zoo . . .

Part B Rewrite each step b so it does not have unnecessary words.

Directions 1

a. Make a vertical line that is half an inch long just to the right of a vertical line that is one inch long.

b. Make a dot just below the vertical line that is half an inch long.

Directions 2

a. Make an **L** so that both lines are half an inch long.

b. Make a dot just below the vertical line that is half an inch long.

Directions 3

a. Make a vertical line that is half an inch long.

b. Make a dot just below the vertical line that is half an inch long.

Part C

For some summaries, you have to be careful with the number.

- Here's what Mrs. Jones said:

  "I bought potatoes, carrots and tomatoes at the market."

- Here's a summary that may be confusing:

  Mrs. Jones said that she bought three vegetables at the market.

- She said that she bought potatoes. That means she bought more than one potato. She bought more than one carrot and more than one tomato.

You can summarize the sentences accurately by using the words **kinds of** or **types of.**

- Here are two good summaries:

  Mrs. Jones said that she bought three types of vegetables.

  Mrs. Jones said that she bought three kinds of vegetables.

- Remember, if the number may be confusing, use the words **kinds of** or **types of** to keep the summary accurate.

Part D

Write a summary sentence for each item.

1. Ben said, "I played with pigs. I played with horses. I played with cows."
2. A TV commercial said, "People are buying boats, cars, pickups and motorcycles at great savings."
3. Dan said, "I collect old pennies. I collect old dimes."

Part E For each argument, write a sentence that explains why the argument is faulty. Start the sentence with the words: **Other conclusions are possible because.**

Argument 1: The voters in Billtown should elect an honest person for mayor.
Jim Gardner is an honest person.
Therefore, the voters in Billtown should elect Jim Gardner for mayor.

Argument 2: People who love the outdoors should own a good truck.
Thumpo is a good truck.
Therefore, people who love the outdoors should own a Thumpo.

Part F Follow the rules for the X box. Tell whether each claim is **misleading** or **inaccurate.** Then write a sentence that tells why.

Claim __ states that ______ ________________________,	but that claim is __________. [Tell why.]

Claim	Fact
1. Creamo Supreme costs less than $15 a gallon.	Cost of Creamo Supreme per gallon: $15.88
2. A Tropic Fun vacation lasts more than three weeks.	How long a Tropic Fun vacation lasts: 21 days and 1 hour
3. A Dreamland vacation lasts more than three weeks.	How long a Dreamland vacation lasts: 20 days

Part G Write an argument that starts out the same way as the argument below but draws a different conclusion.

Argument: You should play a ball game.
Soccer is a ball game.
Therefore, you should play soccer.

Lesson 38

Part A

Follow the rules for the X box. Tell whether each claim is **misleading** or **inaccurate.** Then write a sentence that tells why.

Claim __ states that ______ ____________________________,	but ____________________. [Tell why.]

Claim	Fact
1. Creamo Supreme dries in less than 8 hours.	Time to dry: 7 hours 55 minutes
2. Creamo Supreme costs much less than $5 a pint.	Cost: $4.98 a pint
3. A pint of Creamo Supreme covers 100 square feet.	Area covered by a pint: 68 square feet

Part B

Rewrite each step b so it does not have unnecessary words.

Directions 1

a. Make an **H** with vertical lines one inch long and a horizontal line one inch long.

b. Make a dot just to the right of the horizontal line that is one inch long.

Directions 2

a. Make a **C** that is backward just below an **A.**

b. Make a **B** just to the left of the **C** that is backward.

Part C

Write sentences that start with the words **The only.** Tell why each claim is misleading.

Claim	Fact
1. Bumpos have a free sunroof.	These Bumpos cost $65,000.
2. Riders went 65 miles per hour.	These riders were going downhill.
3. NC houses cost less than $20,000.	These houses are the size of a garage.

Part D

Write a summary sentence for each item.

1. Mrs. Taylor said, “James got an A in math, reading, science and social studies.”
2. Mr. Jackson said, “I repair fire trucks, pickup trucks, garbage trucks and delivery trucks.”
3. The advertisement was in the paper Wednesday, Friday and Saturday.
4. Apples, bananas, pears, oranges and grapefruits were on sale.

Part E

Here's a new kind of X box:

Argument __ concludes that ______________.	Other conclusions are possible ______________.

The letters **OC** in the middle show you that the X box will tell about other conclusions. That's what **OC** stands for: **O**ther **C**onclusions.

You start your X box by telling what the argument concludes. You write a **period.** Then you write a sentence that tells about other conclusions. Other conclusions are possible because . . .

Argument 1: You should vacation in a place with sandy beaches.
Florida is a place with sandy beaches.
Therefore, you should vacation in Florida.

Argument 2: All children should play a musical instrument.
The piano is a musical instrument.
Therefore, all children should play the piano.

Part F Write general directions for each item. Write specific directions for making the first figure shown in each item.

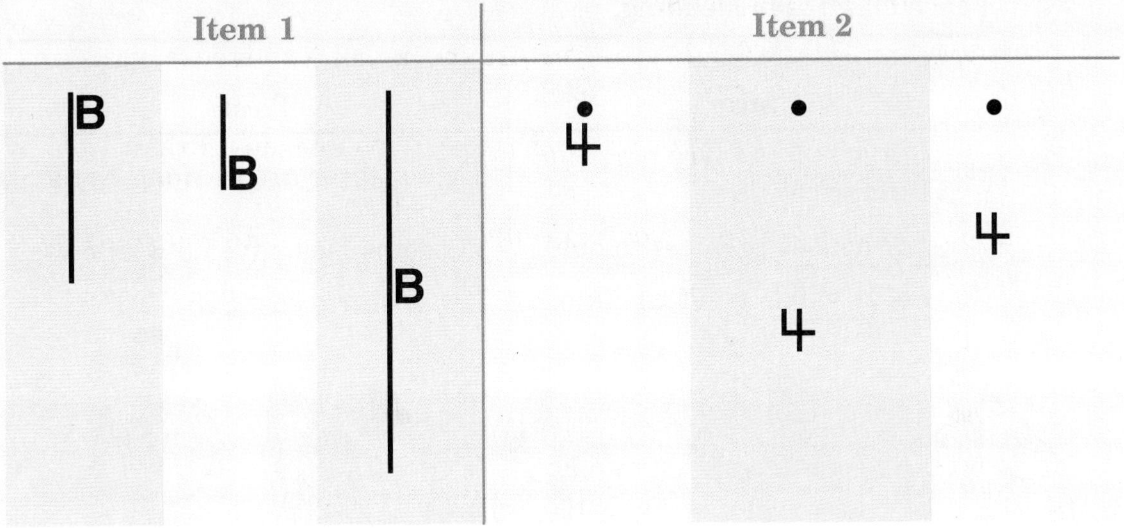

Item 1	Item 2
B B B	• 4 • 4 • 4

Lesson 39

Part A Write sentences that start with the words **The only.** Tell why each claim is misleading.

Claim	Fact
1. Large stores carry parts for Bumpo cars.	These stores are in Hong Kong.
2. NC houses cost less to heat.	These houses have no windows.
3. Sassy shirts don't wrinkle.	These shirts cost $75.

Part B Rewrite any step that has a problem.

Directions	Figure
1. a. Make a circle that is one inch wide. b. Make a dot in the middle of the circle. c. Make an **R** just above the dot in the middle of the circle.	R
2. a. Make a circle that is one inch wide. b. Make a dot in the middle of the circle. c. Make the letter just above it.	
3. a. Make a circle that is one inch wide. b. Make a dot in the middle of the circle that is one inch wide. c. Make an **R** just above the dot.	

Part C

For each argument, write the sentences for the X box.

Argument __ concludes that ______________________.	**OC** X	______________ are possible because ______________________.

Argument 1: You should eat fruit with every meal.
Grapefruit is a fruit.
Therefore, you should eat grapefruit with every meal.

Argument 2: You should do things to save energy.
Shutting off your furnace is a way to save energy.
Therefore, you should shut off your furnace.

Part D

Write a summary sentence for each item.

1. Jane said, "I saw eagles and hawks."
2. In Burtown it is cold during October, November, December, January, February, March and April.
3. Mr. Jones, Mr. Torres and Mr. Anderson rescued Baby Sarah.

Part E

Follow the rules for the X box. Tell whether each claim is **misleading** or **inaccurate.** Then write a sentence that tells why.

Claim __ states that ______ ______________________,	X	but______________________. [Tell why.]

Claim	Facts
1. Speedoo bikes go more than 40 miles per hour.	Speed of bikes: Speedoo – 40 miles per hour Dino – 39 miles per hour
2. Speedoo bikes go faster than Dino bikes.	
3. Dino bikes go much slower than Speedoo bikes.	

Part F

Rewrite each item so it is clear and specific.

1. The store is on Main Street.
2. The factory is next to the store.
3. Mary's house is between two of them.

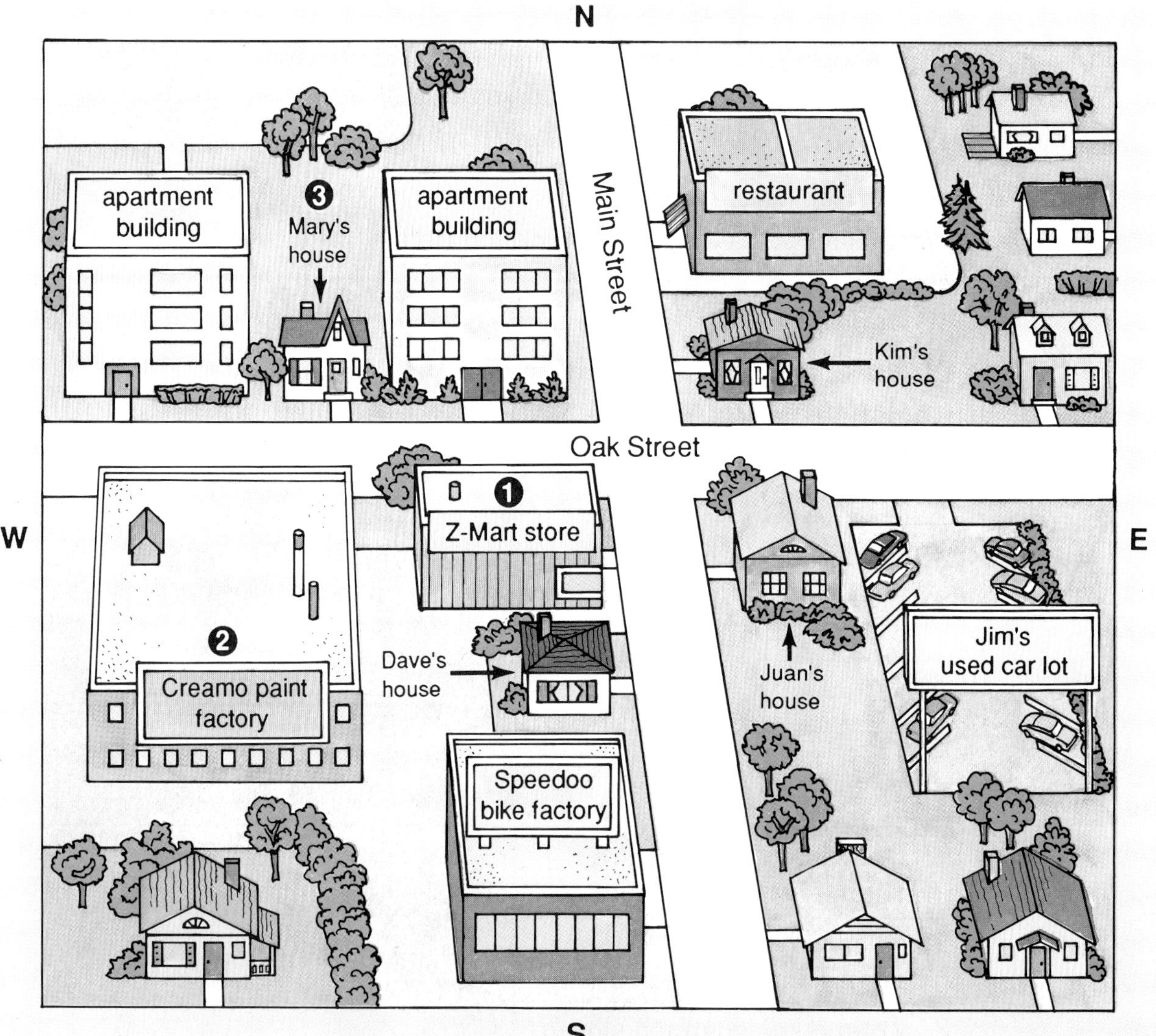

Write a story about the first picture, the missing picture and the last picture.

Rules:

1. Write one paragraph for each picture.
2. For the first picture, tell who had the problem and what the problem was. Give the facts the reader needs to get a clear picture. Write a sentence that tells the exact words Carlos said.
3. For the missing picture, write a paragraph that tells all the things that Carlos and Nelson must have done to solve their problem.
4. For the last picture, tell how the story ended. Tell what the last picture shows. Write a sentence that tells the exact words Mrs. Nolasco said.

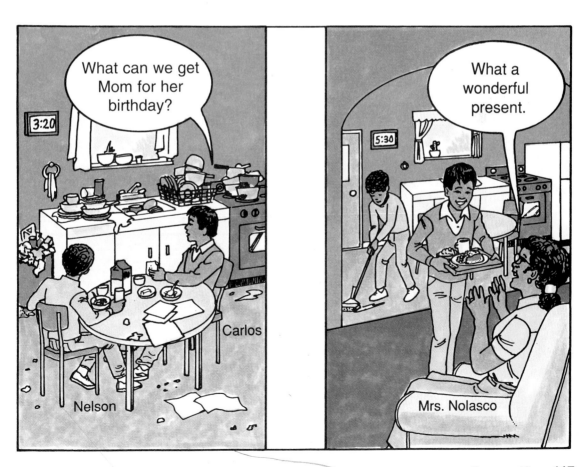

What can we get Mom for her birthday?
3:20
Carlos
Nelson

What a wonderful present.
5:30
Mrs. Nolasco

Test 4

Part A

Follow the rules for the X box. Tell whether the claim is **misleading** or **inaccurate.** Then write a sentence that tells why.

The claim states that _____ ____________________,	X	but that claim is __________. [Tell why.]

Claim	Fact
Snappy apple juice costs much less than $5.00 a gallon.	Cost of Snappy apple juice: $4.99 a gallon

Part B

Directions

a. Make a vertical line that is one inch long.
b. Make a dot in the middle of the vertical line that is one inch long.

Part C

1. Mrs. Perez said, "I took pictures of robins, bluebirds and eagles."
2. Mr. Hale said, "I went fishing on Friday, Saturday and Sunday."

Part D

For each argument, write a sentence that explains why the argument is faulty. Start the sentence with the words: **Other conclusions are possible because.**

Argument 1: Children should play a team sport.
Volleyball is a team sport.
Therefore, children should play volleyball.

Argument 2: Parents should drive safe cars.
A Bumpo is a safe car.
Therefore, parents should drive a Bumpo.

Lesson 41

Part A

Claim	Fact
a. Z-Brand insurance costs only pennies a day.	The insurance costs $2.00 a day.
b. A vacation at Cat's Mountain is an experience.	The experience is horrible.

Write **true** or **false.**

Claim	Fact
1. Creamo paint dries in less than 24 hours.	Time it takes paints to dry: Creamo – 24 hours Splatto – 28 hours
2. Splatto paint takes longer to dry than Creamo paint.	
3. Creamo Supreme dries in minutes.	Time it takes Creamo Supreme to dry: 300 minutes
4. Creamo Supreme dries in less than 300 minutes.	
5. You'll lose pounds on a Blimpo diet.	Pounds you'll lose each week on a Blimpo diet: 2 pounds
6. You'll lose 5 pounds every week on a Blimpo diet.	

Part B

Write sentences that start with the words **The only.** Tell why each claim is **misleading**.

Claim	Fact
1. People lost 20 pounds in one week.	These people weighed more than 400 pounds.
2. People earn $500 a week selling Sticko candy.	These people work 12 hours a day.
3. Test drivers prefer Bumpo cars.	These test drivers work for the Bumpo Car Company.

Part C

Write a summary sentence for each item.

1. Mr. Smith made a phone call to his wife, a phone call to his friend Jim, a phone call to the doctor, a phone call to his mother and a phone call to Mrs. Grady.
2. The store on the corner sells chairs, tables and beds.
3. Fran said, "I had quarters, nickles, dimes and half dollars."

Part D

Follow the rules for the X box. Tell whether each claim is **misleading** or **inaccurate.** Then write a sentence that tells why.

Claim __ states that ______ ____________________________,	but ____________________. [Tell why.]

Claim	Facts
1. Seemore TVs cost a lot less than Tyrone TVs.	Cost of TVs: Seemore TVs – $299 Tyrone TVs – $300
2. Seemore TVs cost much less than $300.	
3. Tyrone TVs cost more than Seemore TVs.	

Part E

Rewrite each step that has a problem.

Directions	Figure
Directions 1 a. Make a square one inch high. b. Make a dot in the middle of the right line. c. Make a **J** just left of the dot.	
Directions 2 a. Make a square one inch high. b. Make a dot in the middle of the bottom line. c. Make a **J** just left of the dot in the middle of the bottom line.	J•
Directions 3 a. Make a square one inch high. b. Make a dot in the middle of the bottom line. c. Make a letter just left of it.	

Part F For each argument, write the sentences for the X box.

Argument __ concludes that ________________________.	OC ✕	________________ because ________________________.

Argument 1: You should study a foreign language.
French is a foreign language.
Therefore, you should study French.

Argument 2: All children should eat a lot of food that is good for them.
Spinach is a food that is good for them.
Therefore, all children should eat a lot of spinach.

Part G The sentences are supposed to tell about the picture, but the sentences are too general. Rewrite each sentence so it is **specific** and **accurate.**

1. They sat on it.
2. They stood next to the barn.
3. They were in the barn.

Lesson 42

Part A

Write sentences to tell why each claim is misleading. Use the word **only.**

Claim	Fact
1. You'll save when you buy a new Bumpo car.	How much you'll save: $7.00
2. Zappo batteries last for months.	How long the batteries last: two months.
3. Dentists prefer Tino toothpaste.	These dentists are over 85 years old.
4. Athletes prefer Tino toothpaste.	These athletes are not experts on dental care.

Part B

Maps are usually shown with north at the top. When north is at the top, south is at the bottom. West is on the left. East is on the right.

When something moves on a map, its direction is the side of the map it approaches.

- This arrow shows something moving west on a map.

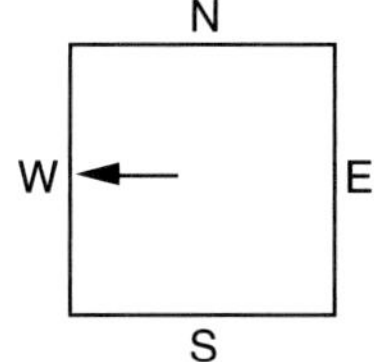

- This arrow shows something moving east.

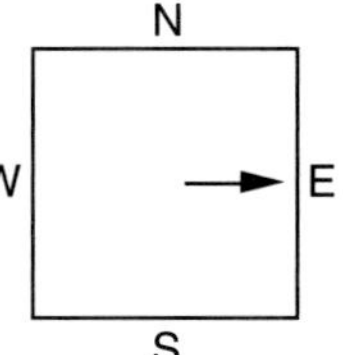

- This arrow shows something moving north.

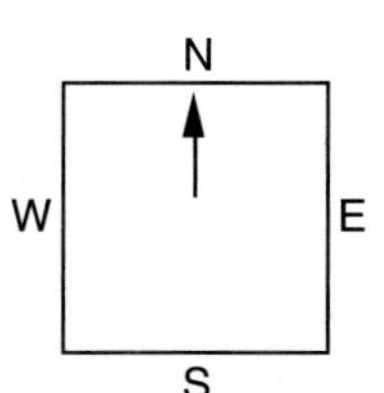

Part C

- Descriptions are general if they could tell about more than one thing. Descriptions are specific if they tell about only one thing.
- Here's a map:

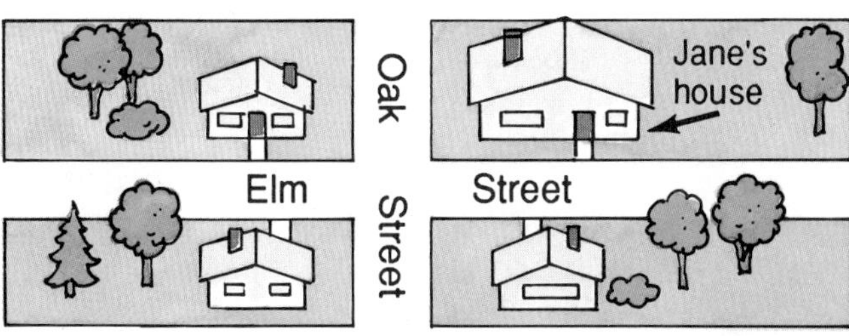

- Here's a statement about Jane's house on the map: **Jane's house is on the corner.** The statement could tell about more than one house. So the statement is **general.**
- Here's another statement about Jane's house: **Jane's house is the big house on the corner of Elm and Oak.** That statement could tell about only one house. So the statement is **specific.**
- Remember, if the statement could tell about more than one house, the statement is general.

Part D

Write the letter of each house each description tells about.

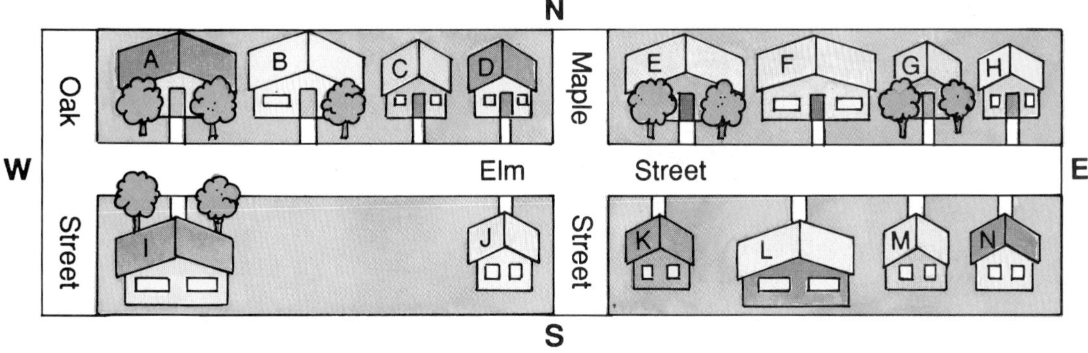

1. Bill's house is on the corner of Elm and Maple.
2. Bill's house is a big house on the north side of Elm Street.
3. Bill's house has two trees in the front yard.
4. Bill's house is east of Maple Street.
5. Bill's house is the big house on the corner of Elm and Maple.
6. Bill's house is the big house east of Maple with two trees in front.

Part E Write **true** or **false** for each item.

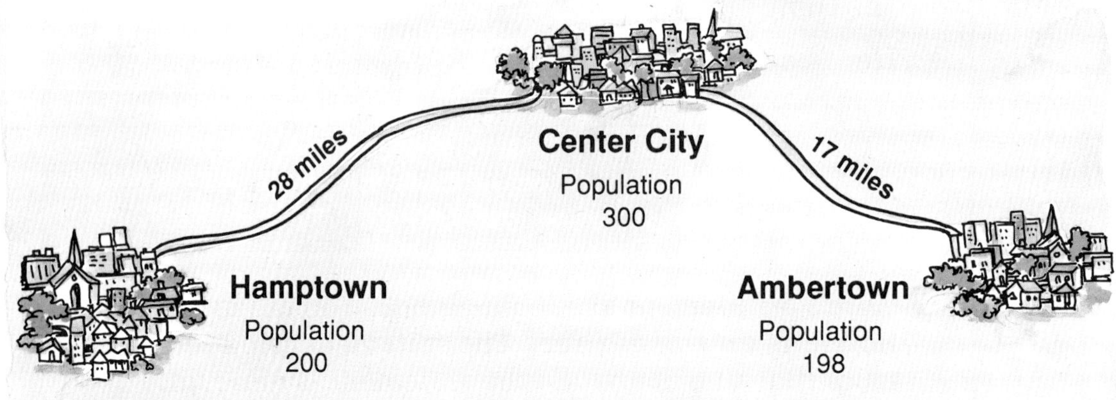

1. Hamptown is only miles from Center City.
2. More than 199 people live in Hamptown.
3. Hamptown has a much larger population than Ambertown.
4. Hamptown is as close to Center City as Ambertown is.
5. Hundreds of people live in Hamptown.
6. Fewer than 198 people live in Ambertown.

Part F Rewrite each step that has a problem.

Directions	Figure
Directions 1 a. Make a line. b. Make it just over it. c. Make a **J** just above the dot that is over the line.	J
Directions 2 a. Make a vertical line one inch long. b. Make a dot just under the vertical line that is one inch long. c. Make it above it.	C

Part G

For each argument, write the sentences for the X box.

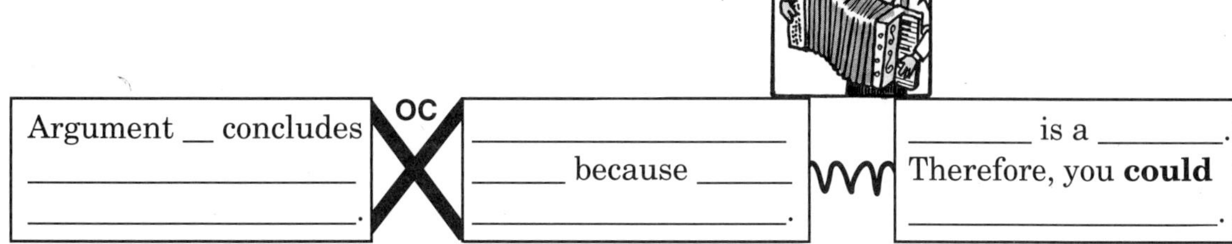

Argument __ concludes
OC
because
is a
Therefore, you could

Argument 1: You should read from a book every day.
A dictionary is a book.
Therefore, you should read from a dictionary every day.

Argument 2: You should eat good food for breakfast.
Liver is good food.
Therefore, you should eat liver for breakfast.

Part H

The sentences are supposed to tell about the picture, but the sentences are too general. Rewrite each sentence so it is **specific** and **accurate.**

1. She waited there.
2. He sat on it.
3. He leaned against it.

Lesson 43

Part A

Follow the rules for the X box. Tell whether each claim is **misleading** or **inaccurate.** Then write a sentence that tells why.

Claim __ states that ______ ______________________________,	but ______________________. [Tell why.]

Claim	Fact
1. Z-Mart stores are open until 9 p.m.	These stores are in Hawaii.
2. Z-Mart stores are giving away free pies.	These stores are in Kansas.
3. Beachfront Lodge is only steps from the ocean.	How far from ocean: about 2000 steps.
4. Freedom Lodge is a very short walk from the ocean.	Distance from ocean: 4 miles.

Part B

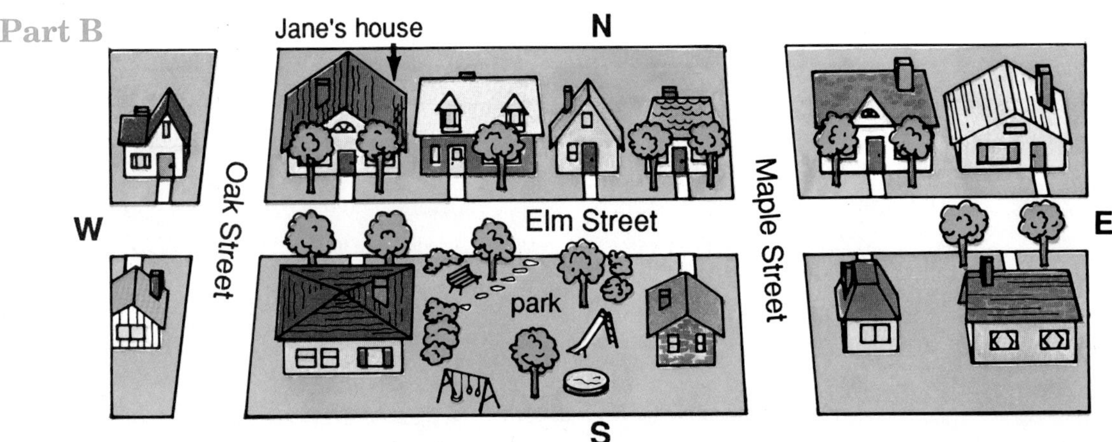

1. Jane's house is a big house on the corner of Elm and Oak.
2. Jane's house is four houses west of Maple Street.
3. Jane's house is west of Maple Street.
4. Jane's house has one tree in the front yard.
5. Jane's house is on the corner.
6. Jane's house is on the northeast corner of Elm and Oak.
7. Jane's house is on the south side of Elm Street.

Part C

Rewrite each step that has a problem.

Directions	Figure
a. Make a square about one inch high. b. Make an **R** on the bottom line. c. Make a dot just above the **R** that is on the bottom line.	

Part D

Write the sentences for the X box and the accordion box.

The argument concludes ____________________ ____________________.	OC	____________________ ____ because ______ ____________________.		______ is a ________. Therefore, you **could** ____________________.

Argument: You should visit a place that is quiet.
The North Pole is a place that is quiet.
Therefore, you should visit the North Pole.

Part E

Write a summary sentence for each item.

1. The president of Bumpo Car Company said, "Bumpo is introducing a new sports model; Bumpo is introducing a new two-door model; Bumpo is introducing a new all-purpose model; Bumpo is introducing a new off-road model."
2. Mary earned money by cleaning yards. Mary earned money by washing cars. Mary earned money by painting the fence.

Lesson 44

Part A

Follow the rules for the X box. Tell whether each claim is **misleading** or **inaccurate.** Then write a sentence that tells why.

Claim __ states that ______ ____________________________,	but ____________________. [Tell why.]

Claim	Fact
1. Metro Zoo is open for hours every day.	Hours for each day: Monday – not open; Tuesday through Sunday – 9 a.m. to 11 p.m.
2. A Dino battery gives you power hour after hour.	Hours a Dino battery lasts: 2
3. Lace Less shoes are on sale for half price.	Lace Less shoes on sale for half price: baby shoes

Part B

1. Directions to Jan's house:
   a. Go north on Main to Oak Street.
   b. Turn west.
   c. Go to the second house on the left.
2. Directions to Fran's house:
   a. Go north to the first corner.
   b. Turn left on the first corner.
   c. Go to the last house on the north side of the street.

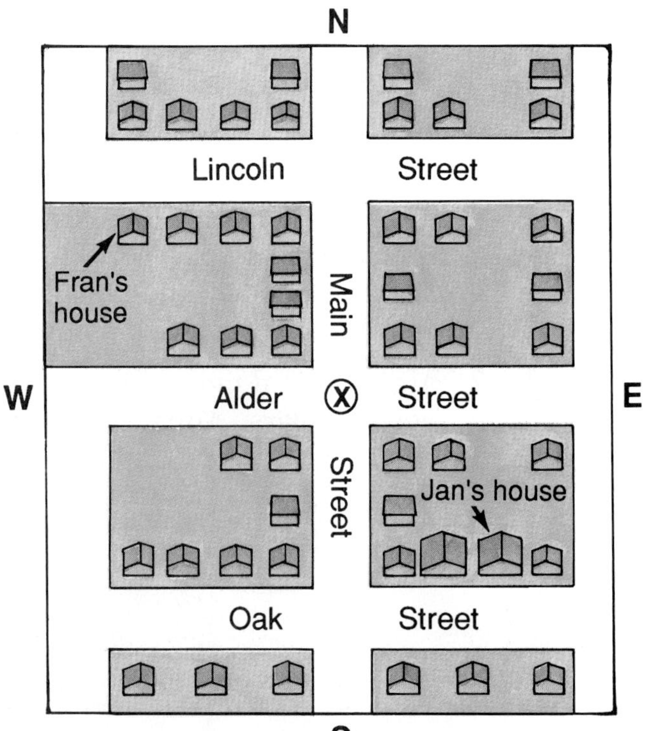

Part C Write the sentences for the X box and the accordion box.

The argument ________ ______________________ ______________________.	OC ✕	______________________ ______________________ ______________________.	∿∿∿	________ are__________. Therefore, people could ______________________.

Argument: People should wear jackets that are brightly colored.
Red jackets are brightly colored.
Therefore, people should wear red jackets.

Part D Write **general** or **specific** for each description.

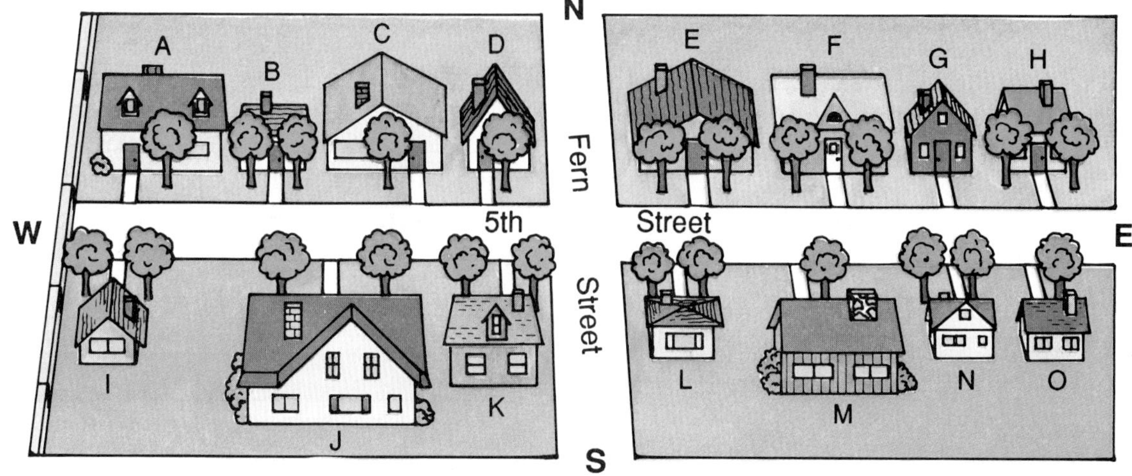

1. Tony's house is a small house.
2. Jan's house has no trees in the front yard.
3. Dan's house is on the corner of Fifth Street and Fern Street.
4. Fran's house is the big house on the west end of Fifth Street.
5. Greg's house is a small house west of Fern Street.
6. Greg's house has one tree in the front yard.

Part E Copy each name below. After each name write the letter of the house the person lives in.

Jan Fran Greg

Part F

- You can figure out missing parts of a deduction by looking at the parts of each statement that are not the same.
- If you combine the parts that are not the same, you'll have the missing part of the deduction.

Windows are things made of glass.

Therefore, windows break.

- Here's the whole deduction:

Windows are things made of glass.
Things made of glass break.
Therefore, windows break.

1. Trucks are vehicles.

   Therefore, trucks move.

2. You should eat the food that has the most fiber.

   Therefore, you should eat Flako.

3. Poodles are dogs.

   Therefore, poodles don't sweat through their skin.

4. People prefer cars with high-performance engines.

   Therefore, people prefer Bumpos.

Part G Write at least three sentences to tell what must have happened in the missing picture.

Part A

New Bumpos cost less than Heapers.

New Bumpos are roomier than Heapers.

BUMPO

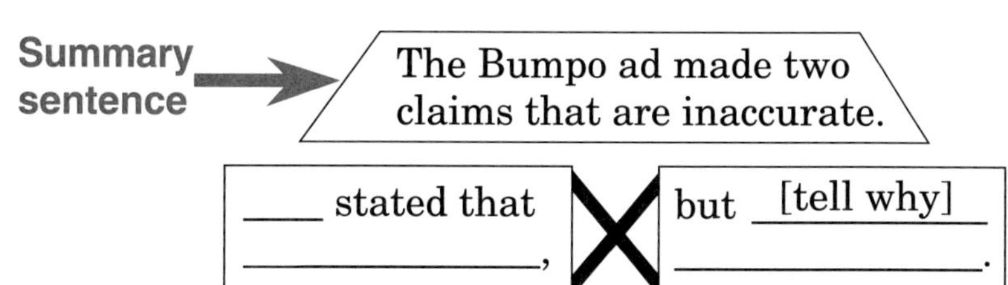

Summary sentence
The Bumpo ad made two claims that are inaccurate.
____ stated that ________________,
but [tell why] ________________.

Part B

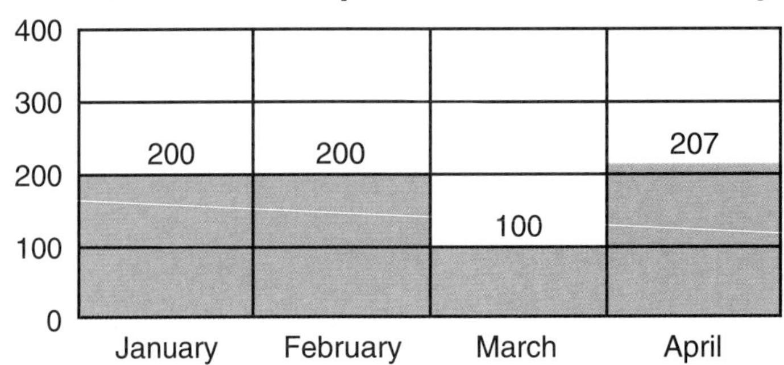

The president of Bumpo made these statements:

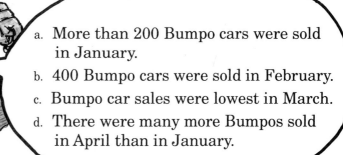

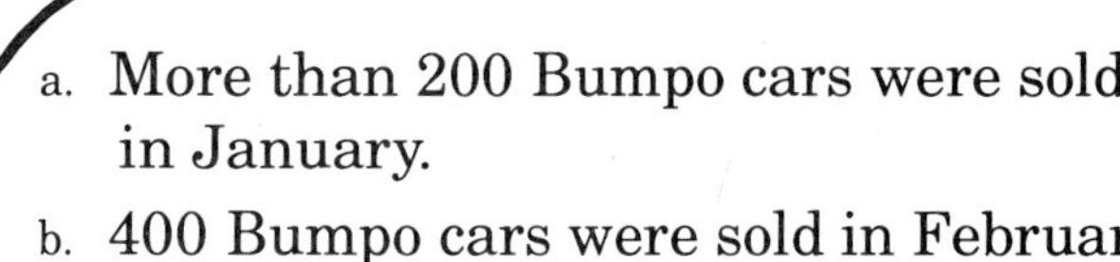

a. More than 200 Bumpo cars were sold in January.
b. 400 Bumpo cars were sold in February.
c. Bumpo car sales were lowest in March.
d. There were many more Bumpos sold in April than in January.

____________ made ___ statements that are inaccurate.

__________ stated that ____________________,	but [tell why] __________________________.

Part C

Write the missing sentence for each deduction.

1. People prefer items that are expensive.

   ____

   Therefore, people prefer Dinto shoes.

2. Every person who works at the spa is in good shape.

   ____

   Therefore, Linda is in good shape.

3. Cars that have a Flub engine break down a lot.

   ____

   Therefore, Bumpos break down a lot.

Part D

Write the sentences for the X box and the accordion box.

The argument ________ ________________ ________________.	OC	________________ ________________ ________________.		________________. Therefore, children **could** ________________.

Argument: Children should make pretty things.
Pictures are pretty things.
Therefore, children should make pictures.

Part E Write clear three-step directions for going to Don's house and to Tina's house.

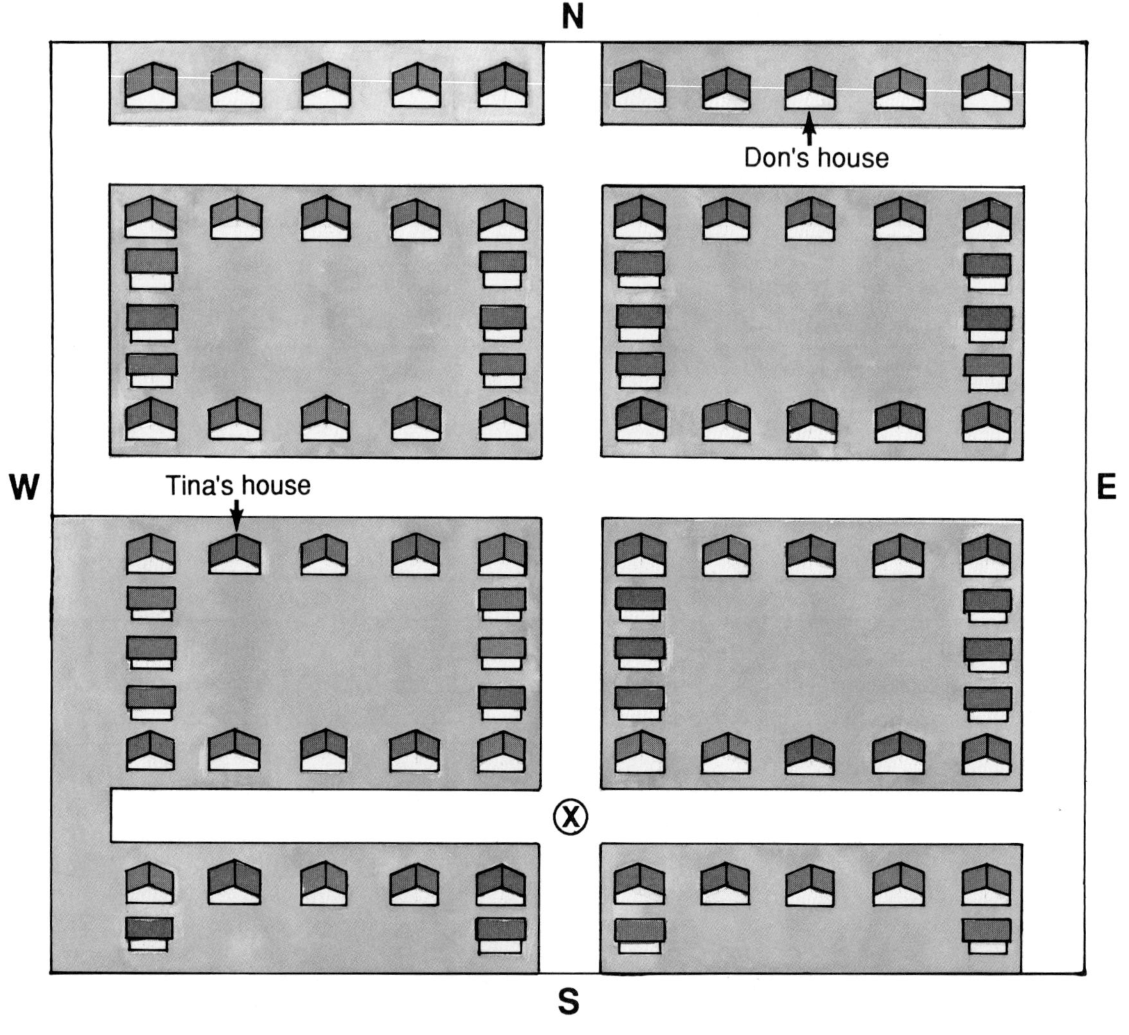

Part F Write a summary sentence for each item.

1. The president of Bumpo said, "Bumpo cars are available in bright red. Bumpo cars are available in bright orange. Bumpo cars are available in bright pink. Bumpo cars are available in bright, bright yellow."
2. Every day the salesman visits grocery stores. Every day he visits department stores. Every day he visits clothing stores.

Part A

- Deductions have sentences that are more **general** and sentences that are more **specific.**
- The **evidence** has a sentence that is more general.
- The **conclusion** has a sentence that is more specific.
- The statement that is more general tells about more things.

- Here are two statements:

Vehicles move. — This statement is **more general.**

Tractors move. — This statement is **more specific.**

- Here are two statements:

Robins have feathers. **Birds have feathers.**

- The more general statement goes in the **evidence.** → **Birds have feathers.**

[Evidence]

- The other statement goes in the **conclusion.** → **Therefore, robins have feathers.**

1. Dogs are warm-blooded. Mammals are warm-blooded.
2. Dogs are warm-blooded. Beagles are warm-blooded.
3. Eagles are warm-blooded. Birds are warm-blooded.

Part B

- Some of the statements below compare something with something else. They tell that one thing is more or less, bigger or smaller, faster or slower, or the same number.
- Some of these sentences do not make comparisons. They don't tell about something being more or less.

a. Bumpo cars hold six people.

b. Bumpo cars hold more people than Dino cars hold.

c. This year's Bumpo cars go just as fast as last year's Bumpos.

d. Bumpos go 130 miles per hour.

e. Bumpo cars go twenty miles an hour faster than Zermo cars.

Part C

Write the number of each sentence that compares.

1. Z-Mart stores carry more shoes than they ever carried.
2. Z-Mart stores carry more shoes than H-Mart stores.
3. You'll find 500 types of greeting cards at Z-Mart.
4. All jackets are priced $12 less than their regular price.
5. Z-Mart is open 12 hours a day.
6. There are 13 Z-Mart stores in this area.

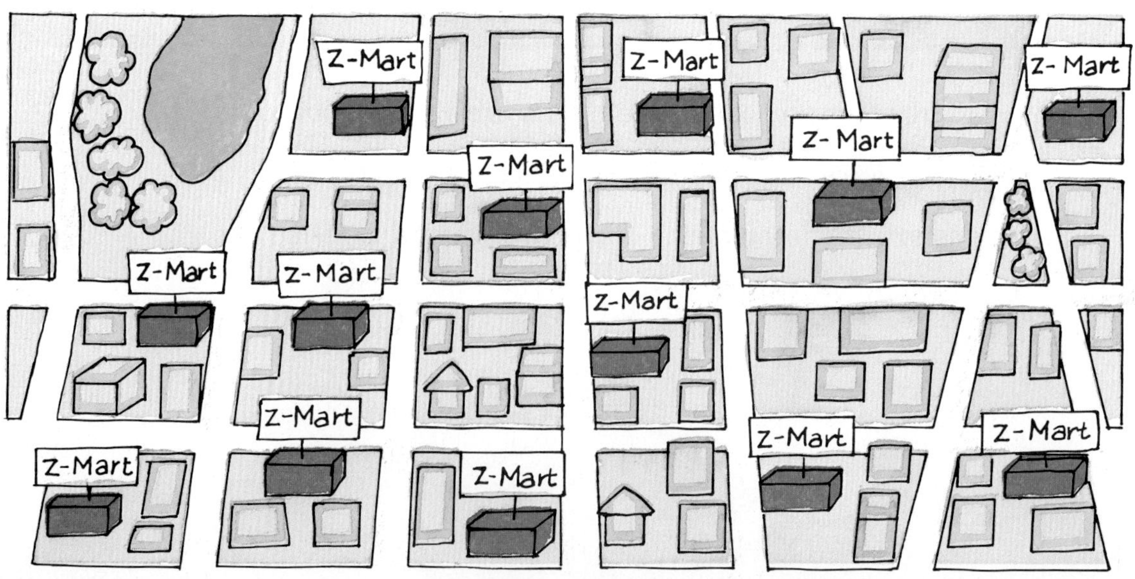

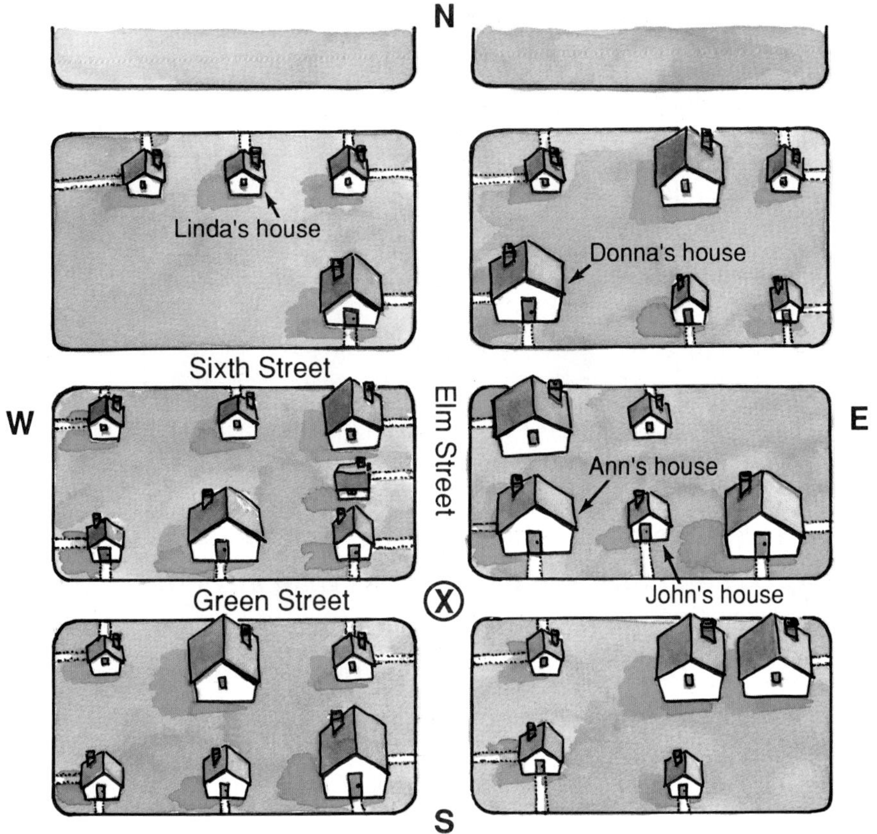

Part D

Follow the rules for the X box and tell about each description.

Description a: Donna's house is on the corner of Sixth and Elm.

Description 1: John's house is between two small houses.

Description 2: Ann's house is on the corner of Green and Elm.

Part E

Write directions for the best way to go from the starting point to Linda's house. Write three sentences.

1. First tell the direction and the distance to go.
2. Then tell which way to turn.
3. Then tell how to go from that corner to Linda's house.

Part F

Number of Games That Different
Baseball Teams Won

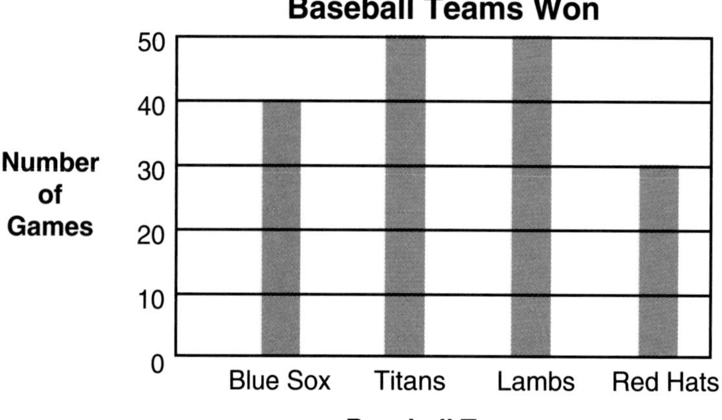

Here are statements from **a newspaper article**:

1. The Titans won more games than any other team.
2. The Blue Sox won 40 games.
3. The Blue Sox won twice as many games as the Red Hats.
4. The Titans and the Lambs won the same number of games.

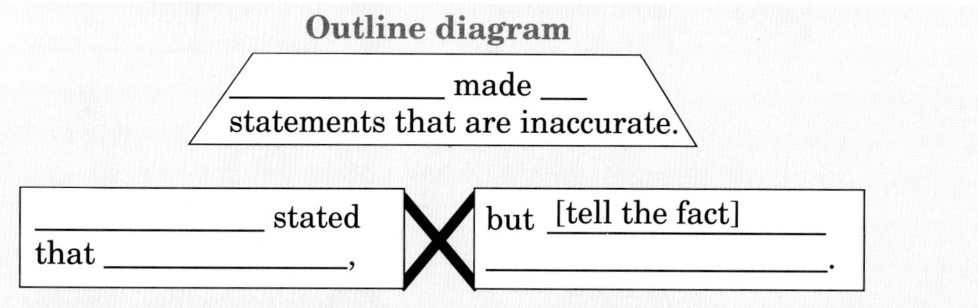

Part G

Write X box sentences to tell about the problem with this deduction.

The argument ________________.

OC ________________.

________ is a ________. Therefore, people could ________.

Argument: People should use a toothpaste that has fluoride.
Glinto is a toothpaste that has fluoride.
Therefore, people should use Glinto.

Lesson 47

Part A For each item, write a sentence that gives specific and accurate information. Use the word **only.**

Claim	Fact
1. Bumpos go miles and miles on a gallon of gas.	How far Bumpos go on a gallon of gas: 4 miles
2. Zee Boo toy cars are guaranteed.	How long cars are guaranteed: 3 days
3. You'll save when you buy Flip shirts on sale.	How much you save: 7 cents
4. Doctors prefer TT vitamins.	These doctors live at the North Pole.

Part B Write directions for the best way to go from the starting point to Ann's house. Write three sentences.

1. First tell the direction and the distance to go.
2. Then tell which way to turn.
3. Then tell how to go from that corner to Ann's house.

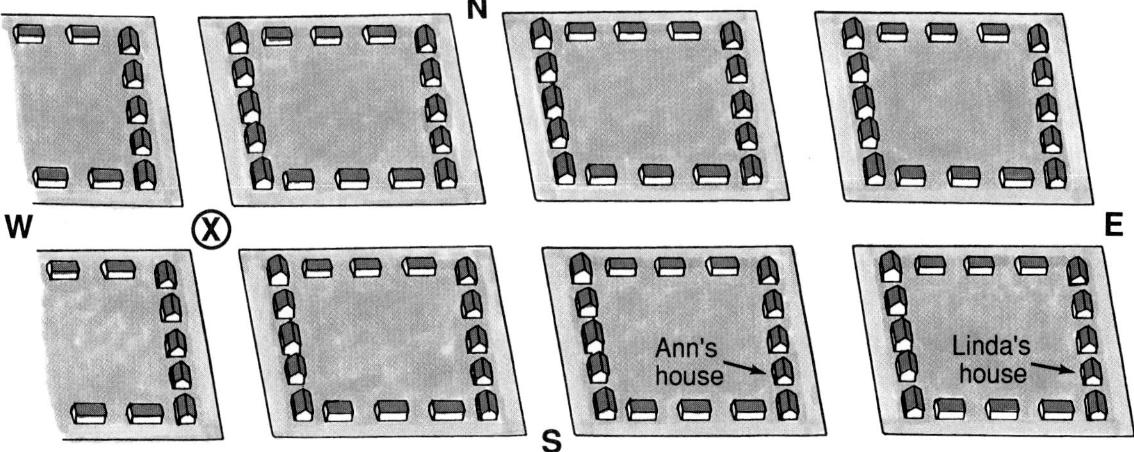

Part C

1. Nancy is nice to her friends. Nancy is nice to Ginger.
2. The weather is nice during October. The weather is nice during the months in the fall.

Part D

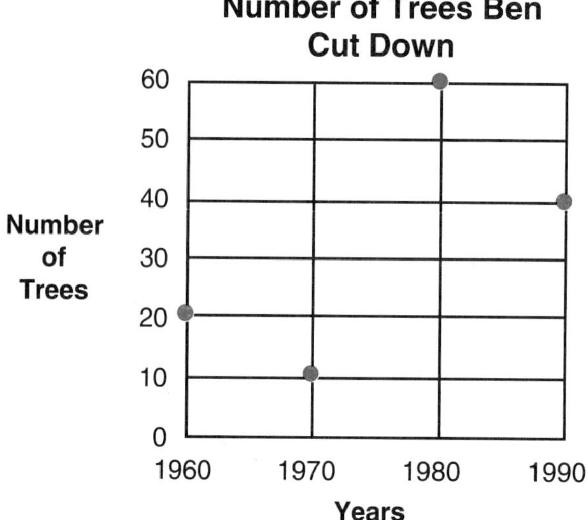

Ben made these statements:

- I cut down 20 trees in 1960.
- I cut down 50 trees in 1970.
- I cut down 60 trees in 1980.
- I cut down more trees in 1980 than in any other year.
- I cut down 10 more trees in 1980 than in 1990.

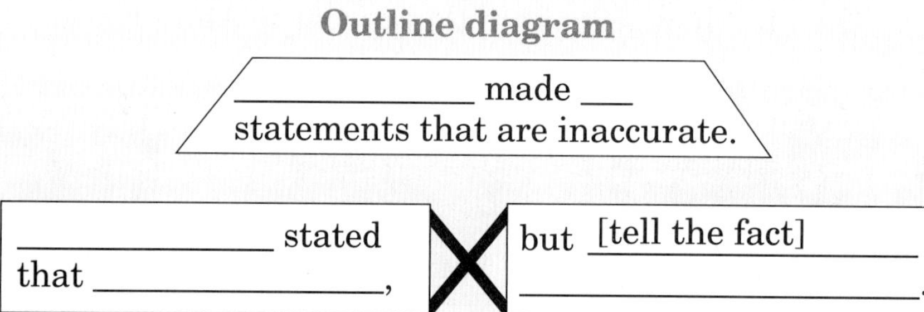

Part E

Lefty's directions	Accurate directions
1. Turn left.	Go straight ahead.
2. Stop.	Go faster.
3. Turn north on Elm.	Turn west on Elm.

Lefty's directions state that you should _______________,	but you should _______________ _______________.

Part F Write the number of each sentence that compares.

1. Zee Boo toys last for years.
2. Zee Boo racers cost $3 less than Dooley racers.
3. Zee Boo toys last longer than they ever did.
4. Zee Boo racers are guaranteed for three years.
5. Zee Boo racers go 200 miles on one battery.
6. Zee Boo racers require fewer repairs than Flash Brand racers.
7. More kids choose Zee Boo racers than any other racers.

Part G Read the directions. Write the letter of each step that has a problem. Rewrite each step that has a problem. Make sure your steps are clear and that they do not have unnecessary words.

Directions	Figure
a. Make a square that is about one inch high. b. Make a dot in the middle of the square that is one inch high. c. Make a backward **J** near the dot that is in the middle of the square that is one inch high.	

Lesson 48

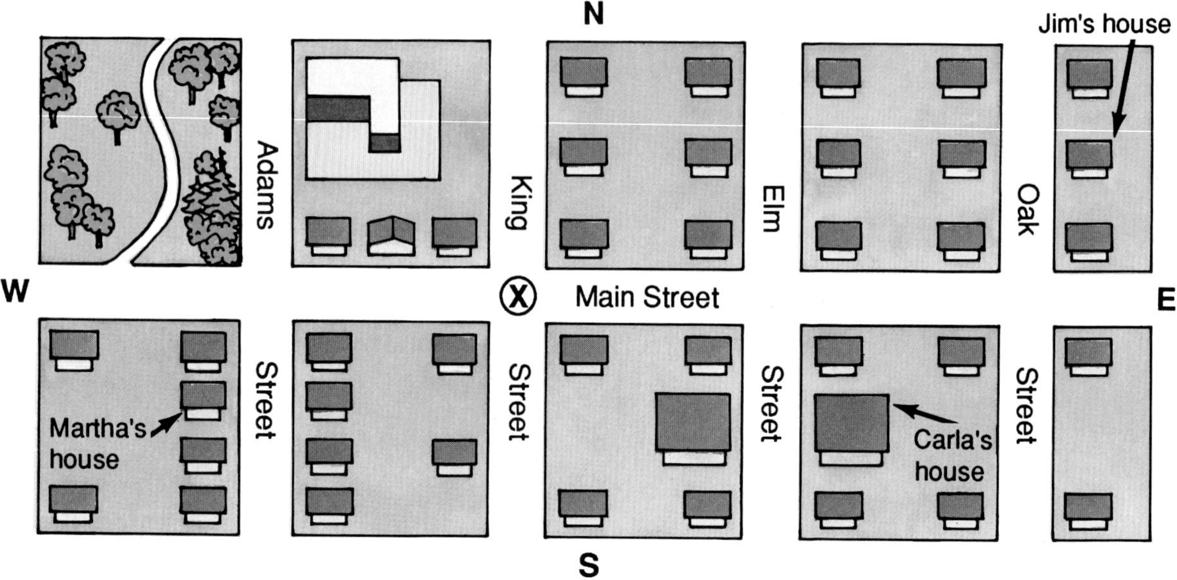

Part A

Tell whether the directions are **inaccurate** or **too general.** Then tell what you should do.

Item 1. Directions to get to Jim's house:
Go east on Main Street.
Turn left at the corner of Main and Elm.
Go to the second house on your right.

Item 2. Directions to get to Carla's house:
Go east on Main Street.
Turn right on Elm Street. Go to the big house.

Item __ states that you should ______________,	but that direction ________. You should ______________.

Part B

Write three-sentence directions for going from the starting point to Martha's house.

1. First tell the direction and the distance to go.
2. Then tell which way to turn.
3. Then tell how to go from that corner to Martha's house.

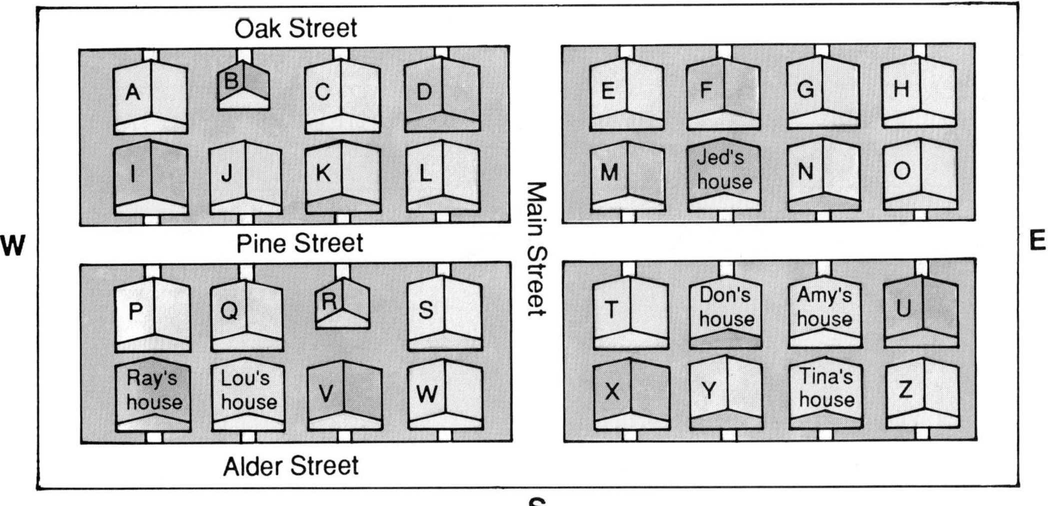

Part C Miss Taylor made these statements:

- Don's house is next door to Amy's house.
- Amy's house is on Oak Street.
- Tina's house is behind Don's house.
- Jed's house is across the street from Don's house.

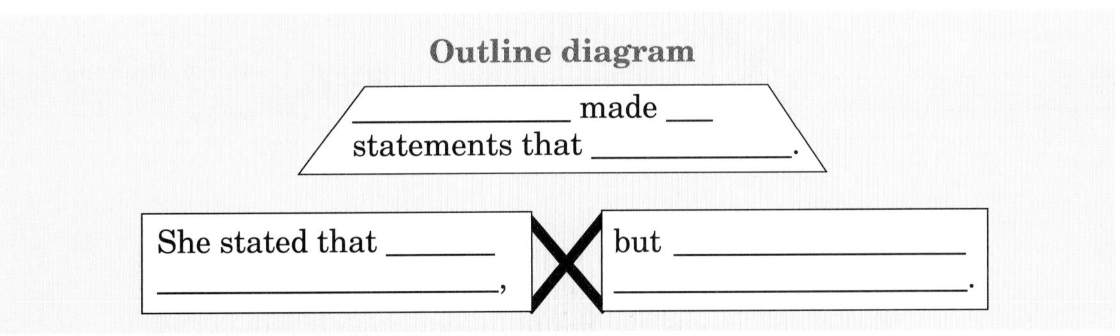

Outline diagram
______ made ___ statements that ______.
She stated that ______ ______,
but ______ ______.

Part D Copy the names: Ted Jill Al Fran Tim.
Write the letter of each person's house.

1. Ted's house is the only small house on Pine Street.
2. Jill's house is the only small house on the street.
3. Al's house is across the street from Amy's house.
4. Fran's house is close to Jed's house.
5. Fran's house is the third house east of the corner.
6. Tim's house is next door to Al's house.

Part E

Lefty's direction	Accurate direction
Go to the second house on the left.	Go to the third house on the right.

Lefty's direction states that you should ______________, ✕ but you should ____________ ____________________________.

Part F

Write the whole deduction.

Jim loves checkers. Jim loves games.

Part G

Write X-box and accordion-box sentences to tell about the problem with this argument.

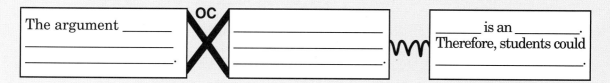

The argument ______ ____________________ ____________________. ✕ (OC) ____________________ ____________________ ____________________. ∿ ______ is an ________. Therefore, students could ____________________.

Argument:

Students should have experiences that are educational.
Working in a coal mine is an educational experience.
Therefore, students should work in a coal mine.

Lesson 49

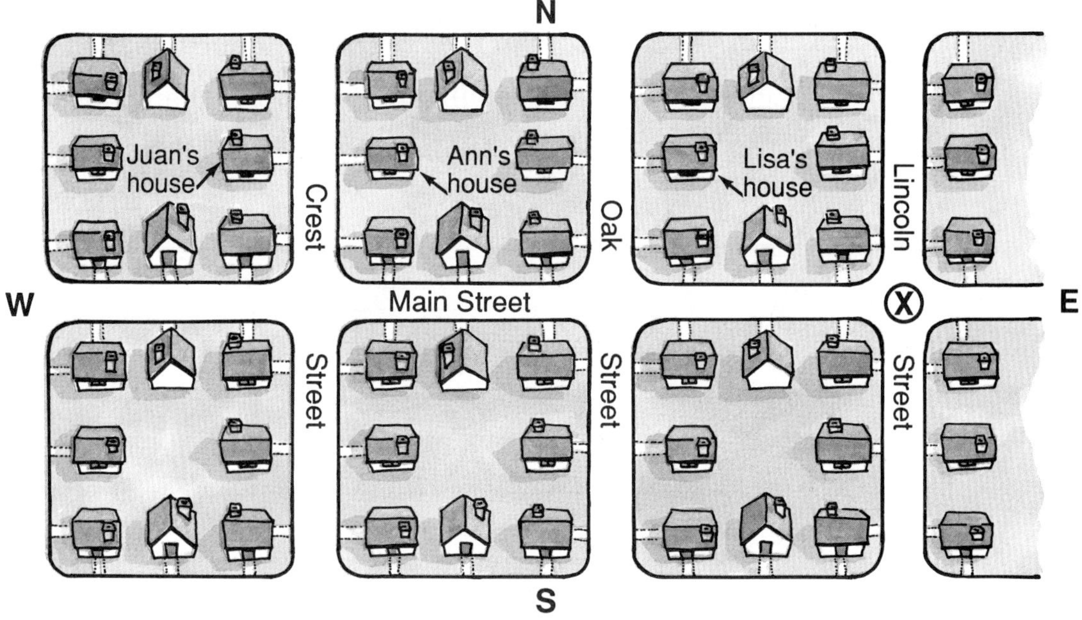

Part A

Tell whether the directions are **inaccurate** or **too general.** Then tell what you should do.

Item 1. Directions to get to Ann's house:
Go east. Turn north at the corner of Main and Crest. Go to the second house on the east side of the street.

Item 2. Directions to get to Juan's house:
Go west on Main Street. Turn right at the corner. Go to the second house on the left.

Item __ states that you should ______________________,	but that direction __________.
	You should ______________.

Part B

Write three-sentence directions for going from the starting point to Lisa's house.

1. Tell the direction and the distance to go.
2. Tell which way to turn.
3. Then tell how to go from that corner to Lisa's house.

Part C

Write the whole deduction for each item.

1. Fomo cleans fast. Any soap that contains pumice cleans fast.
2. Hard stones are formed deep inside the earth. Diamonds are formed deep inside the earth.

Part D

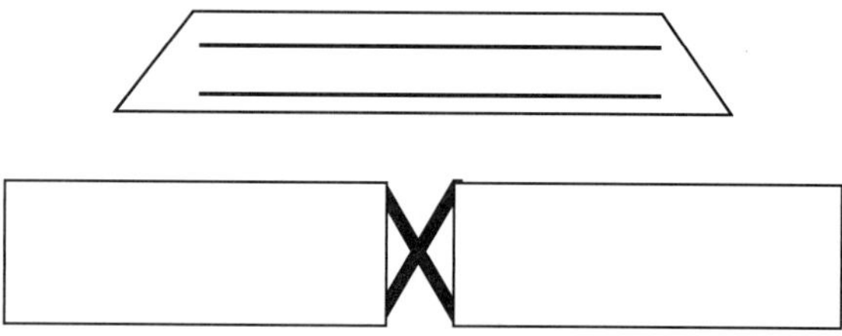

- Here's a new symbol:

- Your source is a graph or a table or a map that gives you accurate information. When there is a source circle behind a summary box, it tells you **to indicate your source.**

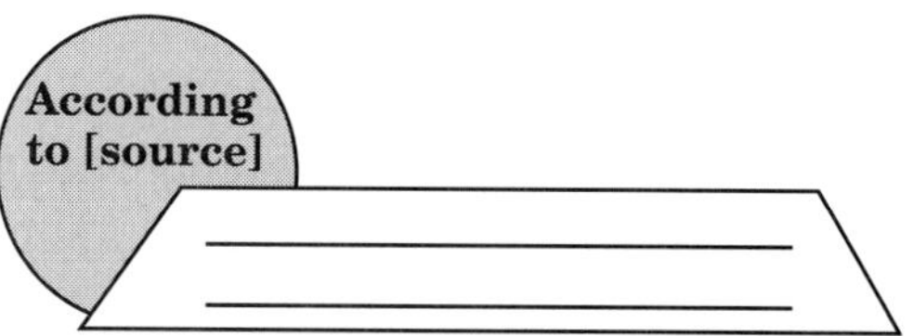

- If you got your facts from a source labelled Graph D7, here's the summary sentence you'd write:

  According to Graph D7, Ben made two statements that are inaccurate.

Part E

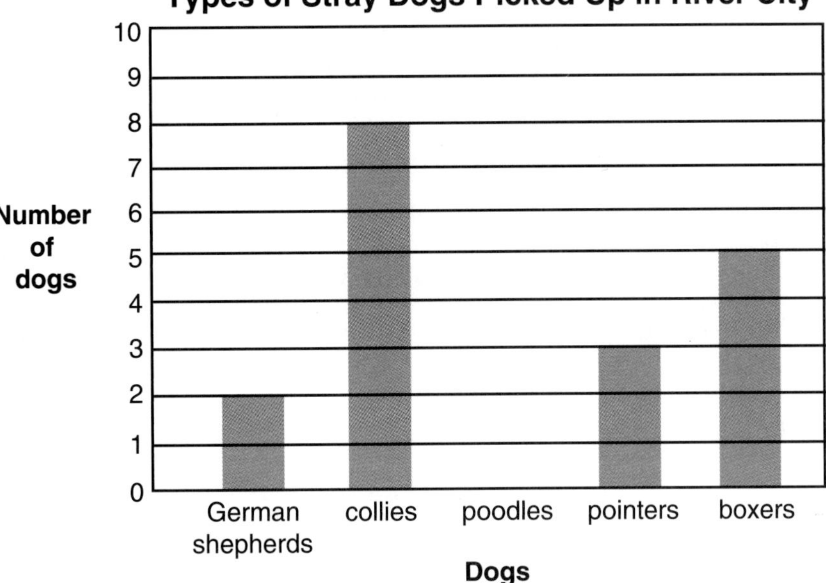

Miss Taylor made these statements:

1. There were three more boxers than pointers.
2. Five boxers were picked up.
3. One German shepherd was picked up.
4. Five types of dogs were picked up.
5. No poodles were picked up.

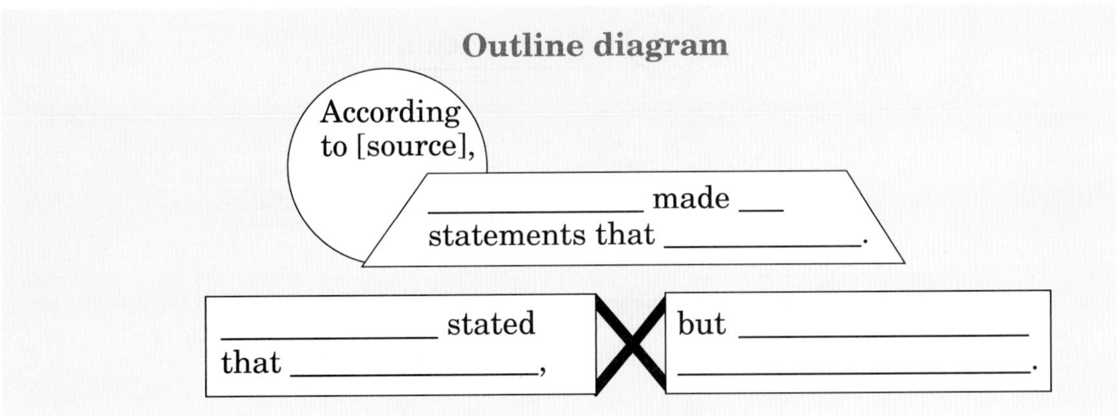

Part F

- Here's a sentence:

She was planting seeds.

That sentence is called a **statement.** It doesn't ask. It tells.

- You can use the same words to make a question:

She was planting seeds.

Was she planting seeds?

The question has the same subject as the statement. And it has the same predicate.

- Here's a different sentence:

That dog was barking loudly.

- The question and the statement have the same subject and the same predicate:

Was that dog barking loudly?

- You can also go the other way and write statements from questions. Here's a question:

Will she go with us?

The subject is **she.** The rest of the sentence is the predicate.

- Here's the statement:

She will go with us.

Part G

1. Were the boys happy when they came home?
2. Are those ducks bigger than chickens?
3. Wasn't your sister crying?
4. Have those horses been running?

Part H

Rules:

1. Write three paragraphs.
2. Set the scene in the first paragraph. Tell who the characters were and where they wanted to go.
3. For your second paragraph, tell what must have happened in the middle picture.
4. For the third paragraph, tell what happened in the last picture. Remember to tell the exact words Liz said.

Part A Rewrite each question as a statement. Then circle the subject and underline the predicate.

1. Was she in good shape for the race?
2. Have those dogs and cats been in the woods all morning?
3. Will the people eat all that food?

Part B Write whether each statement is **general** or **specific.**

Statement 1. Mike's house is on Cherry Street.
Statement 2. Greg's house has two trees in the front yard.
Statement 3. Don's house is the only small house on Cherry Street.
Statement 4. Donna's house is right across the street from Don's house.
Statement 5. Fran's house is the second house from the corner.
Statement 6. Mike's house has one tree in the front yard.
Statement 7. Fran's house is next door to Mike's house.
Statement 8. Greg's house is east of Snow Street.

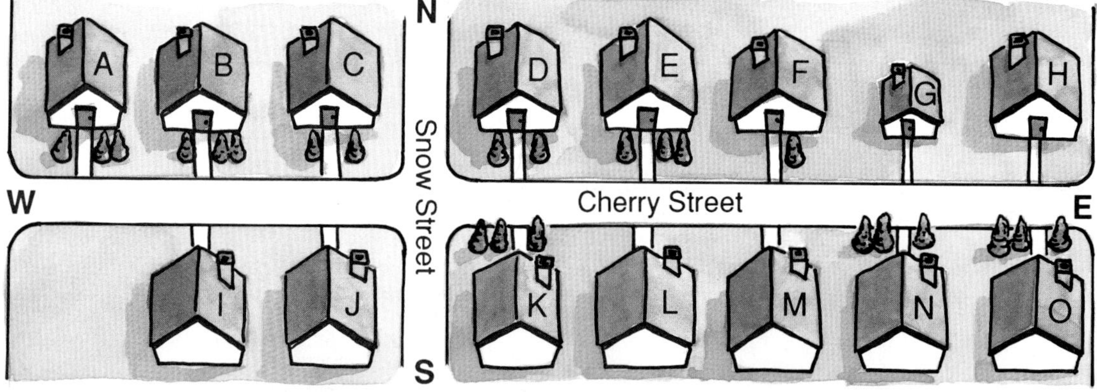

Part C Write simple sentences that tell about the squares and the lines. Begin each sentence with **the square** or **the squares.** End each sentence with **the line** or **the lines.**

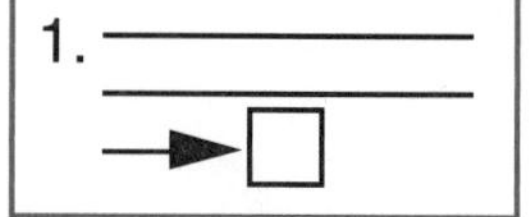

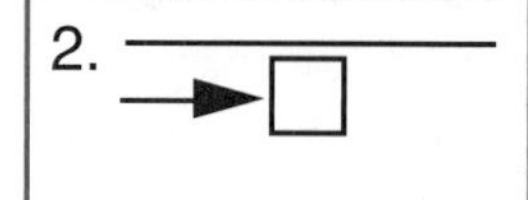

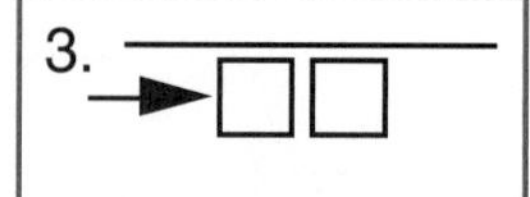

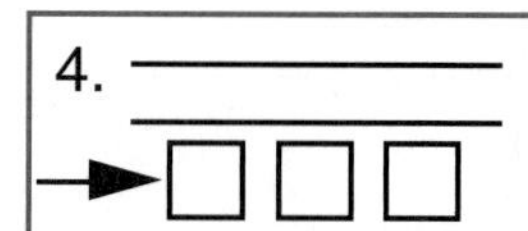

Test 5

Part A Write three-sentence directions for going from the starting point to Kevin's house.

1. Tell the direction and the distance to go.
2. Tell which way to turn.
3. Then tell how to go from that corner to Kevin's house.

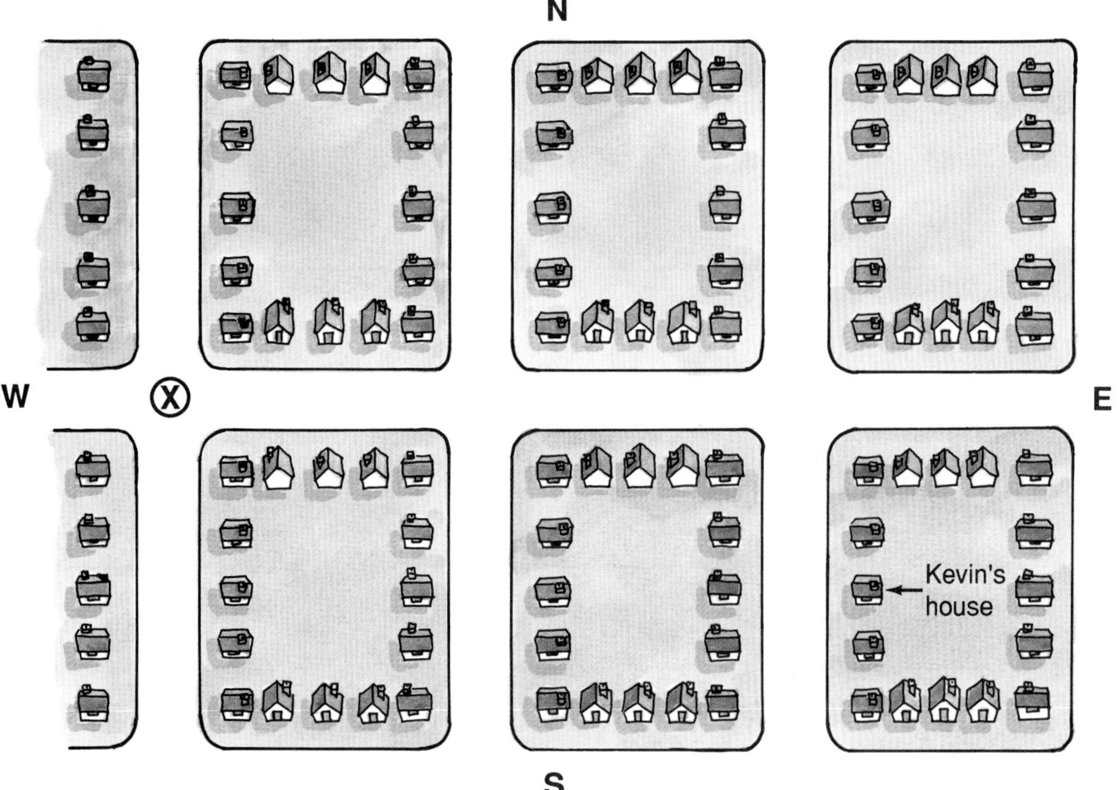

Part B Read the directions. Write the letter of each step that has a problem. Rewrite each step that has a problem. Make sure that your steps are clear and that they do not have unnecessary words.

Directions	Figure
a. Make a square that is one inch high. b. Make a dot just under the middle of the square that is one inch high. c. Make a letter near the dot that is just under the square.	R

Part C Make a complete deduction.

Linda loves all vegetables. Carrots are vegetables.

Part D Write X-box and accordion-box sentences to tell about the problem with this argument.

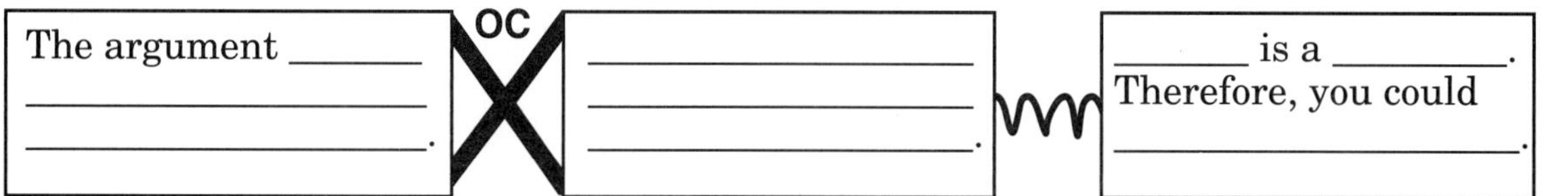

Argument: You should visit a big city.
New York is a big city.
Therefore, you should visit New York.

Lesson 51

Part A

- You've worked with claims that compare. Some of those claims are misleading.
- Sometimes claims that do not compare are misleading.
- Here's a claim that is true: Zee Boo racers go 200 miles on a battery.

  The statement does not tell about a comparison. But when we compare Zee Boo racers with Flash racers, we discover that Flash racers go **600 miles** on a battery.
- Here are the X-box rules for telling about these sentences:

Claim __ states ________________ ________________.	X	That claim is misleading when you compare ______________. [Give specific fact.]

- First indicate the claim: **Claim 1 states that Zee Boo racers go 200 miles on a battery.**

  Next tell about the comparison that makes the claim misleading: **That claim is misleading when you compare Zee Boo racers with Flash racers.**

  Next give the specific fact: **Flash racers go 600 miles on a battery.**

Part B

Claims

1. Bumpo has a 125 horsepower engine.
2. Bumpo gets 26 miles per gallon.

Table D1

Car	Horsepower	Miles per gallon
Bumpo	125	26
Zermo	165	41

Part C

- Some arguments have the conclusion at the beginning, not at the end. Arguments that have the conclusion at the beginning do not start with the word **therefore.** In some arguments, the evidence tells the reasons for the conclusion.
- Here's an argument:

  Panama has warm winters.
  The reason is that Panama is near the equator.
  Countries near the equator have warm winters.
- The first sentence is the conclusion. It is more specific than the sentence: Countries **near the equator** have warm winters.

Write each argument so that it begins with the conclusion.

Argument 1: Poodles are very smart dogs.
Booboo is a poodle.
Therefore, Booboo is a very smart dog.

Argument 2: Jill is good at all sports.
Swimming is a sport.
Therefore, Jill is good at swimming.

Argument 3: Ann can't eat dairy products.
Cheese is a dairy product.
Therefore, Ann can't eat cheese.

Part D

Write an X-box sentence that tells about the problem with each claim.

Claim __ states __________ ______________________,	X	but ______________ ______________________.

Claim	Fact
1. Creamo paint dries in hours.	Time to dry — 75 hours
2. Creamo paint comes in a much larger can.	Can is half filled.

Part E

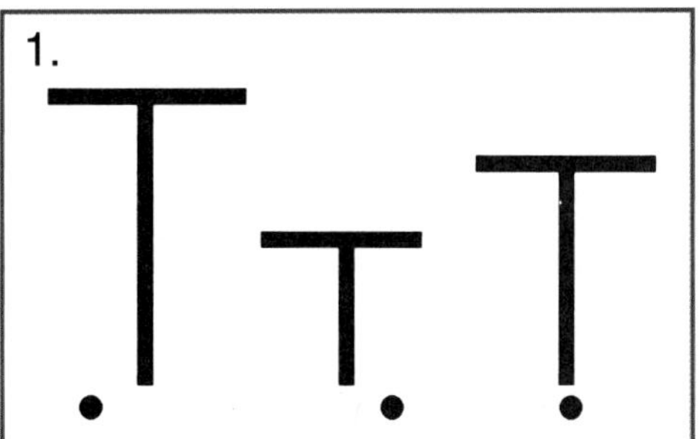

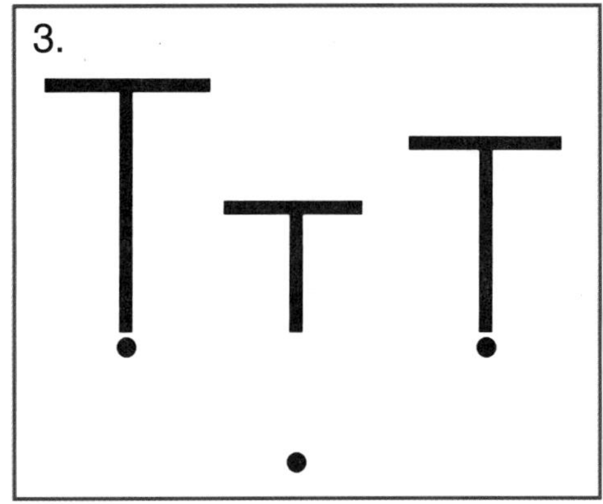

Part F

For each item, the second sentence could have two meanings. Write both meanings. Circle the meaning that you think makes most sense.

1. Vern and his sisters ran from the bees. They were making buzzing sounds.
2. The snow covered the sidewalk. It was white.

Lesson 52

Part A Write the argument so that it begins with the conclusion.

Miami is in Florida.
The weather is very hot in Florida.
Therefore, the weather is very hot in Miami.

Part B

Part C Write a sentence for each diagram. Start with the subject and tell where.

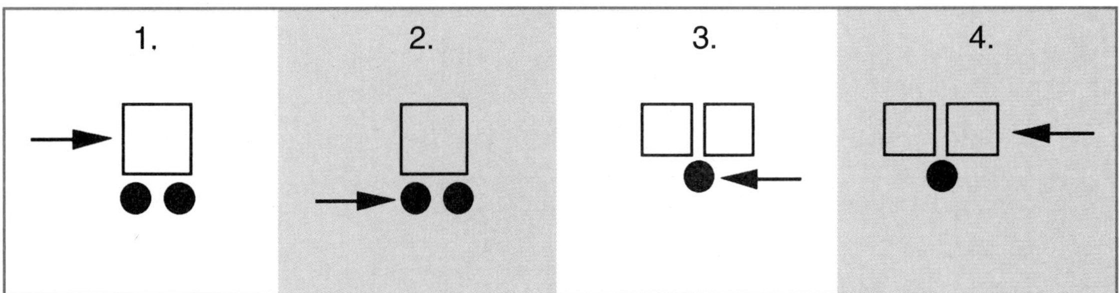

Part D **The EZ Step shoe advertisement made these statements:**

- EZ Step shoes give you the look and feel of leather.
- Even EZ Step shoelaces are parts that are guaranteed.
- EZ Step shoes cost much less than 50 dollars.

Table D2 Facts about EZ Step Shoes

Made of	Price	Parts guaranteed
imitation leather	$21.00	only shoelaces

Outline diagram

According to [source],

the EZ Step ad makes ____ statements that are misleading.

The ad states that _____ _____________________________, but ________________ ___________________________.

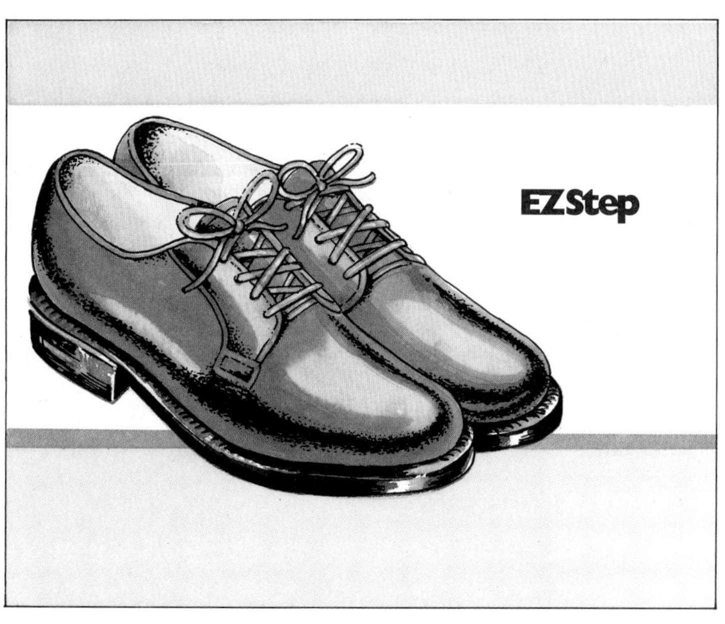

Part E

- Words in sentences have names that tell what parts of speech they are. Every word is a part of speech.
- One part of speech is a **noun.** A noun is the **name** of a person, place or thing.
- You can find nouns in the subjects of sentences. If a subject has more than one word, the last word is almost always a noun.
- Remember, that rule is for subjects with more than one word.
- Here's a sentence with the subject underlined:

N

Five little dogs were playing.

- The last word of the subject is **dogs.** That word is a **noun.**

1. She was very pretty.
2. My mother works hard.
3. An old man sat under a tree.
4. They chased butterflies.
5. The girls in the park were eating lunch.
6. All those bugs ran under her house.

Part F

Write sentences that have the word **who** or **that.** Start each sentence with the words **The only.**

Statement	Fact
1. People enjoyed the movie.	These people did not pay to see it.
2. E-Z shirts will last for years.	These shirts cost $200 each.
3. Athletes recommend Big Top cereal.	These athletes receive money from Big Top.

Lesson 53

Part A

Dino Ad

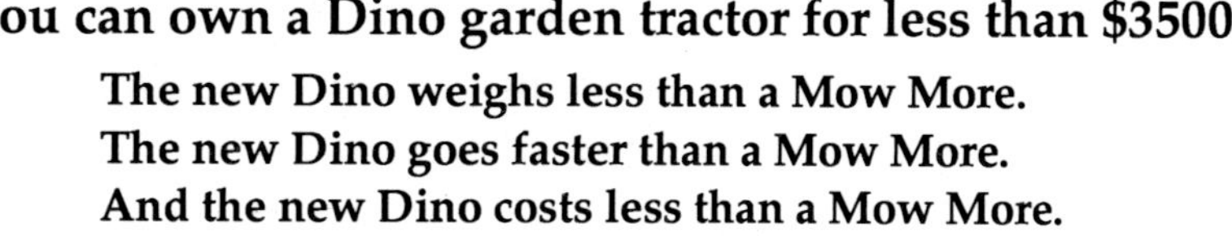

You can own a Dino garden tractor for less than $3500.
The new Dino weighs less than a Mow More.
The new Dino goes faster than a Mow More.
And the new Dino costs less than a Mow More.
DINO GARDEN TRACTOR

Table D3 Facts about Dino and Mow More Tractors

Tractor	Weight	Miles per hour	Cost
Dino	600 pounds	17 miles per hour	$2900
Mow More	602 pounds	16 miles per hour	$2910

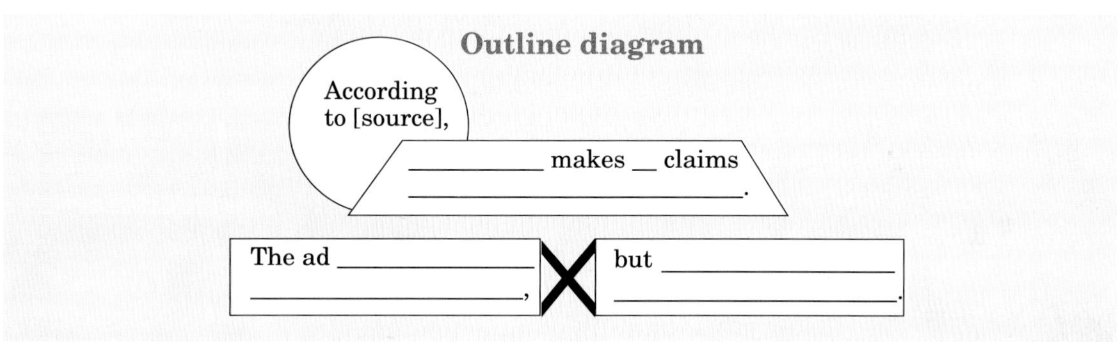

Part B

Claims

1. Creamo paint does not fade for one year.
2. A gallon of Creamo covers 300 square feet.

Table D4 Facts about Paints

Paint	How long before the paint fades	Area a gallon of paint covers
Creamo	1 year	300 square feet
Brite	3 years	520 square feet

Claim __ states ______________ ______________.	That claim is misleading when you compare ____ with ______. [Give specific fact.]

Part C

Use the words she, they, them or it to make sentences that are not clear.

[1] Miss Taylor took her class to a farm. [2] The farm was very quiet. [3] The first thing some of the boys did was chase mice into the barn. [4] The mice hid under piles of straw.

[5] Two girls tried to play with the mice. [6] "Be careful," Miss Taylor said. [7] "Mice that are frightened may bite fingers."

[8] One girl said, "I'll keep my fingers in my pockets."

[9] Just then a horse appeared next to the tractor. [10] The tractor was green and blue.

[11] Ginger wanted to ride another horse named Molly. [12] She walked toward Molly. [13] Suddenly, Molly ran away and jumped over the fence.

[14] A snake appeared in the field. [15] The snake was brown and green.

Part A

Map D1 Lefty's Neighborhood

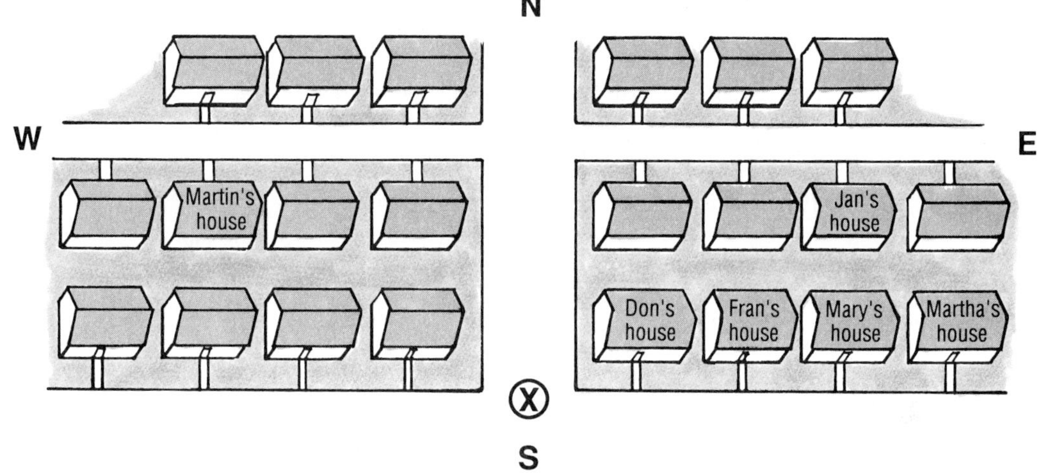

Part B These are statements Lefty made:

- Martha's house is two houses east of Don's house.
- Don's house is bigger than Fran's house.
- Jan's house is next door to Mary's house.

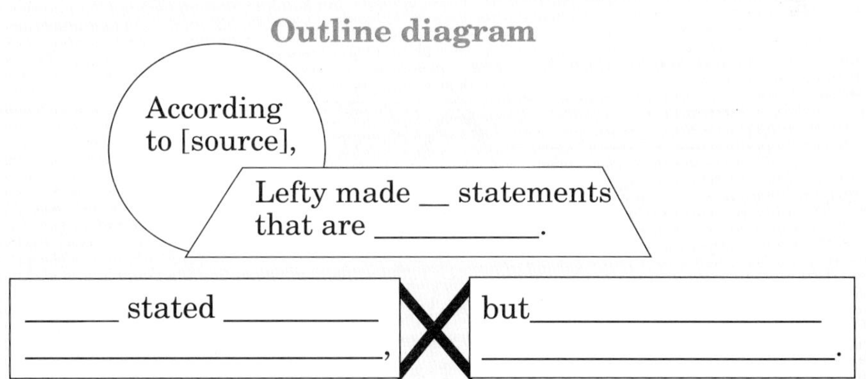

Part C **Rewrite the argument so that it begins with the conclusion.**

A person with health problems shouldn't eat salty foods.
Mr. Jacobs is a person with health problems.
Therefore, Mr. Jacobs shouldn't eat salty foods.

Part D

Write the subject of each sentence. Write N above each noun in the subject.

1. A boy and his sister walked to school.
2. It felt very cold.
3. Martha and four friends came to our party.
4. Their fish were blue and yellow.
5. The horse near the barn started running.

Part E

Claims

1. Z-Mart is open ten full hours every day.
2. You can choose from 120,000 items at every Z-Mart store.

Table D5 Facts about Stores

Store	Hours open each day	Number of items in each store	Number of stores
Z-Mart	10 hours	120,000	13
H-Mart	9 hours	250,000	9
V-Mart	24 hours	114,000	10

Claim __ states ______________ ______________.	That claim is _________ when you _________________________.
	[Give specific fact.]

Part F

For each item, write a good summary sentence. Use numbers.

1. There were cars, trucks, bikes and buses on Oak Street.
2. Mr. Jackson said, "Shirts are on sale in my shop. Also, pants are on sale. Coats are on sale. And underwear is on sale."

Part A

Holt Furniture Ad

SALE

SALE

Holt Furniture is going out of business.

400 items are on sale.

You can buy attractive end tables for half their original price.

You can buy full-sized sofas for less than $100.

Table D6 Facts about Sale

When Holt plans to go out of business	12 years from now
Number of items on sale	400 items
Number of items overpriced	263 items
Price of end tables	half price
Sofas that are on sale	used sofas in bad condition

Outline diagram

According to [source],

_______ makes __ claims ____
_______________________________.

The ad states that ______
_____________________________,

but ___________________
_____________________________.

Part B

Construct arguments that have the conclusion first.

1. People feel comfortable in a heavy car. People feel comfortable in a Bumpo.
2. Paper burns. Things made of wood burn.

Part C Write the subject of each sentence. Write **N** over each noun in the subject.

1. Greg and Linda can run very fast.
2. The bug on that tree is chasing a snake.
3. He was getting very tired.
4. The biggest button on his shirt was red and white.
5. All those horses and cows belong to Ms. James.

Part D

Claims

1. Z-Mart stores have very convenient hours.
2. There are lots of Z-Mart stores in your area.

Table D7 Facts about Stores

Store	Hours open each day	Number of items in each store	Number of stores in your area
Z-Mart	10 hours	120,000	6
H-Mart	9 hours	250,000	2
V-Mart	24 hours	114,000	3
R-Mart	8 hours	110,000	12

Claim __ states ______________ ______________.	That claim is __________ when you ______________ ____.
	[Specific fact], but [specific fact].

Part E Write the regular-order sentence for each question. Circle each subject and underline each predicate.

1. Are you satisfied with Debby's work?
2. Didn't they notice the truck near the corner?
3. Could all those workers fit in a Bumpo?

Lesson 56

Part A

- You've learned that regular-order sentences start with a subject and end with a predicate.
- You've learned that the last word of a subject with more than one word is a noun.
- Here's a new rule: The first word of the predicate is almost always a verb. Some verbs tell about actions.
- Here's a sentence with the predicate underlined:

That cat <u>runs very fast.</u>

- The first word of the predicate is **runs.** That's a **verb.** It tells about an action—running.
- Here's a different sentence:

N V
My older brother <u>is 14 years old.</u>

1. The dog followed us home.
2. Our roof leaked all day.
3. Two girls were very sick yesterday.

Part B

Write an argument that ends with the conclusion.

People enjoy inexpensive entertainment. People enjoy TV.

Part C

Claim: You can select from lots of items in every Z-Mart store.

Table D7 Facts about Stores

Store	Hours open each day	Number of items in each store	Number of stores in your area
Z-Mart	10 hours	120,000	6
H-Mart	9 hours	250,000	2
V-Mart	24 hours	114,000	3
R-Mart	8 hours	110,000	12

The claim states ______________ ______________.	That claim ____________ when you ____________ ______________________________________. [Specific fact], but [specific fact].

Part D

a. It was on a vehicle.

b. A squirrel was on a vehicle.

c. A small animal was on a vehicle.

d. A squirrel was on a car.

e. An animal was on a vehicle.

Part E Bill's Account of What Happened

The lights went out at 3 o'clock. I was doing my homework at the time. A truck had run off the road and into the tree in our front yard.

I went outside and helped the driver out of the truck. The driver was hurt. So I helped him over to the front steps.

Then I noticed that a broken tree branch had snapped a power line. People had gathered in my yard. I took charge and told everybody to move back and keep away from the broken power line. I grabbed one kid who was too close to the broken line.

When the police came, I was busy with them for two hours answering questions. If they hadn't stayed so long, I would have been able to finish my homework.

Table D8 Facts about What Happened

Questions	What really happened
What was Bill doing when the lights went out?	He was watching TV.
How badly was the driver injured?	The driver had a small cut on his cheek.
Who gathered in his yard?	three little kids
Who grabbed the kid who was too close to the broken power line?	the driver

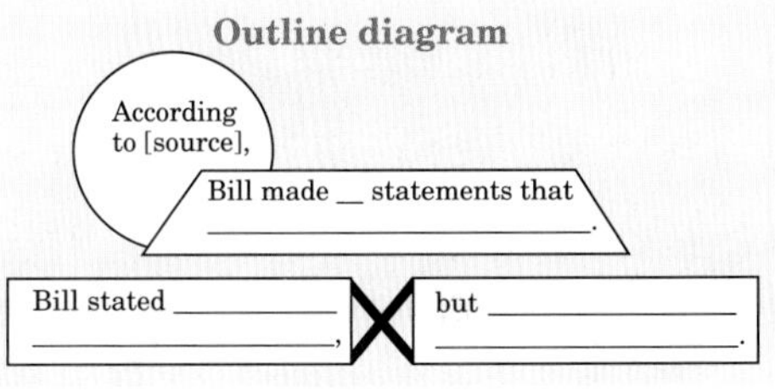
Outline diagram
According to [source],
Bill made __ statements that
Bill stated
but

Part F Write the sentences for the X box.

The argument ______ ______________ ______________.

OC

______________ are possible because ____ ______________.

______ is a ______. Therefore, ____ could ______________.

Argument: Mary should play a team sport.
Basketball is a team sport.
Therefore, Mary should play basketball.

Part A Outline diagram

According to [source],

the Bumpo ad makes __ claims ______________________.

The ad states ____ ______________ ______________.

______________ ________, but ________ ______________.

BUMPO cars are a favorite in your part of the country.

Bumpos are selling like mad because people love them.

One thing people love is the money they save on gas. Bumpos get excellent gas mileage.

Another thing people love is the smooth ride. How could anybody not fall in love with Bumpo performance? Bumpo cars have a powerful engine.

When you add up all the things that Bumpos deliver, the answer is just:

Table D9 Facts about Cars

Car	Gas mileage	Engine
Bumpo	34 miles per gallon	125 horsepower
Heaper	21 miles per gallon	126 horsepower
Miser	58 miles per gallon	117 horsepower
Dancer	29 miles per gallon	280 horsepower

Part B Rewrite the argument so it starts with the conclusion.

Every small bird has a heart that beats very fast.
A robin is a small bird.
Therefore, a robin has a heart that beats very fast.

Part C For each sentence, write the noun that is in the subject. Then write the verb.

1. Their tent had a big rip in it.
2. Nancy gave me some paper.
3. Four baby birds were in the nest.
4. My dream had some strange pets.
5. Her father's office called us.

Part D

a. A woman stood in front of a store.

b. An old woman stood in front of a grocery store.

c. A woman stood in front of a grocery store.

d. A person stood in front of a building.

Part E Turn to lesson 56, part E.

Part F Write the sentences.

The argument ______ ______________ ______________.	OC		______ is a ______. Therefore, _____ could ______________.

Argument: Smart students should have goals.
Climbing a dangerous mountain is a goal.
Therefore, students should climb a dangerous mountain.

Lesson 58

Creamo Ad

What a beautiful house.
It's a Creamo house.

CREAMO paint is just wonderful.

- A gallon of Creamo costs less than a gallon of Brite.
- Creamo dries faster than Z-Brand.
- And Creamo comes in many colors.

CREAMO

Part A

Outline Diagram

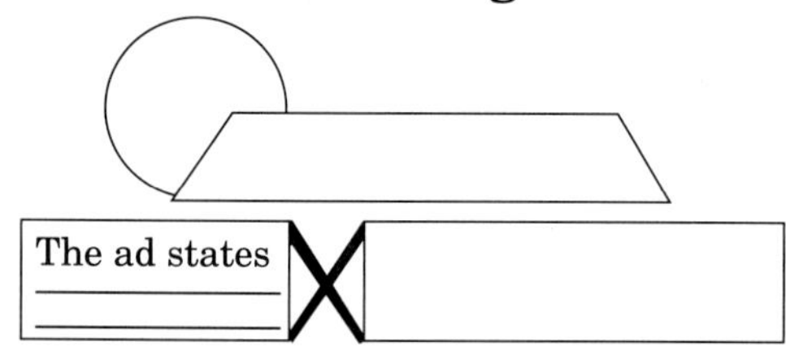
The ad states

Table D10 Facts about Paints

Paint	Number of colors	Cost	How long it takes to dry
Creamo	28	\$11.99 a gallon	12 hours
Brite	20	\$12.00 a gallon	8 hours
Z-Brand	49	\$9.00 a gallon	$12\frac{1}{2}$ hours

Part B

1. A rabbit (a) stopped (b) next to our fence.
2. The cat (c) in that tree belongs (d) to Fran.
3. My mother (e) and Bob took (f) the wrong road.
4. A meeting at school lasted (g) for three hours.
5. That evening was (h) very cool.

Part C

First, write the answer to each question. Then write **M**, **P** or **MP**.

- Write **M** if the source of information is only the map.
- Write **P** if the source of information is only the passage.
- Write **MP** if the source of information is both the map and the passage.

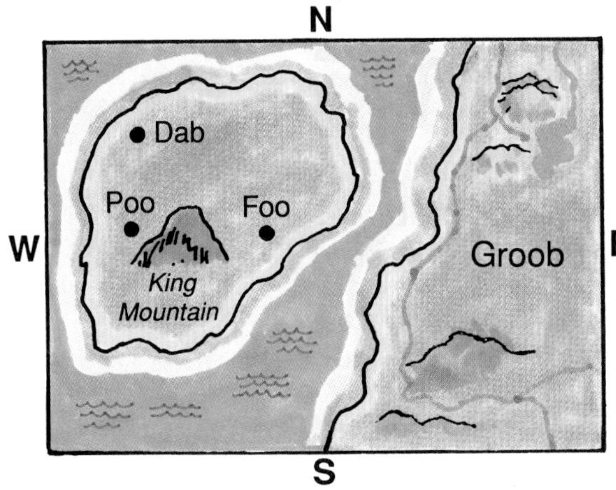

Passage

The city of Poo is on a small island that is close to Groob. The city of Poo is south of another city named Dab. The distance between these cities is about 10 miles. There is a small lake between these cities. Hundreds of people from Poo and Dab visit the lake. They boat and fish and have fun.

1. What is the name of the large land mass that's close to the island?
2. What is the name of the mountain that is east of Poo?
3. What popular place is between Dab and Poo?
4. What is the name of the city that is north of Poo?
5. What's the name of the town that is east of Poo?
6. What direction would you go to get from the mountain to the town of Poo?

Part D

Ann was on the front porch of her house. Ann's mother was sitting. Ann's younger brother was using his ax.

Lesson 59

Part A

- You've worked with sentences that have one-word verbs. In some sentences, the verb has more than one word.
- Here's a sentence:

  Tom runs fast.

  Any combination of words that replaces the word **runs** is a verb.
- Here are some sentences with underlined verbs:

  Tom can run fast.

  Tom could run fast.

  Tom would run fast.

  Tom will run fast.

  Tom was running fast.

  Tom will be running fast.

  Tom might have been running fast.

  The underlined parts are verbs because they replace the word **runs** in the first sentence.
- Remember, any words that replace a verb are verbs.

1. Tom and Donna were on the porch.
2. Two dogs were in the front yard.
3. Mary was on a ladder.
4. Robert and Dawn were in the pool.

Part B

First, write the answer to each question. Then write **M, P** or **MP.**
- Write **M** if the source of information is only the map.
- Write **P** if the source of information is only the passage.
- Write **MP** if the source of information is both the map and the passage.

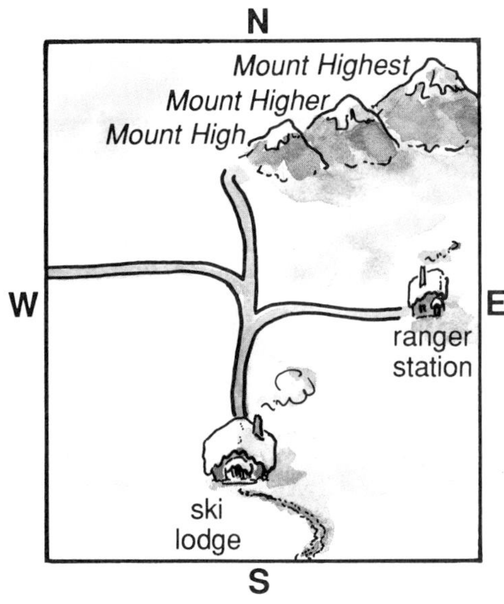

Passage

There are three mountains that are north of the ski lodge. The tallest of these mountains is Mount Highest. Mount Highest is over 10,000 feet high.

It is possible to go from the ski lodge to the town of Done. You can go north, then turn west before you get to the mountains.

You can also get to one of the mountains from the ski lodge by going north to the end of the road.

South of the ski lodge is the town of Hoost. A small trail leads from the lodge to Hoost.

1. What's the name of the smallest mountain just north of the ski lodge?
2. What's the name of the tallest mountain?
3. How tall is that mountain?
4. What direction is Mount Highest from the ranger station?
5. What's the name of the town that is south of the ski lodge?

Part C

Write sentences that tell the problem with the argument.

What Lefty Said

I know that Jerry walked to Hoost. The reason I know is that Jerry walked to a place that is near the ski lodge. And Hoost is near the ski lodge.

Lefty's argument concludes ____________ ____________.	OC		______ is ____________. ______ could have ___ ____________.

Part D

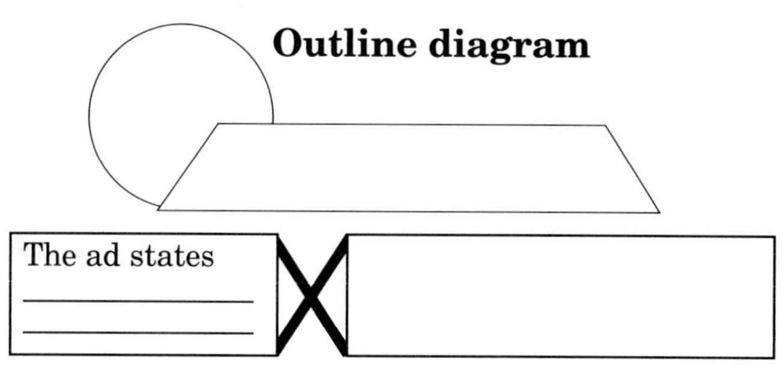

Zee Boo Ad

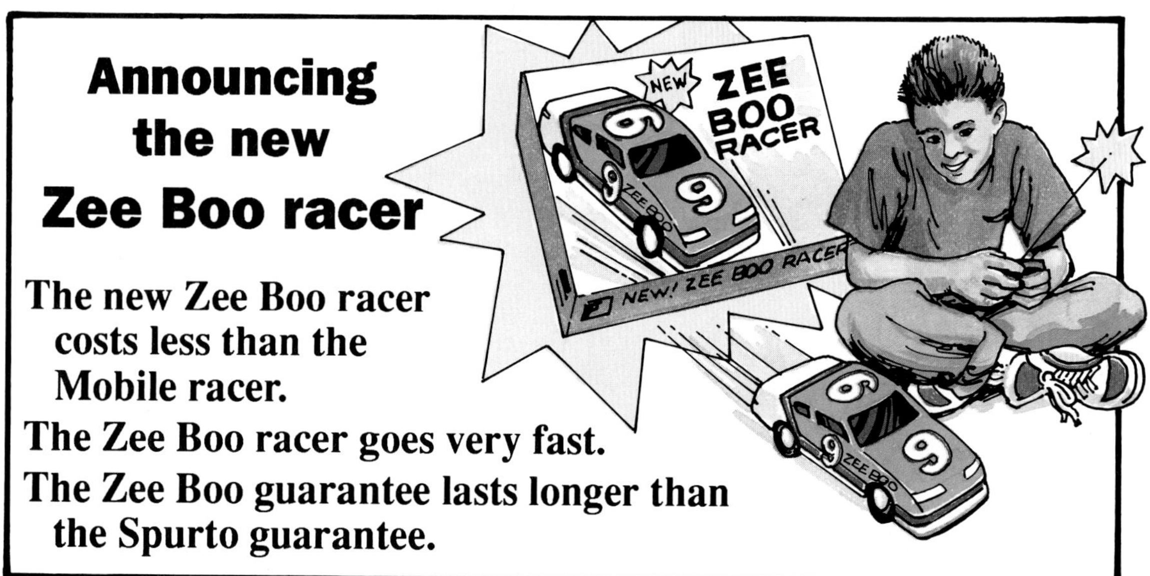

Announcing the new Zee Boo racer
The new Zee Boo racer costs less than the Mobile racer.
The Zee Boo racer goes very fast.
The Zee Boo guarantee lasts longer than the Spurto guarantee.
NEW
ZEE BOO RACER
NEW! ZEE BOO RACER

Table D11 Facts about Toy Cars

Racer	Cost	Guaranteed for how long	Top speed
Zee Boo	$39.00	13 months	35 miles per hour
Spurto	$32.00	12 months	30 miles per hour
Mobile	$40.00	36 months	60 miles per hour

Independent Work

Turn to lesson 53, part A. Write a paragraph that tells about the misleading claims in the Dino ad.

Lesson 60

Part A

1. The dog was in the shade.
2. Ginger's mother was in the pool.
3. The neighbors were on a diving board.

Part B

- You've worked with different kinds of sentences. A sentence is a group of words that begins with a capital letter and ends with an ending mark.
- Most of the sentences you've worked with are called **statements.**

  A statement has a subject and a predicate. The usual ending mark for a statement is a period.
- The second type of sentence is a **question.**

  A question has a subject and a predicate, but the ending mark for a question is a question mark, not a period.
- The third type of sentence is a **command.**

  A command is strange. It does not have a subject, just a predicate. The ending mark is a period. The command tells somebody to do something.
- Here are some **commands:**

  Go to the second house from the corner.
  Stop talking.
  Hold up your left hand.
  Stay on your side of the street.
  Pick up your dirty clothes.

1. was going to the store
2. can we go to the store
3. is not at the store
4. go to the store
5. fold your paper down the middle
6. that girl folded her paper
7. will that girl fold more paper

Test 6

Part A Every day has 24 hours.
Monday is a day.
Therefore, Monday has 24 hours.

Part B

1. A girl (a) in our class won (b) the contest.
2. James (c) and his sister (d) were in the park.
3. The moon (e) seemed (f) very small.

Part C

The argument concludes ______________________. | OC | | ______ is a ______. Therefore, ______ ______.

You should visit a big city.
New York City is a big city.
Therefore, you should visit New York City.

Part D **Claim:** Z-Mart has very convenient hours.

Table D7 Facts about Stores

Store	Hours open each day	Number of items in each store	Number of stores in your area
Z-Mart	10 hours	120,000	6
H-Mart	9 hours	250,000	2
V-Mart	24 hours	114,000	3
R-Mart	8 hours	110,000	12

The claim states ______________________. | That claim ______________________.

Part A For each sentence, write **statement, question** or **command.**

1. Does Billy have a brother
2. Who is that tall masked man
3. Take off that mask
4. The horse did not have a saddle
5. Jump on that horse and get out of here
6. Early in the morning, the rain started to fall

Part B

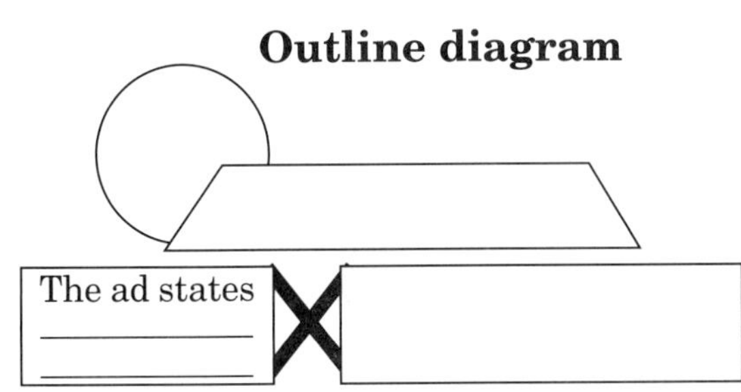

Sleep Rite Ad

People choose Sleep Rite hotels for good reasons.

- Rooms at Sleep Rite cost less than rooms at Dozer.
- You get free meals at Sleep Rite.
- Sleep Rite hotels are in lots of major cities.

Table D12 Facts about Hotels

Hotel	Room price	Meals included	Locations
Dozer	\$130 per night	breakfast, lunch, dinner	7 major cities
Sleep Rite	\$129 per night	breakfast	18 major cities
Snore More	\$65 per night	none	27 major cities

Part C **Lefty's first argument:**

We know that Tom carried a small object. A baseball is a small object. Therefore, Tom carried a baseball.

Lefty's second argument:

We know that Jenny bought a beverage. Milk is a beverage. Therefore, Jenny bought milk.

Lefty's _____ argument concludes ___________ ________________.	**OC**		_______ is a __________. _______ could have ___ _________________.

Part D

- If you have a source of information that is accurate, you can tell whether statements are true, misleading or false.
- However, if you don't know whether your source is accurate, it's impossible to judge statements that don't agree with the source. All you can say is that the statement doesn't agree with the source.

Passage

Off the coast of Costa Ruma are three islands. They are Gluck, Glom and Glib.

Glib is to the west of the other two islands. Gluck is to the north of Glom. Gluck is the largest of the three islands.

Map

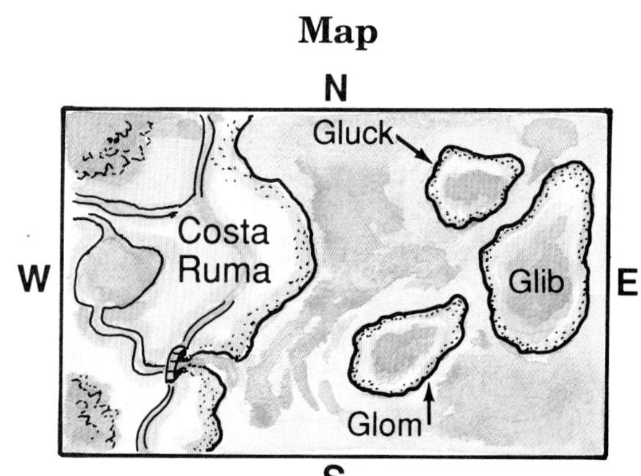

The passage states that _____________ _______________,	but the map contradicts that statement. The map indicates that ______________________.

Independent Work

Turn to lesson 51, part C. Write each argument so that it begins with the conclusion. Remember, the second sentence begins with: **The reason is that . . .**

Lesson 62

Part A For each item, write the verb.

1. My mother could dance very well.
2. People should protect wildlife.
3. The man in the red car was my friend.
4. Mary is a very smart woman.
5. They will talk in the morning.
6. The man in the red car was singing.

Part B

The ad states ________ ________________________,	but that claim is ______. [Tell why.]

Claims from an advertisement:

The new Bumpo Sportster holds four people.

The Sportster has a powerful engine.

Facts about the New Bumpo Sportster

- The Sportster comes in nine attractive colors.
- The Sportster has a five-year guarantee.
- The Sportster's engine breaks down frequently.
- The Sportster comes with bucket seats.
- The Sportster can't hold people who are taller than three feet.

Part C If an item is a sentence, write the first word with a capital letter, the last word and the ending mark.
Then write **statement, question** or **command** to tell what kind of sentence.

1. the bug on the leaf is sick
2. could be going to the lake
3. Bob, his younger sister and four little kids
4. stop teasing the cat
5. could they help us lift this log
6. put one hand on your head and the other hand behind your back
7. what is she trying to say
8. the insects and the frogs made a terrible sound

Part D For each item, write a summary sentence.

1. Hilda said, "My family went to the farm and looked at cows, horses, goats, sheep and chickens."
2. Greg said, "I smiled, I jogged, I ate, I walked, I turned and I took a bath."

Part E

- Some arguments lead to faulty conclusions because they start with a faulty rule.

  If the rule at the beginning of the argument is faulty, the conclusion will be faulty.
- Here's an argument:

  Going to college is the only way to get rich.
  Billy isn't going to college.
  So he must not care about getting rich.
- The rule for this argument is: **Going to college is the only way to get rich.**

  The rule is not accurate because there are other ways to get rich.

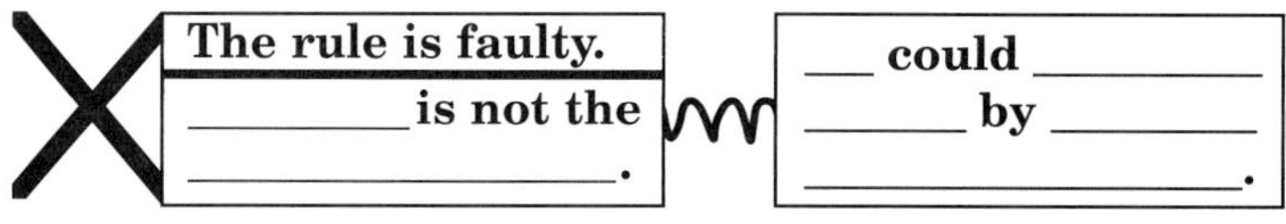

The rule is faulty.
_________ is not the
_________________.
___ could _________
_______ by ________
_________________.

Argument 1: Wearing fancy clothes is the only way to become popular.
Fran wants to be popular.
So Fran should wear fancy clothes.

Argument 2: Using Shino toothpaste is the only way to reduce cavities.
Linda isn't using Shino.
So Linda will have a lot of cavities.

Independent Work Turn to lesson 52, part D. Follow the outline diagram and write a paragraph that tells the problem with the statements from the advertisement.

Lesson 63

Part A

Map

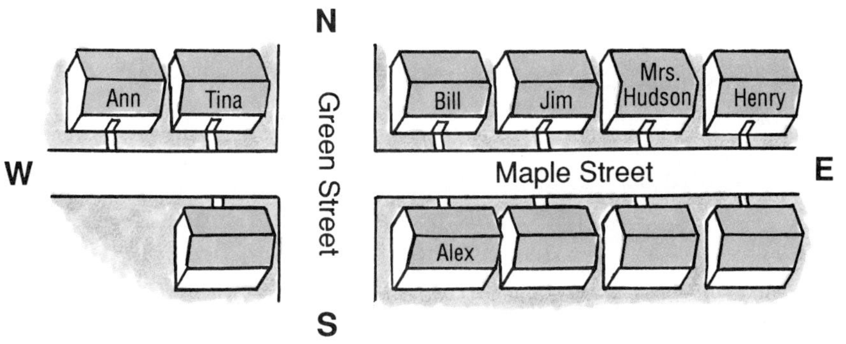

N

W Maple Street E

S

Green Street

Ann | Tina | Bill | Jim | Mrs. Hudson | Henry | Alex

Passage

Ann lives in the house that is farthest to the west.
Jim lives between Mrs. Hudson and Henry.
Henry lives in the house that is farthest to the east.
Bill lives across the street from Jim.
Green Street runs north and south.
Maple Street runs east and west.

The map contradicts __ details of the passage.

The passage states that ____________ ________________,	but the map indicates that ________________ ________________.

Part B

For each item, write the verb.

1. I should go home.
2. Martha's teacher met us in the hall.
3. That apple might become rotten.
4. Ginger has been running a long distance.
5. The little dog has a long tail.
6. The runner could break the record.
7. Mr. Jones and his son might deliver the package.

Part C Write X-box sentences to tell about the problem with the arguments.

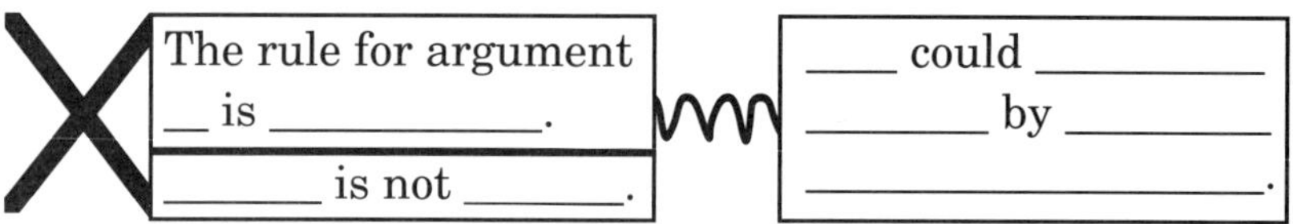
The rule for argument
__ is ___________.
_______ is not _______.
____ could _________
_______ by _________
_________________.

Argument 1: Asking a lot of questions is the only way to get good grades. James doesn't ask many questions.
So James will not get good grades.

Argument 2: Taking the bus is the only way to get to school fast.
Linda never takes the bus.
So Linda must spend a lot of time getting to school.

Part D If an item is a sentence, write the first word with a capital, the last word and the ending mark.
Then write **statement, question** or **command** to tell what kind of sentence it is.

1. not going to the park
2. stop talking and start working
3. help me lift this thing
4. in the park with the rest of us
5. does she like me
6. four of the puppies started playing
7. did her homework in the kitchen

Part E

At Dove's Nest you'll live in
comfort and convenience.
A shopping mall is within walking distance of your home.
Every home has a swimming pool that is shared with only one other home.
The cost of renting smaller homes is less than $200 a week.
Each home comes with free cable TV.

Facts about Dove Nest Village

- The cable TV picks up only 2 channels.
- Some of the pools are shared by 20 homes.
- To get to the shopping mall, you would walk over 4 miles.
- The cost of renting smaller houses is $180 per week.
- Medium-sized houses rent for $400 per week.

The ad states ________ ________________________,	but ________________. [Tell why.]

Independent Work

Turn to lesson 54, part B. Write a passage that tells about the inaccurate statements Lefty made.

Part A

Zee Boo toy cars are winners!

The new Zee Boo Super has outstanding performance.
The Zee Boo Standard guarantees parts longer than Mobile does.
All Zee Boos run for two hours on a battery charge.
You can own a Zee Boo for less than a Mobile.

Car	How long parts are guaranteed	Speed	Hours of running on a battery charge	Cost
Zee Boo Super	2 years	65 miles per hour	2 hours	$450.00
Zee Boo Standard	5 months	24 miles per hour	12 minutes	$45.00
Mobile	6 months	50 miles per hour	1 hour	$66.00

The ad states ________ ________________________,	but ____________________.
	[Tell why.]

Part B

a. The little girl started[1] running across the street.

b. Old people[2] are a lot of fun.

c. The fastest horse had[3] a short tail.

d. Those math problems[4] were[5] terrible.

e. She lost[6] her coat.

Part C

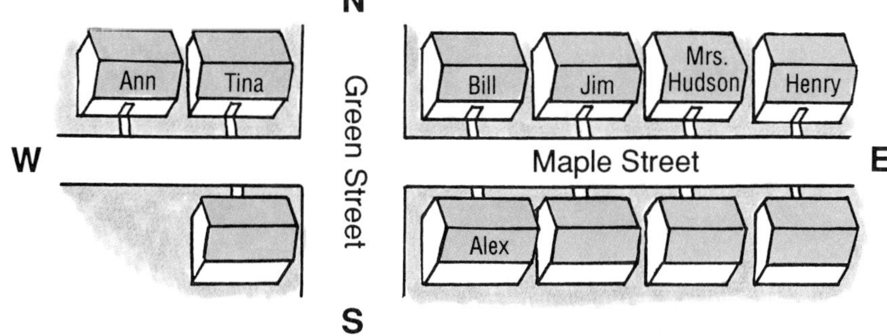

Passage Ann's house is two houses from Green Street.
Ann's house is next door to Henry's house.
Ann's house is the second house west of Green Street.
Bill's house is on the corner of Maple and Green.
Mrs. Hudson's house is just west of Jim's house.
Mrs. Hudson's house is three houses east of Green Street.

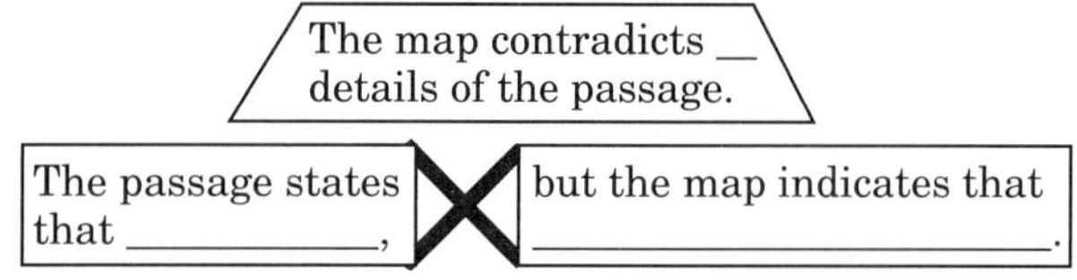

Part D

1. Write general directions that would work for any rectangle.
2. Write general directions for the pink box.
3. Write specific directions for making one of the figures inside the pink box. Tell how high and how wide the **rectangle** is.

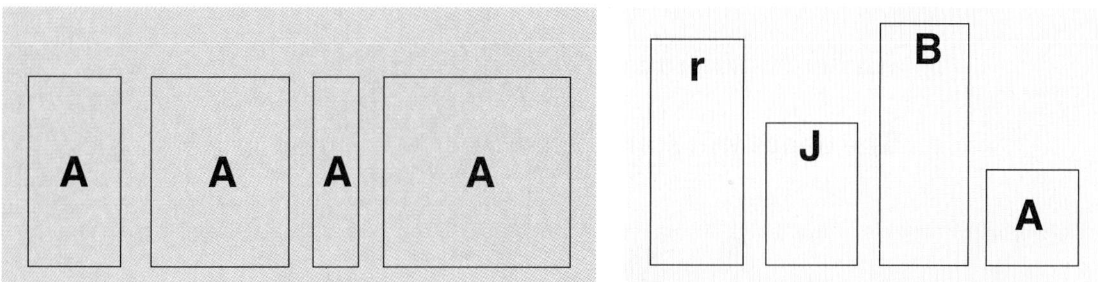

Independent Work

Turn to lesson 39, part C. Write sentences that tell the problem with each argument.

Lesson 65

Part A

Turn to lesson 64, part A. You're going to write about the last two claims in the Zee Boo ad.

Part B

Write X-box sentences to tell about the problem with the arguments.

X	The rule for argument __ is faulty.		___ could ___________ ________ by __________ __________________________.
	_______ is not _______.		

Argument 1: Eating lemons is the only way to get vitamin C. Jerry doesn't eat lemons. So Jerry doesn't get any vitamin C.

Argument 2: Running every day is the only way to get in good shape. Debbie does not run every day. So Debbie is not in good shape.

Part C

Number your paper 1-7. After each number, write **N** for noun or **V** for verb.

a. The little kitten[1] jumped[2].

b. All her sisters can[3] dance[4] very well.

c. The dance[5] will[6] start[7] after dinner.

Part D

Lefty's Report

At 7:00 p.m., I was on the corner of Oak and Maple. I saw two mean-looking guys running down Maple Street toward me. One of them was carrying a gun. I tried to stop those guys. They overpowered me and threw me in a garbage can.

Police Report

At 7:00 p.m., Lefty Nelson was on the corner of Oak and Maple. Two teenagers were walking down Maple Street on their way to a costume party.

One of them was dressed like Bugs Bunny. The other was dressed like a cowboy. He was carrying a gun. It looked real, but it was a squirt gun.

Lefty Nelson must have thought that these boys were dangerous because when he saw them he jumped inside a garbage can and got stuck there. A rescue unit was sent out at 7:20 p.m. to remove him from the garbage can.

The police report contradicts
__ sentences of Lefty's report.

Lefty's report indicates ____,	but the police report indicates ____.

Independent Work

Turn to lesson 43, part A. Write sentences that tell the problem with each claim.

Lesson 66

Part A For each argument that starts with a **faulty** rule, write sentences that tell about the problem.

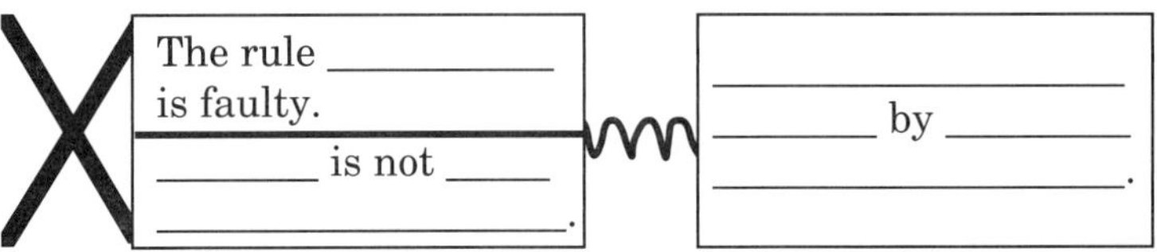
The rule ________ is faulty.
________ is not ________
________.
____
________ by ________
________.

Argument 1: Plants are the only living things that grow more than 200 feet tall.
Farmer Brown has living things that are more than 200 feet tall.
So Farmer Brown must have plants.

Argument 2: Taking a shower is the only way to get clean.
Jan wants to get clean.
So she must take a shower.

Argument 3: The only living things that can write books are humans.
Fran and Greg write books.
So Fran and Greg are humans.

Argument 4: Watching television is the only way to learn about wild animals.
Donna watches television a lot.
So she must know a lot about wild animals.

Part B

- You've worked with commands. Commands are directions.

  Commands are different from statements in an important way. The subject of commands is **you,** but the subject is not usually written.

- Here are commands with the subject written:

  You, stand up.
  You, help me with this ladder.

  The **you** in each sentence is the person you're talking to.

- For most commands, the subject is not written. So the command is just a predicate.

  Stand up.
  Help me with this ladder.

- It's easy to find verbs in commands because commands are regular-order predicates. Regular-order predicates start with verbs. So commands start with verbs.

1. She is very happy.
2. Stop that thief.
3. That puppy looks sick.
4. Sit next to Milly.
5. Eat more slowly.
6. The man in the jacket worked on my mother's car.
7. Walk with me to the store.
8. That walk was long and hard.

Part C

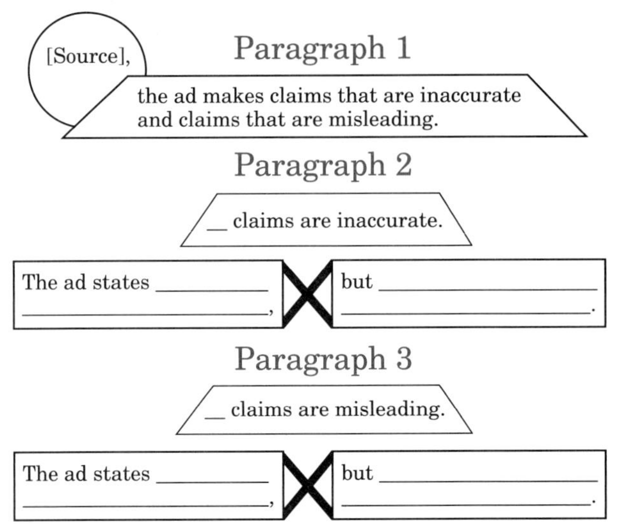

Paragraph 1
[Source],
the ad makes claims that are inaccurate and claims that are misleading.
Paragraph 2
__ claims are inaccurate.
The ad states ___________ ___________,
but ___________ ___________.
Paragraph 3
__ claims are misleading.
The ad states ___________ ___________,
but ___________ ___________.

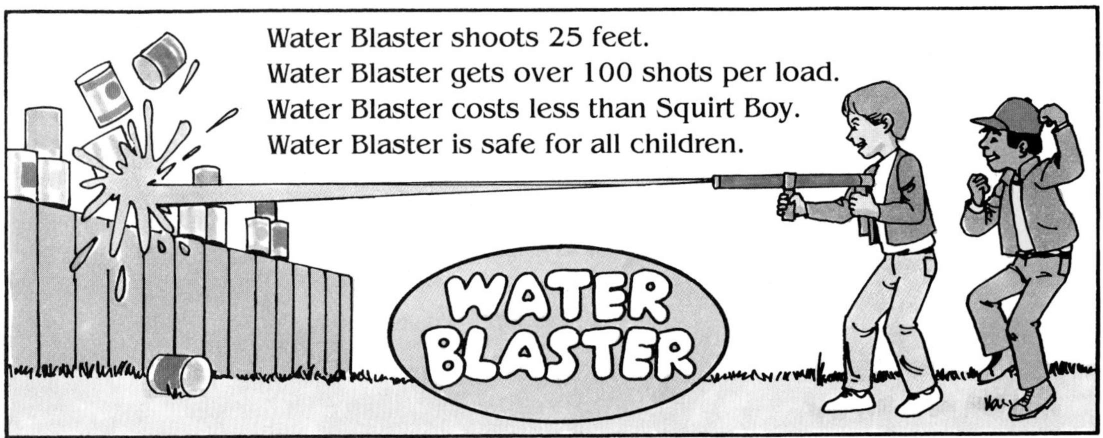

Water Blaster shoots 25 feet.
Water Blaster gets over 100 shots per load.
Water Blaster costs less than Squirt Boy.
Water Blaster is safe for all children.
WATER BLASTER

Table D14 Facts about Water Guns

Water gun	Safe for (ages)	Shots per load	Distance (shooting)	Colors	Price
Water Blaster	Children over 9 years old	101	20 feet	red or blue	$2.49
Squirt Boy	Children over 9 years old	100	20 feet	red, yellow, blue, black or green	$2.50

Independent Work

Turn to lesson 48, part A. Write sentences that tell the problem with each direction.

Lesson 67

Part A Write the verb for each sentence.

1. Water those flowers right away.
2. The water feels cold.
3. My uncle and his neighbor went to Texas.
4. Put your coat on.
5. The step looked wet.
6. Step on the gas.
7. Hold the baby.
8. A bird on our roof makes a lot of noise.

Part B

Outline diagram

[Source], the Bumpo ad makes __ claims that are ________.

The ad states ____________ ____________

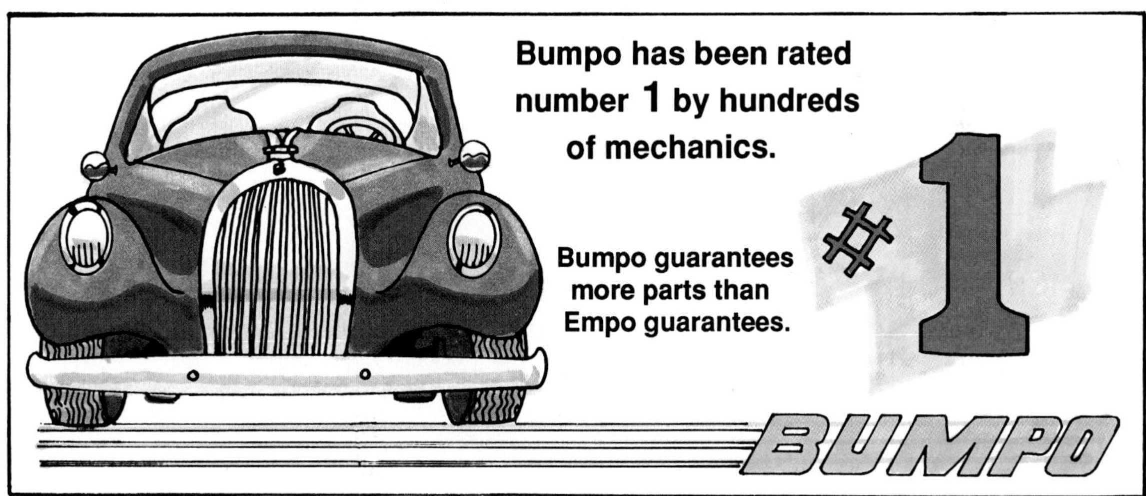

Bumpo has been rated number 1 by hundreds of mechanics.
Bumpo guarantees more parts than Empo guarantees.
#1
BUMPO

Table D15 Facts about Cars

Car	Gas mileage	How many mechanics rated the car number 1	How many parts are guaranteed
Bumpo	38 miles per gallon	462	228
Empo	51 miles per gallon	13,890	227

Part C

Write about the arguments that start with faulty rules.

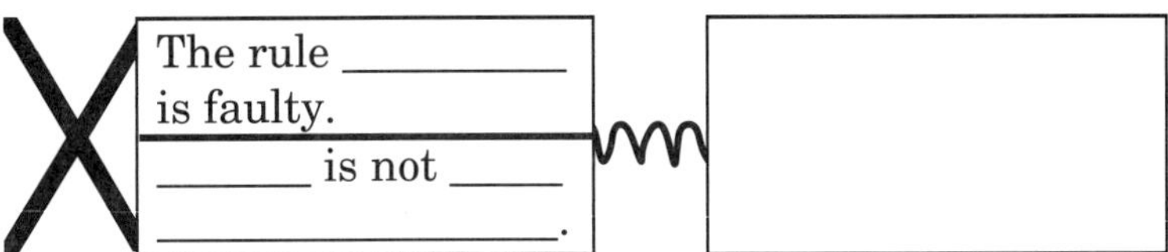

The rule ________ is faulty.
______ is not ______
________________.

Argument 1: Running is the only way to stay in good shape.
Ginger does not run.
Therefore, Ginger must not be in good shape.

Argument 2: You should keep tools that will rust in a dry place.
The desert is a dry place.
Therefore, you should keep tools that will rust in a desert.

Argument 3: You should avoid people who are different from you.
Derrick is different from me.
So I'm not going to have anything to do with Derrick.

Argument 4: Living on a dairy farm is the only way to learn about dairy products.
Fran doesn't live on a dairy farm.
So she must not know much about dairy products.

?
MILK
MILK
CHEESE

Part D

Lefty's Report

I was visiting my Uncle Al's house. There was a leak in the kitchen. Uncle Al asked if I could fix it. I said that I would try.

I turned off the water to the house. Then I worked on the pipes for a while. The job was very difficult. So I told Uncle Al to call a plumber.

Uncle Al turned the water back on, and the kitchen flooded. I don't know why he turned the water back on.

Uncle Al's Report

Lefty was visiting me. I told him that I had a leak under the kitchen sink. I asked him if he could fix leaks. He said that he'd try.

I went outside and turned off the water to the house. Then he worked on the pipes for a while. He called out at me and said, "Okay, the pipes are fixed. Turn on the water."

So I turned on the water. When I got back to the kitchen, there was water everywhere and Lefty was soaking wet.

Uncle Al's report contradicts __ sentences of ___________.

Lefty's report indicates ______________________ ______________________, but ______________ indicates ______________________ ______________________.

Independent Work

Turn to lesson 47, part B. Write directions that tell how to get to Ann's house.

Lesson 68

Part A Write a good summary sentence for each item.

Directions 1:

To get to Ginger's house, go north past the first house, past the second house, past the third house, and then you stop at the next house. That is Ginger's house.

Directions 2:

To get to Tom's house, go east past the first house. Then go past the next house and the next house. Tom's house is the next house.

Part B

- You know that the first word in a command is usually a verb. Not all verbs can be used as the first word in commands.
- Here are some verbs that can't be the first word:

  is have can did would could should will did

  These are not main verbs, but they are verbs. They are **helping verbs.**
- Questions that are answered with **yes** or **no** start with helping verbs.
- Here are some questions that start with helping verbs:

  Have you read that book?
  Will Ginger pass the test?
  Can we catch those butterflies?
  Did Henry come home yet?
- Each question starts with a helping verb. Then it has the subject. Then it has another verb just after the subject.
- Not all questions work this way, just questions that can be answered with **yes** or **no.**

1. What is that?
2. Who is carrying that package?
3. Why are you so sad?
4. Did you open the door?
5. Will she come to the party?
6. Which student is named Martha?
7. Have we put enough gas in the car?
8. Is Martha feeling better?
9. Can you fix my car?

Part C

Tell about the problem with each argument.

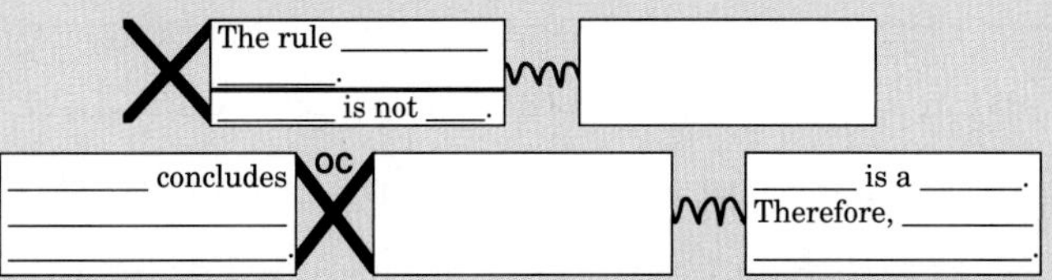

Argument 1:
You should keep tools that will rust in a dry place.
The desert is a dry place.
Therefore, you should keep tools that will rust in the desert.

Argument 2:
Using suntan lotion is the only way to keep from getting sunburned.
Greg never uses suntan lotion.
Therefore, he's going to get a bad sunburn.

Part D

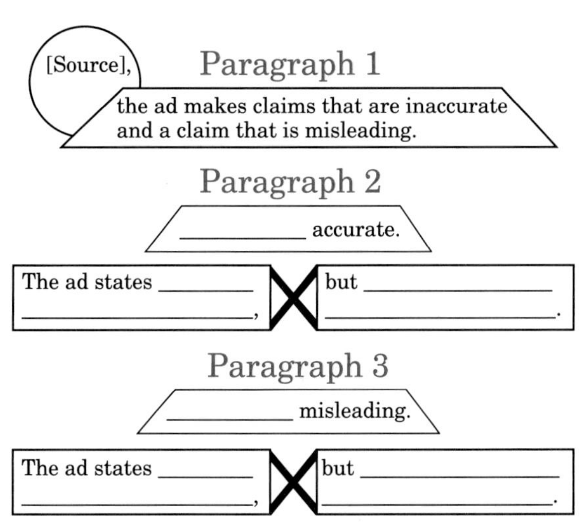

The Rolling Rock album has **5 more songs** than the Twanger album.
The Rolling Rock album has been on the **hit chart** for almost a year.
You can **dance** as you listen to **the Rolling Rock album.**

Table D16 Facts about Albums

Name	Number of songs in album	Months on the hit chart	Number of songs not good for dancing
Rolling Rock	26	5	22
Twanger	24	12	22

Independent Work

Turn to lesson 55, part D. Write sentences that tell the problem with each claim.

Lesson 69

Part A

- Here's a new kind of claim that is misleading:

  No running shoe lasts longer than BK Runners.

- The table shows why the claim is misleading:

Running shoe	How long the shoe lasts
BK Runners	900 miles
Pump-Its	850 miles
Hot Feet	900 miles
Cheetahs	900 miles
Zippy	900 miles
Aces	900 miles

- Here are sentences that tell about the problem:

  The claim states that no running shoe lasts longer than BK Runners, but the claim is misleading. Four other brands of running shoes last as long as BK Runners.

Claims:

1. Zee Boo racers have 200 parts guaranteed.
2. No racer has a longer frame than Zee Boo.
3. No other racer goes faster than Zee Boo.
4. No other racer has tires better than those on a Zee Boo.

Table D17 Facts about Toy Racing Cars

Racers	Number of parts guaranteed	Top speed	Length of frame	Type of tires
Zee Boo	25	30 miles per hour	7 inches	RF20
Speed Freak	27	30 miles per hour	11 inches	RF20
Go Go Go	200	24 miles per hour	6 inches	RF20
Performo	104	30 miles per hour	9 inches	RF20

Claim __ states ________ ____________________,	but ____________________. [Tell why.]

Part B — Write about the problem with each argument.

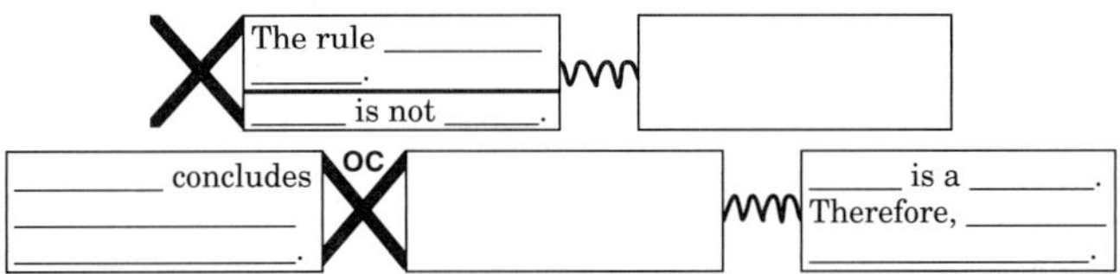

The rule ________ ________.
______ is not ______.
________ concludes ________ ________.
OC
______ is a ______.
Therefore, ________ ________.

Argument 1:
You should study in a quiet place.
A dungeon is a quiet place.
Therefore, you should study in a dungeon.

Argument 2:
Driving a small car is the only way to use less gas.
Mr. Johnson doesn't drive a small car.
Therefore, Mr. Johnson must be using a lot of gas.

Part C — Write a summary sentence for each paragraph.

In a recent test, over 1000 people who tried different brands of toothpaste said that they liked the taste of Tinko best. They said that it left their mouth feeling fresh and that they preferred the lemon-mint flavor of Tinko to the flavor of other brands.

Tinko toothpaste has more than good taste. It also is very effective in helping you keep your teeth in good condition. Tinko toothpaste has been shown to be very effective in reducing the number of cavities that people have. In fact, no other brand is better than Tinko at preventing cavities.

There's one more good reason for using Tinko toothpaste. That reason has to do with the cost of keeping your mouth fresh and your teeth healthy. You'll be happy to know that, although Tinko toothpaste has a marvelous taste and fights cavities, Tinko toothpaste is less expensive than any other major brand of toothpaste. You get much, much more by paying less for Tinko.

Part D — Write the verb or the two verbs for each sentence.

1. Did your sister buy that candle?
2. Stand in the shade.
3. Should they eat so much?
4. Would she sell her bike?
5. Turn at the corner.
6. Take us in the car.
7. Will Ann write us soon?

Part E

Lefty's Account

To get to Bill's house, go one block north. Then go another block north. Then go another block north. Then go one more block north. Then turn to the right and go two blocks. Bill's house is on the northeast corner.

To get to Amy's house, go two blocks to the east on Hill Street. Turn north. Go past the first house. Then go past the second house. Then go past the third house. Amy's house is the next house on the right side of the street

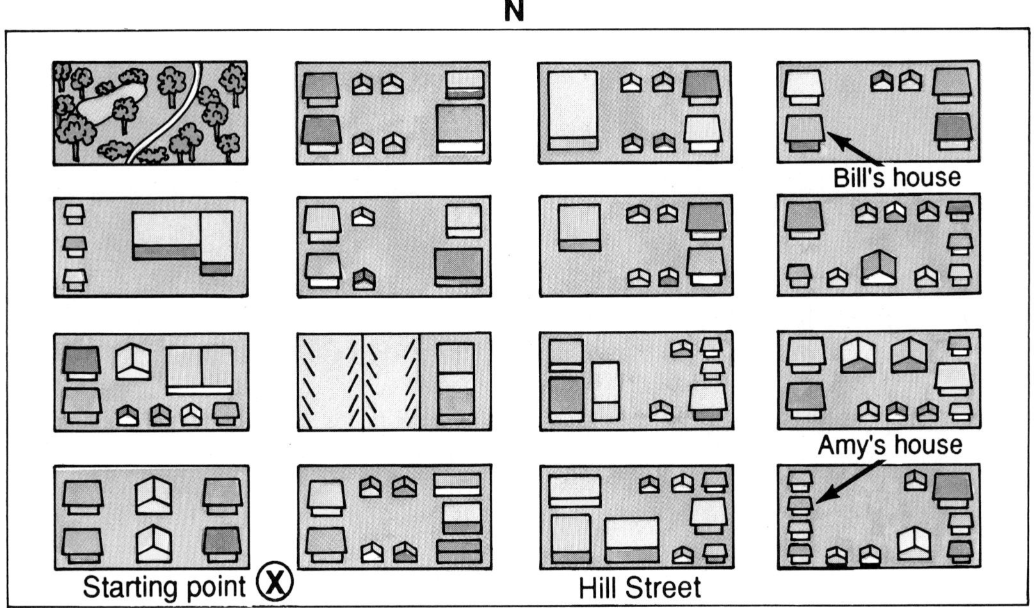

The map contradicts ____ details of ______________.

Lefty's account indicates that _____ house is __________, but _______ indicates ____ ______________________________ ______________________________.

Independent Work

Turn to lesson 56, part C. Write sentences that tell the problem with the claim.

Test 7

Part A

1. Did my sister fix the radio?
2. Change the channel please.
3. Have you eaten lunch?
4. Paint the wall blue.

Part B

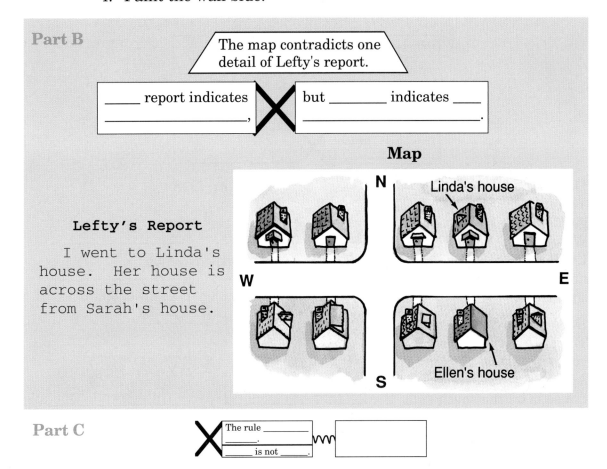

The map contradicts one detail of Lefty's report.

_____ report indicates _____________________,

but ________ indicates ____ _____________________.

Map

N

Linda's house

W

E

Ellen's house

S

Lefty's Report

I went to Linda's house. Her house is across the street from Sarah's house.

Part C

The rule ________ ______.

______ is not ______.

Argument C: Running 5 miles every day is the only way to lose weight.
Kevin wants to lose weight.
So he should run 5 miles every day.

Part D

Argument D: Children should eat food that has lots of vitamins.
Carrots have lots of vitamins.
Therefore, children should eat carrots.

Lesson 70

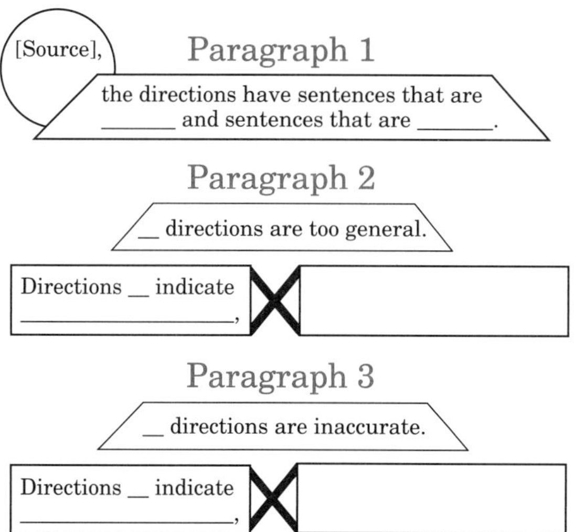
[Source],
Paragraph 1
the directions have sentences that are ______ and sentences that are ______.
Paragraph 2
__ directions are too general.
Directions __ indicate ______________,
Paragraph 3
__ directions are inaccurate.
Directions __ indicate ______________,

Directions A:
To get to Linda's house, go north. Turn west on Washington Avenue. Linda's house is the big house on the left side of the street.

Directions B:
To get to Jerry's house, go north. Turn east on Adams Avenue. Jerry's house is on the south side of the street.

Directions C:
To get to Megan's house, go north. Turn west on Lincoln Avenue. Megan's house is the last house on the south.

Directions D:
To get to Brenda's house go north. Turn west on Adams Avenue. Brenda's house is the last house.

Map D18

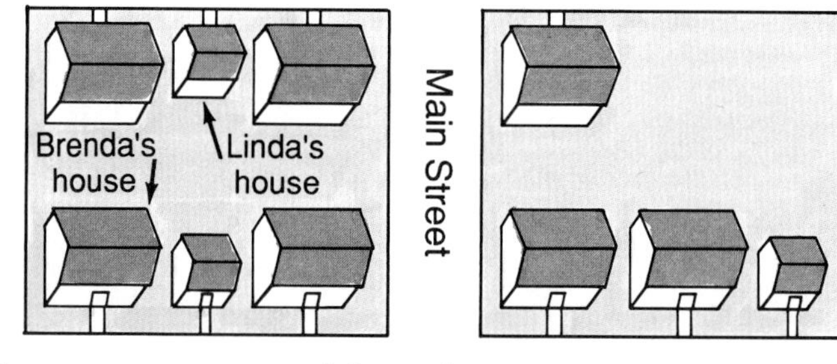
N
Washington Avenue
Main Street
Brenda's house
Linda's house
W
Adams Avenue
E

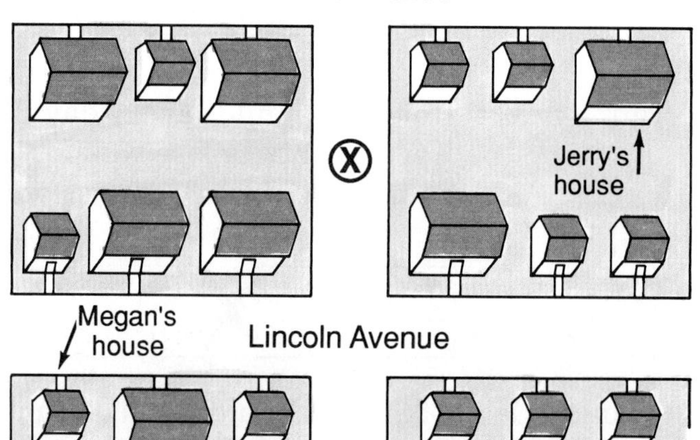
Jerry's house
Megan's house
Lincoln Avenue
S

Lesson 71

Part A

Write a summary sentence for each paragraph. Start each sentence with **Zippo paint.**

Zippo paint is popular today. It also was a leading brand ten years ago. And it was popular fifty years ago. Remember, the Zippo Paint Company was making Zippo paint long before most paint companies had a can to put paint in. And Zippo has always been popular.

If you paint something with Zippo today, it will look good for a long time. A recent test showed that Zippo paint kept its color better than other paints. After one year, Zippo paint hadn't faded at all. Other leading paints had faded. Remember, when you buy Zippo paint, you buy paint that lasts.

Builders and painters agree about which brand they prefer. More builders and painters have used Zippo paint than any other paint, and more builders and painters say that they will buy Zippo again.

Part B

SunDial Ad

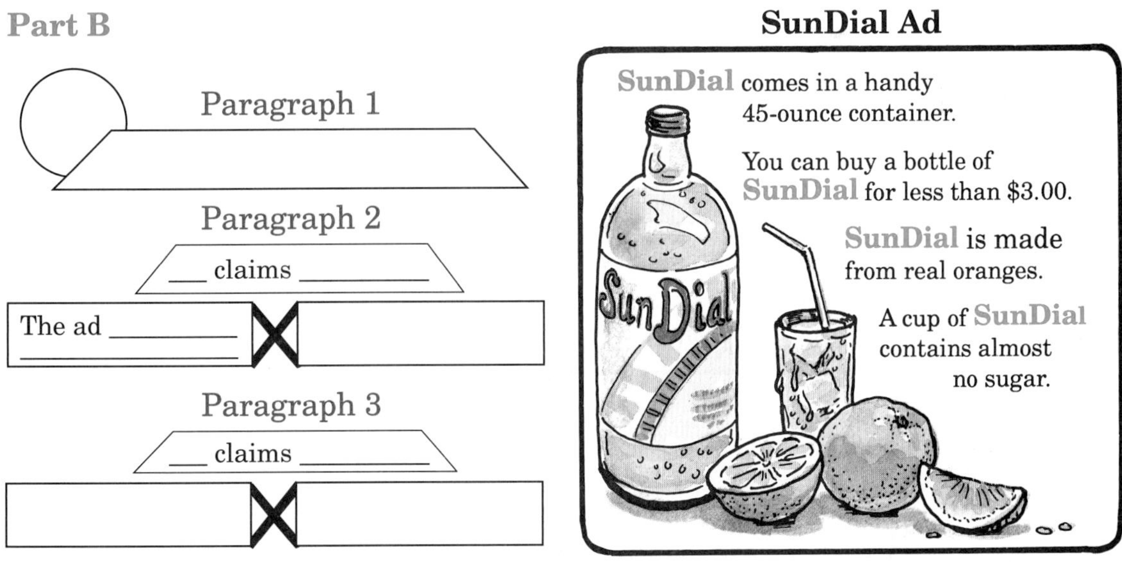

Paragraph 1
Paragraph 2
___ claims ___________
The ad ___________
Paragraph 3
___ claims ___________
SunDial comes in a handy 45-ounce container.
You can buy a bottle of SunDial for less than $3.00.
SunDial is made from real oranges.
A cup of SunDial contains almost no sugar.
SunDial

Table D18 Information about SunDial Orange Drink

Size of container	Cost	How much real orange juice in each bottle	How much sugar in each cup
31–ounce size	$2.99	2 ounces	3 tablespoons

Part C

Lefty's Account

I went fishing for perch and sunfish.

I caught a sunfish that was too small. So I threw it back.

Then I caught a perch that was big enough. And I kept it.

Then I caught another perch that was big enough. And I kept it.

Then I caught five sunfish that were big enough. And I kept them.

Then I caught two more perch that were too small. And I threw them back.

Then the game warden came by and gave me a ticket.

Game Warden's Report

Lefty Nelson was fishing off the south pier.

He had two perch, and both of them were too small.

He had five sunfish, and all of those were too small.

Fortunately, all the fish were alive. So I ordered Lefty to let all of them go.

Then I gave him a $50 ticket.

The game warden's report contradicts two details of ________.

Lefty's account indicates ____________________ ____________________,	but the ____________________ ____________________ ____________________.

Part D

Write questions that begin with these verbs.

1. have
2. did
3. was

Independent Work

Turn to lesson 48, part G. Write sentences to tell the problem with the argument.

Lesson 72

Part A

Lefty's Account

To get to Fran's house, you go north to Green Street. Then you go to Amy's house. Then you go to Tina's house. Then you go three more houses north. That's Fran's house.

To get to Jerry's house, you go to the west. You go to the first house on the north side of the street. Then you go to the next house. And then you stop at the next house. That's Jerry's house.

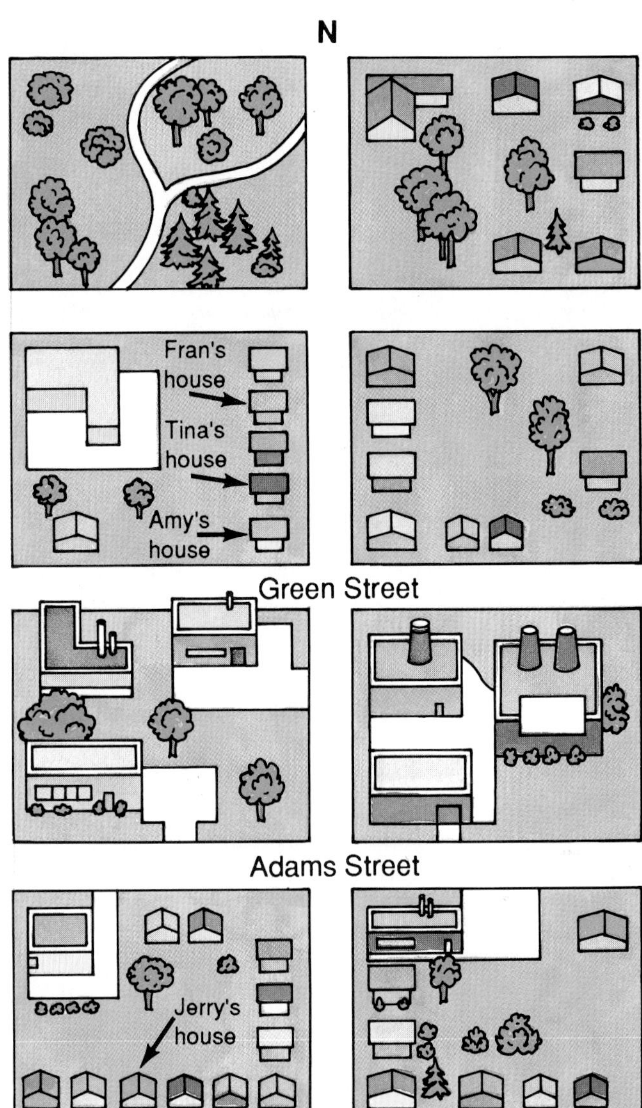

The map contradicts two details of Lefty's account.

Lefty's account indicates ________________,	but ________________.

Part B ***Sample:*** He has worked for three days.

1. She was walking very fast.
2. Those dogs are chasing a rabbit.
3. Your brother should help us.

Part C

Playgrounds

by Mrs. Johnson

We all know how much children love libraries. What some of us may not know is how safe libraries are compared to playgrounds.

In our city, seven children were injured on playgrounds. Only one child was injured in a library. Clearly, playgrounds are far more dangerous than libraries.

Children should avoid places that are more dangerous than libraries. Playgrounds are more dangerous than libraries. Therefore, children should avoid playgrounds.

Table D19 Children Injured in Our City

Place	Number of children injured
libraries	1
playgrounds	7
bathrooms	15

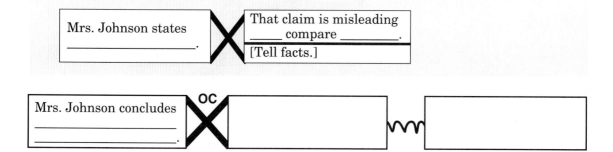

Mrs. Johnson states ____________________.

That claim is misleading _____ compare _________.

[Tell facts.]

OC

Mrs. Johnson concludes ____________________ ____________________.

Independent Work

Turn to lesson 52, part F. Write sentences that have the word **who** or **that.**

Lesson 73

Part A

Write a summary sentence for each paragraph. Then write the conclusion the person who wrote this passage intends you to draw.

Rock City has the friendliest people in the whole state. Come join the picnic every afternoon in the park, or make friends at the Saturday barn dance. Soon you'll be smiling, and you'll feel like Rock City is home.

The beauty of Rock City is breathtaking. Come fish in our clear streams and enjoy the golden sunsets. See for yourself the purple mountains' majesty made famous in a song. There is no finer scenery anywhere.

We also have the world's greatest collection of rocks—large ones, small ones and bumpy ones. The president has seen this fantastic collection, and so should you. Walk through Rock City and see the most amazing display of rocks in the world.

Part B

You've worked with nouns in the subject. Nouns are the names for persons, places or things.

- Names of persons are nouns: James, Ginger, Wendy, boy, children, Andrew.
- Names of things are nouns: pencil, dog, table, book.

The last word of a subject with more than one word is usually a noun.

Four small golden leaves (N) drifted from the tree (N).

- The noun in the subject is **leaves.**
- There's another noun in the sentence. That noun is **tree. Tree** is the name of a thing; so **tree** is a noun.

Remember, nouns do not have to be in the subject. They can be in the predicate as well.

Part C

1. That little girl lives in a new house.
2. My brother loves to eat tomatoes slowly.
3. Her brand-new shoes were covered with mud.
4. Our old car has two flat tires.
5. The meeting lasted for six hours.
6. That brown dog went under the porch very quietly.

Part D

Write a deduction that ends with the conclusion.

All the boys in my family love popcorn. Billy loves popcorn.

Part E

Why There Should Be Longer School Days

by Mrs. Johnson

School is a wonderful place. It's too bad that our children don't spend more time in school. If children spent more time in school, they would be much smarter. Children who have a longer school day do better on tests.

We want improvement in math and reading. A longer school day improves math and reading. Therefore, children should have a longer school day.

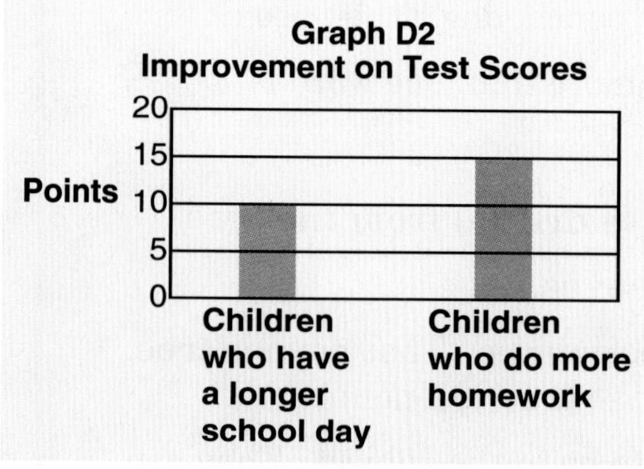

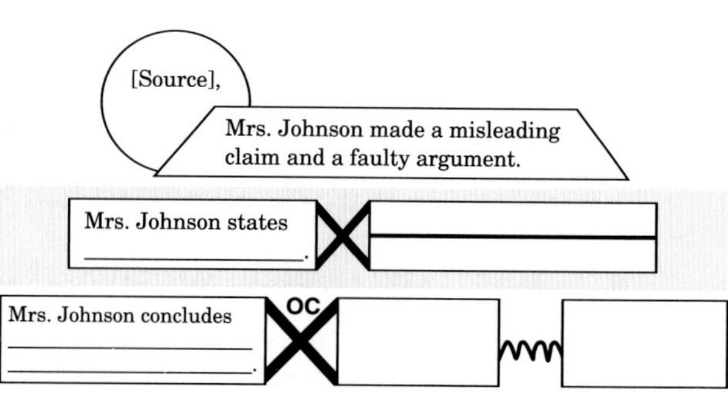

Independent Work

Turn to lesson 15, part F. For each item, write two possible meanings of the second sentence.

Lesson 74

Part A

Write the two nouns that are in each sentence.

1. Robert stood in front of our house.
2. That green boat is full of fish.
3. A tiny black ant ran across our sidewalk very fast.
4. My little sister can read books.
5. The meeting lasted for two hours.

Part B

- Some arguments try to answer a question. These arguments must present evidence.
- Here's a question:

  Did Timmy hit the baseball that went through Mr. Franko's window?

  An argument showing that Timmy **didn't** hit that baseball would have to present evidence that Timmy could not have hit the ball because he was doing something else.
- Here's a different question:

  Did Nancy find $20 in front of her house on Tuesday morning around 10 a.m.?
- Here's a good argument to show that she could not have found the $20:

  Nancy could not have found $20 in front of her house at 10 a.m. on Tuesday because she was in school at the time. She was taking a language test. Her teacher has the test, written by Nancy. Also, the other students in the class saw her in the classroom from 8:30 until lunchtime.

Part C

Here's a question:

Did Fred cheat on the test by copying from Nancy?

Start with the sentence:

Fred could not have copied from Nancy.

Part D

Write a summary sentence for each paragraph. Then write the conclusion the person who wrote this passage intends you to draw.

Movie Star College does such a good job of teaching our students to act that students who graduate are on their way to finding a good job. Our students get lots of work in movies and on TV. In fact, after they take our classes, we promise to find them their first job.

Many famous movie stars came from our college, and you can be one, too. Your face will be seen on the big screen, and the whole country will watch you on TV. People you don't know will recognize you and stop you on the street, even if you wear sunglasses.

If you think it's expensive to go to Movie Star College, consider this fact: You can go to Movie Star College for a lot less than you could imagine. Check our prices. You'll see that Movie Star College is less expensive than any other school of its type.

Part E

Account

Life is not fair to some people. Consider Tim Jerkey. Tim Jerkey is in prison for stealing one piece of paper from a department store. He was arrested by the police for this crime. Right now, Tim is serving a prison sentence of five years.

Facts

- Tim Jerkey entered the department store at 2:15 p.m.
- Tim Jerkey wore a jean jacket and cowboy boots.
- Tim Jerkey lived 2 blocks from the department store.
- Tim Jerkey stole a $1,000 bill from the store.
- Tim Jerkey is 6 feet tall and weighs 157 pounds.

The account gives the impression that ______,	but the account ________.
	[Tell why.]

Independent Work

Turn to lesson 63, part A. Follow the outline diagram and tell about the contradictions.

Lesson 75

Part A

Write a summary sentence for each paragraph. Then write the conclusion.

We need to vote for a senator who will work for us. Jane Baldwin is that person. Jane Baldwin hasn't taken a vacation in years. She likes to start work at seven in the morning and usually comes home around midnight. Her bedroom and her kitchen look just like her office, full of open books and piles of paper. She keeps her reading glasses on a chain around her neck. Her family says they never see her anymore because she's always working.

Important people admire and trust what Jane Baldwin says. The people in her district trust her. "She always says what she thinks," says one. "She doesn't try to hide anything. Even when it could be bad for her, she will always tell you the truth."

Too many senators neglect their jobs because they want to be president. Jane Baldwin is not interested in becoming president. When friends suggested that she should run for president, she told them no. She said, "I'll make a good senator, and that's what I want to be."

Part B

Account

The case of Herbie Bull is an amazing example of unfair punishment. Herbie drove downtown and parked in a no-parking zone. Herbie was ready to drive away when a police officer arrested him. Herbie was thrown in jail and was later sentenced to one year in prison. That's where Herbie is now.

Facts

- Herbie Bull is 5 feet 3 inches tall and weighs 265 pounds.
- Herbie was arrested at 7:35 p.m. on May 9.
- Herbie Bull was in a new Bumpo sports car.
- The car was stolen.
- Herbie later admitted that he stole the car.

The account gives the impression that ____,
but the account ____.
[Tell why.]

Part C

You've combined sentences with **but.** The word **however** can be used in place of the word **but.**

- Here are sentences combined with **however:**

  The account gives the impression that Tim Jerkey was treated unfairly; however, he was guilty.

- The punctuation mark just before **however** is called a **semicolon,** not a comma. Notice the comma after the word **however.**

1. The dog had a big collar. The dog was brown.
2. Yoko was small. She was very strong.
3. She had two jobs. She was very poor.
4. Her mother is tall. Her grandmother is tall.

Part D

Write 1 through 11 on your paper. For each number, write **N** if the word is a noun, or **V** if the word is a verb.

a. She was running[1] across the yard[2].

b. Our three dogs[3] bark[4] every morning[5].

c. The people on the bus were[6] singing[7] and making a lot of noise[8].

d. My mother[9] saw[10] Fran[11] and her sister in the garden.

Part E

Write an argument to show that the answer to a question is **no.**

Did Fran ride her mountain bike through Mrs. Green's garden Friday evening?

Independent Work

Turn to lesson 61, part B. Follow the outline diagram and write about the misleading claims.

Lesson 76

Part A

- Here's a statement:

  That cat was sleeping for two hours.

  When you make a yes-no question from this statement, the question has the same subject and the same predicate as the statement.

- Here's the yes-no question:

  Was that cat sleeping for two hours?

  Remember, for statements and yes-no questions, the subject is the same and the predicate is the same.

1. This rope will break very soon.
2. Her mother was feeling better.
3. Jimmy could help us.

Part B

- Good evidence is called **relevant evidence.** Some arguments do not present relevant evidence. Those arguments do not actually answer the question. They **pretend** to answer it. They answer some other question. Therefore, the evidence is not relevant.
- Here's a question:

  Did Mary go swimming in the pool on Friday?

- Here's an argument with evidence that is **not relevant to the question:**

  On Friday, as we all know, the weather was cool. The sun did not shine all day, and the wind was stiff. Mary is a very wise person. Her friends and teachers know how well she does in school and how smart she is. A wise person would not go swimming when the weather is as poor as it was on Friday. Therefore, we know that Mary did not go swimming at that time.

- That argument doesn't answer the question: **Did** Mary go swimming in the pool on Friday? The evidence answers the question: **Is Mary smart?** Therefore, the evidence is not relevant.

Part C | For each paragraph, write **relevant** or **not relevant.**

Question: Was the zookeeper sleeping when the lion escaped?

1 There are many reasons to believe that the zookeeper was not sleeping. First, the zookeeper had slept well on the night before the lion escaped. His wife knows that he slept soundly because he snored so loudly that he kept her awake.

2 The zookeeper has a good work record. Nobody has ever complained about his work. A person with a good work record would not sleep on the job.

3 Four people saw him shoveling banana peels out of the monkey cages at the time that the lion climbed over the wall.

4 Many interesting things happen at the zoo. The animals are fascinating and are never boring. People sleep when they are bored, but it's difficult for them to sleep when they are fascinated and busy looking at animals. It's ridiculous to think that the zookeeper could have been sleeping!

Part D

Directions A:
To get to Ryan's house, go south. Turn east on Adams. Ryan's house is the second house.

Directions B:
To get to Cindy's house, go north. Turn left on Washington Street. Cindy's house is on the north side of the street.

Directions C:
To get to Debbie's house, go south. Turn west on Franklin. Debbie's house is the second house on the north side of the street.

Directions D:
To get to Michael's house, go south. Turn east on Adams Street. Michael's house is the last house on the right.

Map D20

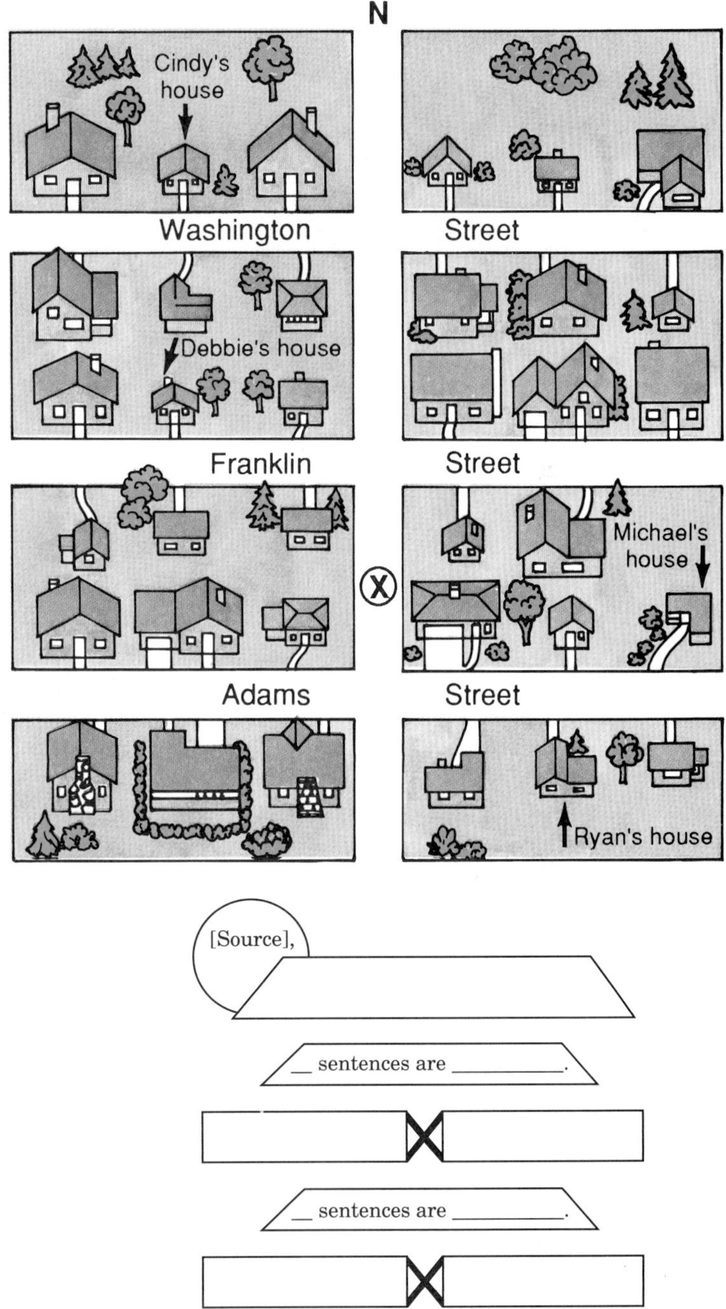

Independent Work

Turn to lesson 25, part G. Tell about the problems with the directions.

Part A

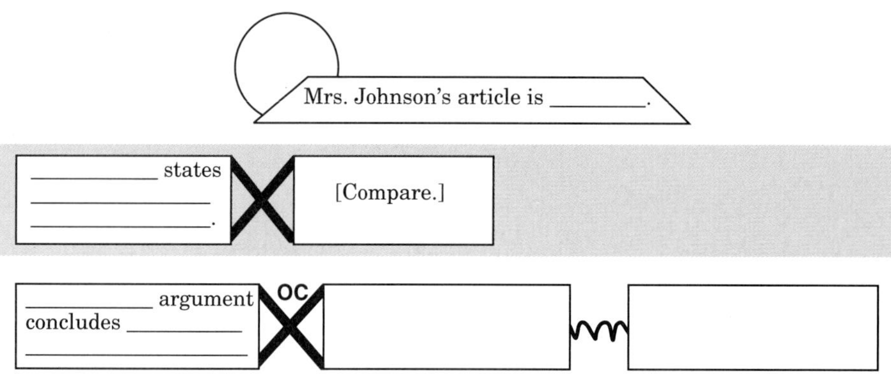

Why Sleeping on a Board Is Healthy

by Mrs. Johnson

Many children sleep in soft beds on soft mattresses. How unfortunate that may be! Children who sleep on boards get taller every year. My, how tall and healthy these children become.

Here is what I would say to any parent: We like our children to get taller and taller. Children who sleep on boards get taller and taller. Therefore, all children should sleep on boards.

Graph D21
How Much Children Grow Each Year

	Inches: 0 1 2 3 4
Children who sleep in beds	
Children who sleep on boards	
Children who sleep on couches	

Part B

1. That ship is sinking.
2. That little bird can fly fast.
3. Your sister could work quickly.

Part C Write directions for making this figure.

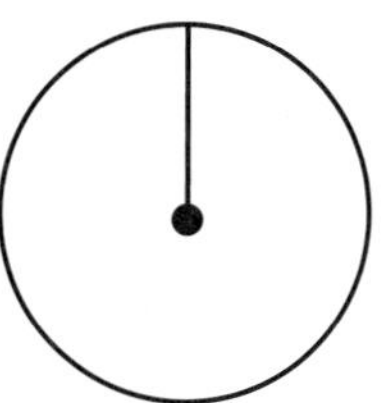

Part D

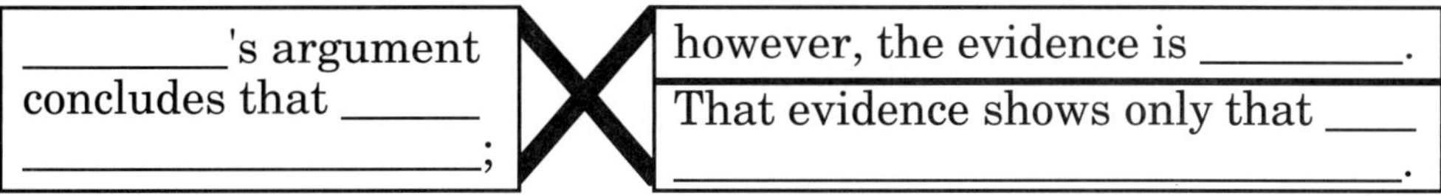
________'s argument concludes that ______ ____________________;
however, the evidence is ________.
That evidence shows only that ____ ______________________________.

1. Ted said, “I know that Milly was in school on December first. The reason is that she was never absent in September, October or November. Why would anybody believe that she would be absent on December first?”
2. Ginger said, “I know that Bill can run faster than Jane. After all, Bill runs faster than any other boy in our school.”

Independent Work Turn to lesson 64, part C. Write a passage that tells about the contradiction.

Lesson 78

Part A Write X-box sentences to tell the problem with the argument.

The argument concludes ______ ______.	OC	______ ______ is not the only ______.	~	______ is ______. Therefore, ______ ______.

Argument: Everybody wants to save money.
New Bumpos are priced so that you can save lots and lots of money.
So buy a new Bumpo now and save, save, save.

Part B Write X-box sentences to tell the problem for each argument.

Argument __ concludes that ______ ______;	X	however, the evidence is ______. That evidence shows only that ______ ______.

Argument 1: Carol did not cheat on the math test. She has always done well in math. Last year she got an A in math. The year before that, she almost got an A. She's such a good math student, why would she cheat?

Argument 2: Rita could not have broken the rules. The reason is that Rita is a good worker. Rita always finishes her work. She works fast. She gets along well with others. So Rita must have followed the rules.

Part C Write each statement as a yes-no question. Then circle the subject and underline the predicate. Write **N** above each noun. Write **V** above each verb.

1. My teacher will call me.
2. That dog is sleeping again.
3. Bill should stop now.

Part D Write a summary sentence for each paragraph. Then write the conclusion.

In most schools, the morning recess is 30 minutes long. The afternoon recess is just as long. Children spend one full hour every day at recess. That is too much time to devote to activities that do not help children read better, work better or learn more.

Recess is a very active time for children. They run; they skip rope and play ball; they shout. Their play often leads to accidents. Big children run over little children. Balls fly through the air and strike children in the head. Feet accidentally kick. Jump ropes become whips that can hurt children. Other things happen that make the playground a most dangerous place.

When children return from recess, they are still very active. They are sweating and yelling and running and pushing. Their teachers try to settle them down, but the children find it hard to think about working. Sometimes, children take 20 minutes or more before they stop sweating and can settle down to start on their arithmetic or reading.

Independent Work Turn to lesson 63, part C. Tell about the problem with each argument.

Lesson 79

Part A

1. The dog was sleeping on that bed.
2. Her brother can jump over our fence.
3. Their long trip has seemed like a bad dream.

Part B

Write X-box sentences to tell about the problem with the argument.

Argument __ concludes ______________________________________;	X	however, ______________________________________. [Tell why.]

Argument 1:

Frankie Hubber could not have stolen the payroll from the Preston Building. Here is why: It would take a person with great athletic skill to climb up the side of the Preston Building all the way to the fifth floor. Only a person with great strength and balance could do that. Then the athlete would have pried open the window, gone inside, opened the safe, taken the money and climbed back down the side of the building.

Frankie Hubber is on trial for committing that crime. But look at Frankie. He doesn't look like an athlete. He's small. He does not have bulging muscles. He's got tiny hands and skinny legs. Frankie could **not** have stolen the payroll.

Argument 2:

Mrs. Johnson is one of the best math teachers in the world! The proof is her students. I've met three of them, and they are sensational at doing math. Carlos can do math problems that most adults can't do. So can Tiffany and so can Fran. If these three students do such a superb job, you know that everybody in the class must do just as well. And that means they must have one of the best teachers in the world. That's Mrs. Johnson.

Part C

Follow the directions and make the figures.

Directions 1:
- Make a capital **H** one inch high.
- Make a dot on each end of both vertical lines.
- Make a dot in the middle of the horizontal line.
- Connect all five dots with an **X.**

Directions 2:
- Make an **X** that is one inch high.
- Make a dot on each end of the slanted lines.
- Make a rectangle that has one of the dots in each corner.
- Make a horizontal line that goes through the middle of the **X** and touches both vertical lines.

Part D

Hotel Fact Guide

Breakfast: Free

Soft drinks: Free

Pool: Free

Horses: Free (between the hours of 4 a.m. and 6:30 a.m.)

Newspaper: Free

Sleeping rooms with kitchens: $45 per night (rooms have dressers, but no beds)

Each bed: $45 extra per night

Bathrooms: $15 extra per night

Advertisement for Clunkbocker Hotel

When you travel, it seems that everything costs a lot. Gas costs a lot. Food costs a lot. Visiting parks and campgrounds can be very expensive.

Well, here's some good news. Clunkbocker Hotel is different: At Clunkbocker, we have your pocketbook in mind. At Clunkbocker, you won't pay one cent for breakfast, because breakfast is free!

We know what you want and we're ready to give it to you. You won't pay for soft drinks, because they are free!

You'll swim in a pool that is free, ride horses that are free, even read daily newspapers that are free!

Oh yes, your room isn't free, but it is very inexpensive. A family-sized room with a kitchen costs only $45 a night. Where could you find a greater bargain?

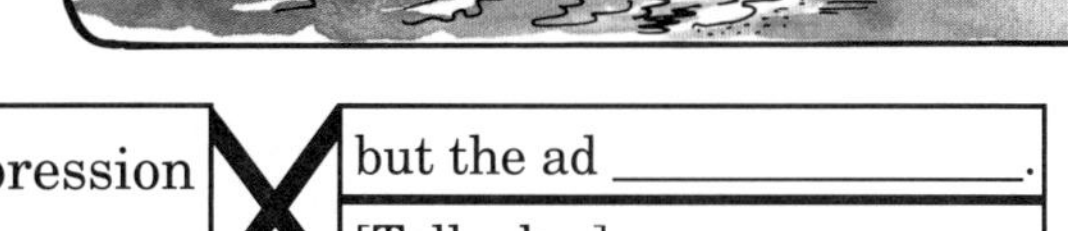

The ad gives the impression ________________________,	but the ad ______________. [Tell why.]

Independent Work

Turn to lesson 24, part H. Tell about the problems with the directions.

Lesson 80

Children under 14 are permitted to ride bikes on roads and streets, but learning to ride a bike is difficult. I know of one youngster who took three years to balance a bicycle. Another little girl took more than four years. Most children require more than one year to learn how to steer and pedal properly.

Another problem has to do with safety rules. Children under 14 do not know how to signal when they turn. They do not know that the rider should watch out for other vehicles on the road. There are many rules. Each one takes time to learn and practice.

Another problem is that younger children ride their bikes when they should be at home having dinner or doing homework. The bike makes it easy for them to ride off to a friend's house or to a park. Late at night, parks swarm with youngsters on bicycles who should be at home! Their parents worry about them because they don't know where they are. Children who are over 14 years old do not have these problems.

Test 8

Part A

Write a yes-no question for each statement. Then circle the subject and underline the predicate. Write **N** above each noun. Write **V** above each verb.

1. Our cat was playing in your yard.
2. Raymond should study more.
3. Her friend will call a taxi.

Part B

The argument concludes ______________________ ______________________;	however, the evidence ________ ______________________________.
	[Tell why.]

Argument:

I know that the movie playing at the Globe theater this week is a great movie. The reason is that the Globe has been playing good movies for a long time. Last week, the Globe played a movie that has won lots of awards. The week before that, the Globe played one of the funniest movies I have ever seen.

Part C The directions have sentences that are inaccurate and sentences that are too general. Follow the outline diagram and write a passage that tells about the problems with the directions.

Directions A:
To get to Ryan's house, go south. Turn east on Adams. Ryan's house is the second house.

Directions B:
To get to Cindy's house, go north. Turn left on Washington Street. Cindy's house is on the north side of the street.

Directions C:
To get to Debbie's house, go south. Turn west on Franklin. Debbie's house is the second house on the north side of the street.

Directions D:
To get to Michael's house, go south. Turn east on Adams Street. Michael's house is the last house on the right.

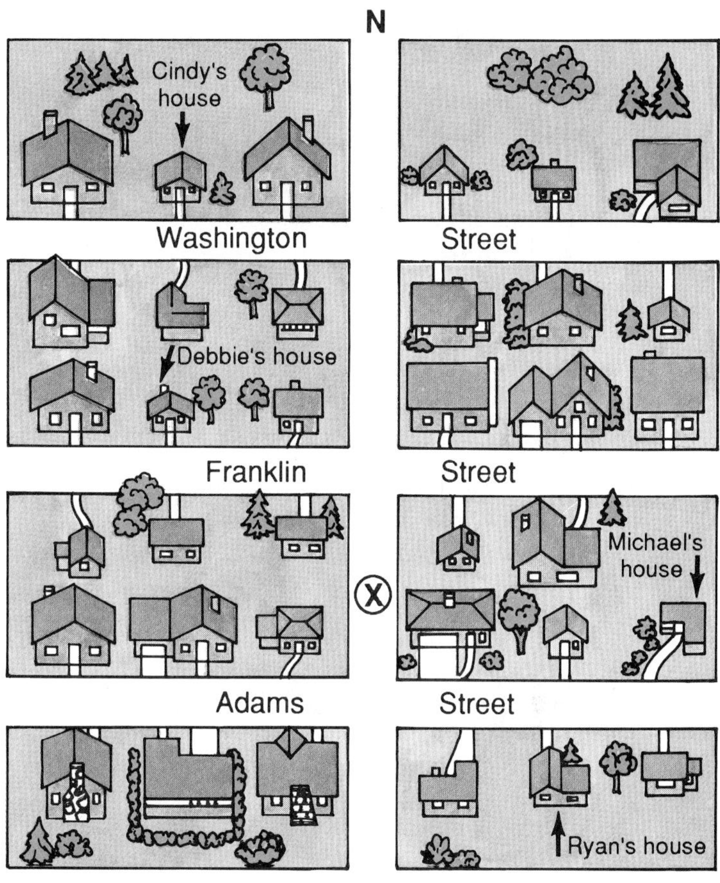

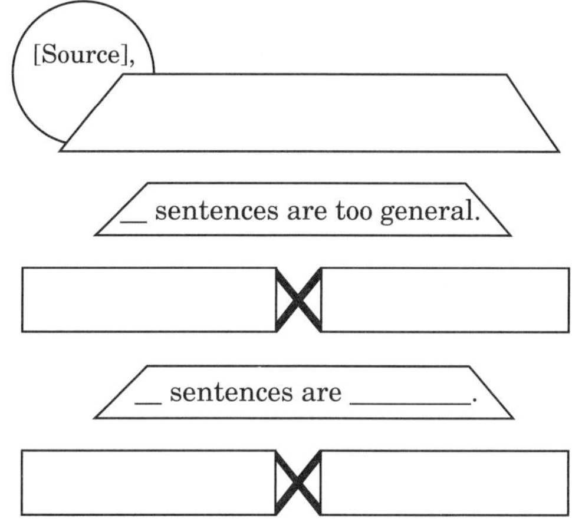

Lesson 81

Part A

- You can use the names of letters and numbers to describe how to make some figures.

a. ∞ Make an **8** that is on its side.

b. △ Make an upside-down **V**. Connect the ends with a horizontal line.

c. ▽ Make a **7**. Connect the ends with a straight line.

d. ∩ Make a **C** with the open part facing down.

e. ⬯ Make an upside-down **V**. Connect the ends of the **V** to a **U**.

Use letters and numbers to tell about the parts. Tell about one letter or number. Then tell how to connect another figure to the ends of the lines. Use the word **connect.**

1. 
2. 
3. 
4. 

Part B

a. A small and red bug was in the yard.
   A small, red bug was in the yard.

b. She had a thick and warm coat.
   She had a thick, warm coat.

Part C

1. The plane flew over the mountain. <u>The plane</u> was big.
2. Four horses hid among the trees. <u>The trees</u> were tall and dark.
3. He watched the butterflies. <u>The butterflies</u> were small and yellow.

Part D

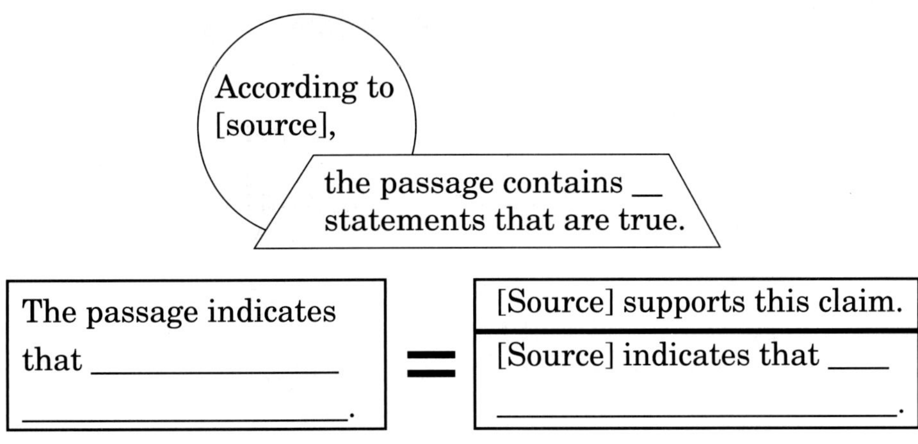
According to [source],
the passage contains __ statements that are true.
The passage indicates that ______________ ______________.
=
[Source] supports this claim.
[Source] indicates that ____ ______________.

Passage

Dentists recommend Blow-Big gum over other leading bubble gums.

Blow-Big contains no sugar. That's why it has been shown to reduce cavities.

And Blow-Big has a wonderful flavor that lasts longer than any other gum. Blow-Big is the best-tasting gum.

Table D24 Leading Brands of Bubble Gum

Brands	Taste	Dentists recommending the gum	Amount of sugar	How long flavor lasts
Blow-Big	excellent	1324	small amount	35 minutes
Choo-Choo	poor	61	none	12 minutes
Big-Bub	pretty good	8	large amount	38 minutes

Independent Work

Turn to lesson 35, part C. Make the figure for each set of directions. Then rewrite the second step so it does not have unnecessary words.

Lesson 82

Part A

Passage

Fran Dent wanted a raise. She told her boss why she deserved a raise. She told the boss that she worked hard, that she worked fast and accurately, and that she was always on time.

Her boss said that he didn't think she should get more money because she wasn't always on time. He said, "You're late most of the time."

She said, "I'm never late to work."

Time Clock Record

Name	Starts working at	Days absent	Latest time of arrival
Alice Bash	8:00 a.m.	0	7:56 a.m.
Fran Dent	8:00 a.m.	0	7:56 a.m.
Tim Donner	8:00 a.m.	27	8:58 a.m.
Bob Gilbert	8:00 a.m.	0	7:58 a.m.

[Person who was right] ______ indicated that ____________________.	=	[Source] supports this claim. [Source] indicates ________.

Part B

Combine the sentences.

1. The car went down a road. The road was hot and dusty.
2. A storm approached the city. The storm was violent.
3. On Saturday, Tina went hiking. The Saturday was cold and clear.

Part C

Lefty's Argument

Are my new neighbors lazy? I haven't met them yet, but they have a yellow car. I've known four families that have yellow cars. Every single one of those families was lazy. So this new family has to be lazy.

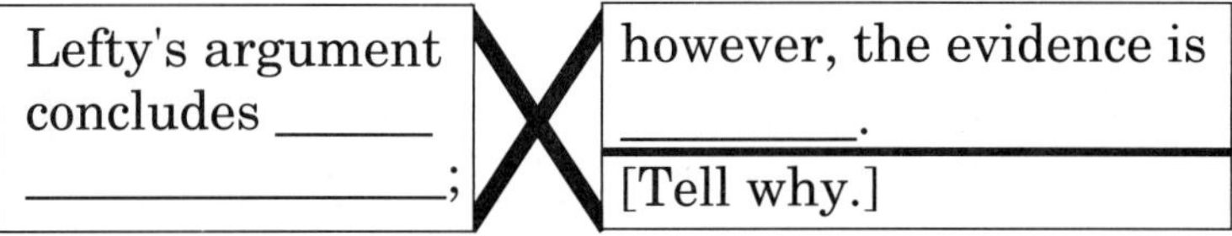

Lefty's argument concludes ______ ______;
however, the evidence is ______.
[Tell why.]

Part D

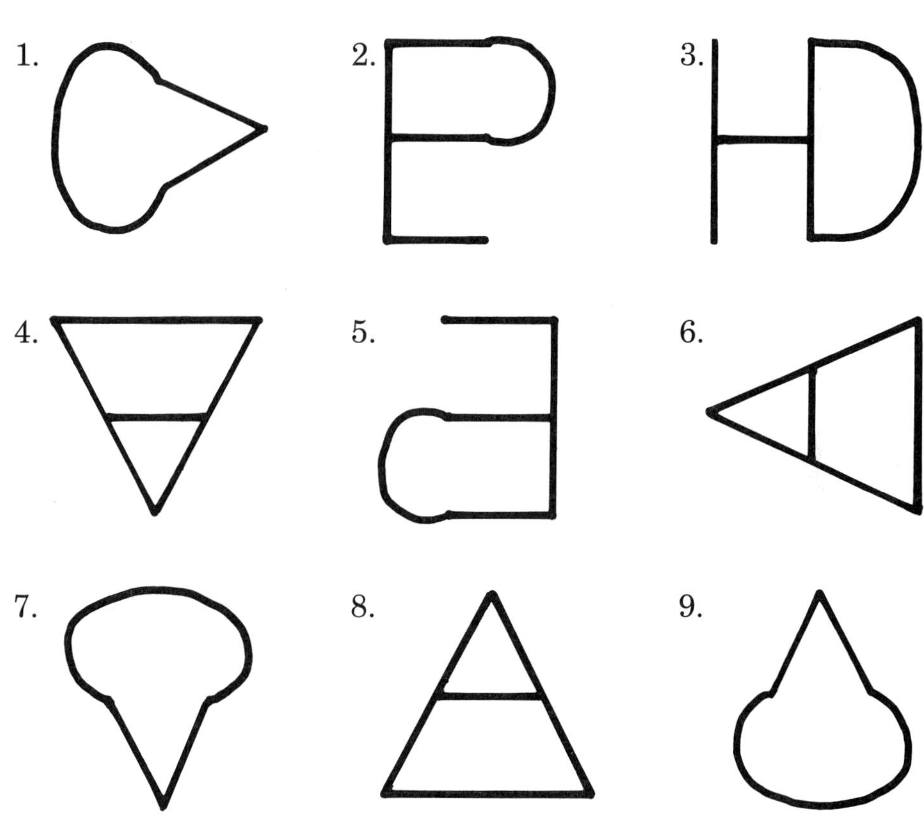

Independent Work

Turn to lesson 38, part D. Write a summary sentence for each item.

Lesson 83

Part A

Creamo Paint Ad

CREAMO paint will brighten up your summer.

Colors, colors and more colors will fill your rooms and make the outside of your house look like summer.

Light colors, dark colors, rich colors. Creamo has them all. **Remember, Creamo paints come in more colors than any other brand.**

But it's summer, and you're planning a lot of things that cost a lot of money. Well, good news again. Creamo paints are priced for the smallest budget.

Right now, at your Creamo dealer, you can buy Creamo interior paint for less than any other major brand of interior paint.

So you can bring the inside of your house to living color and not empty your pocketbook.

Table D25 Facts about Major Brands of Paint

Brands	How many stores sell the paint	Number of colors	When paint starts fading	Cost of interior paint	Cost of exterior paint
Brighto	5200	165	After 15 months	$21 a gallon	$21 a gallon
Creamo	501	236	After 15 months	$13 a gallon	$15 a gallon
Shino	1426	182	After 15 months	$19 a gallon	$19 a gallon
Splat	834	194	After 21 months	$12 a gallon	$17 a gallon

According to [source],

one claim in the Creamo ad is ________, and one claim is ________.

The ad indicates that ________________ ________________.

=

[Source] supports ________.

[Source] indicates ________ ________________.

________________ ________________;

X

however, ____________.

[Tell why.]

Part B

- Words that come before the noun and tell about the noun are **adjectives.**
- Adjectives answer the questions:

  Which one? or
  What kind? or
  How many?

- Here's a subject:

  A A N
  That lazy dog ________.

- Here's a different subject:

  A A N
  Five small bugs ________.

Part C

1. Her brother runs faster than Mark.
2. A little dog followed us.
3. An inaccurate claim appeared in the paper.
4. Their car was yellow.

Part D

Turn to lesson 82, part D. Write clear directions for one figure.

Independent Work

Turn to lesson 42, part F. Rewrite each step that has a problem.

Lesson 84

Part A

- **Adjectives** are words that tell about nouns. It doesn't matter whether the noun is in the subject or the predicate. The noun may have words in front of it that tell about it.
- Here's a sentence with nouns in the subject and the predicate:

N V V A A N
(Flies) were swarming near the broken table.

Part B

1. They had a big dinner[a] on their porch[b].
2. During dinner[c], Don[d] talked about his trip[e].
3. Before recess[f], we finished three papers[g].
4. James[h] spoke to his best friend[i].
5. The broken clock[j] was on sale.

Part C

Splat Paint Ad

Splat paint hits the mark!

SPLAT

You want colors? Splat has them. Splat has more colors than any other brand.

You want convenience? Splat has that, too. More stores sell Splat paint than any other brand of paint in the world!

You want paint that doesn't fade? Splat is your paint. Splat goes longer without fading than any other paint does.

And do you want to save on exterior paint? Once more, you have to select Splat. Splat's exterior paint costs less than any other brand.

Table D25 Facts about Major Brands of Paint

Brands	How many stores sell the paint	Number of colors	When paint starts fading	Cost of interior paint	Cost of exterior paint
Brighto	5200	165	After 15 months	$21 a gallon	$21 a gallon
Creamo	501	236	After 15 months	$13 a gallon	$15 a gallon
Shino	1426	182	After 15 months	$19 a gallon	$19 a gallon
Splat	834	194	After 21 months	$12 a gallon	$17 a gallon

_______ indicates _______ ___________________________.	=	[Source] supports _____. [Source] indicates _____.

Part D Write directions for making the figure. Tell the main shape. Tell the number of **C**s to make and where to make them. Tell the number of **V**s to make and where to make them.

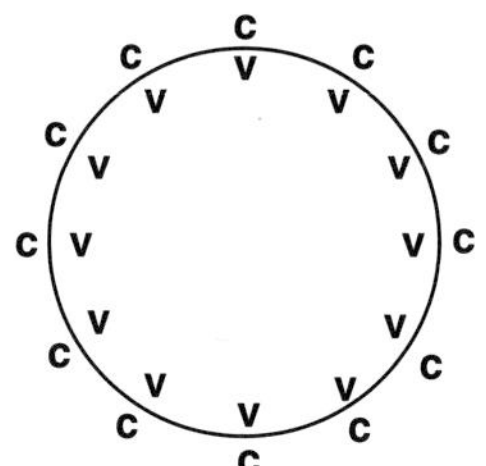

Part E Describe this neighborhood. Start with the words: **From above, Crest Hill.**

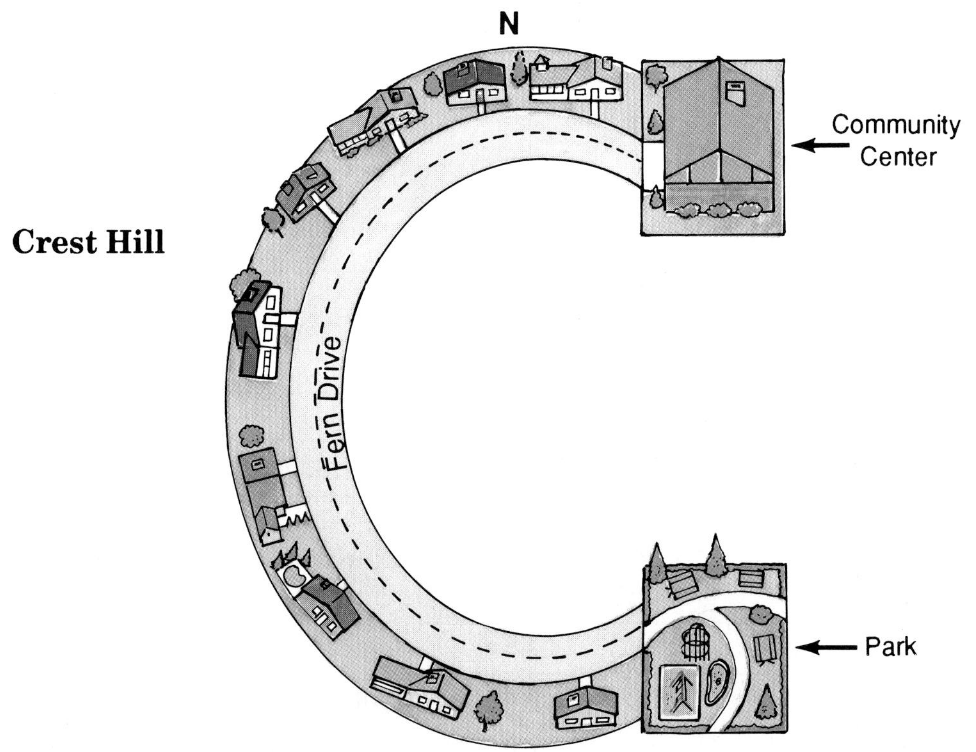

Independent Work Turn to lesson 63, part A. Write a passage that tells about the contradiction.

Lesson 85

Part A

1. Was his sister running in the street?
2. Has Michael finished the paper?
3. Should that little girl sleep?

Part B

Argument

The only way to save money is to spend less when you purchase things.
You'll spend less when you purchase things at Z-Mart.
Therefore, you should do all your shopping at Z-Mart.

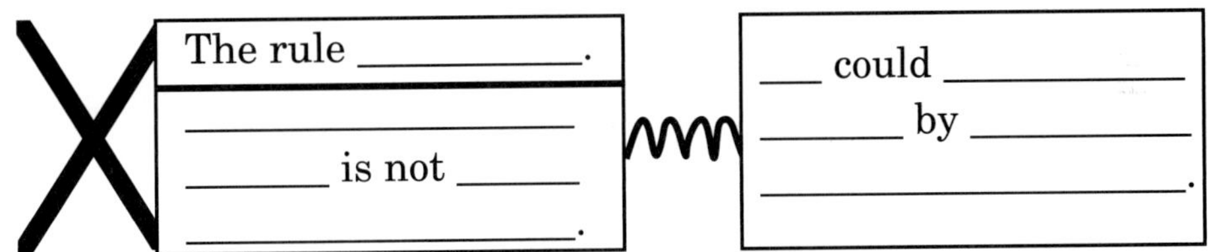

Part C

1. Their new (a) house is very pretty.
2. I lost my favorite (b) book.
3. During (c) breakfast, our (d) cat howled loudly.
4. During the next (e) meeting, we will discuss a (f) problem.

Part D Write a description of Topland. Start by saying: **From above, Topland looks like.**

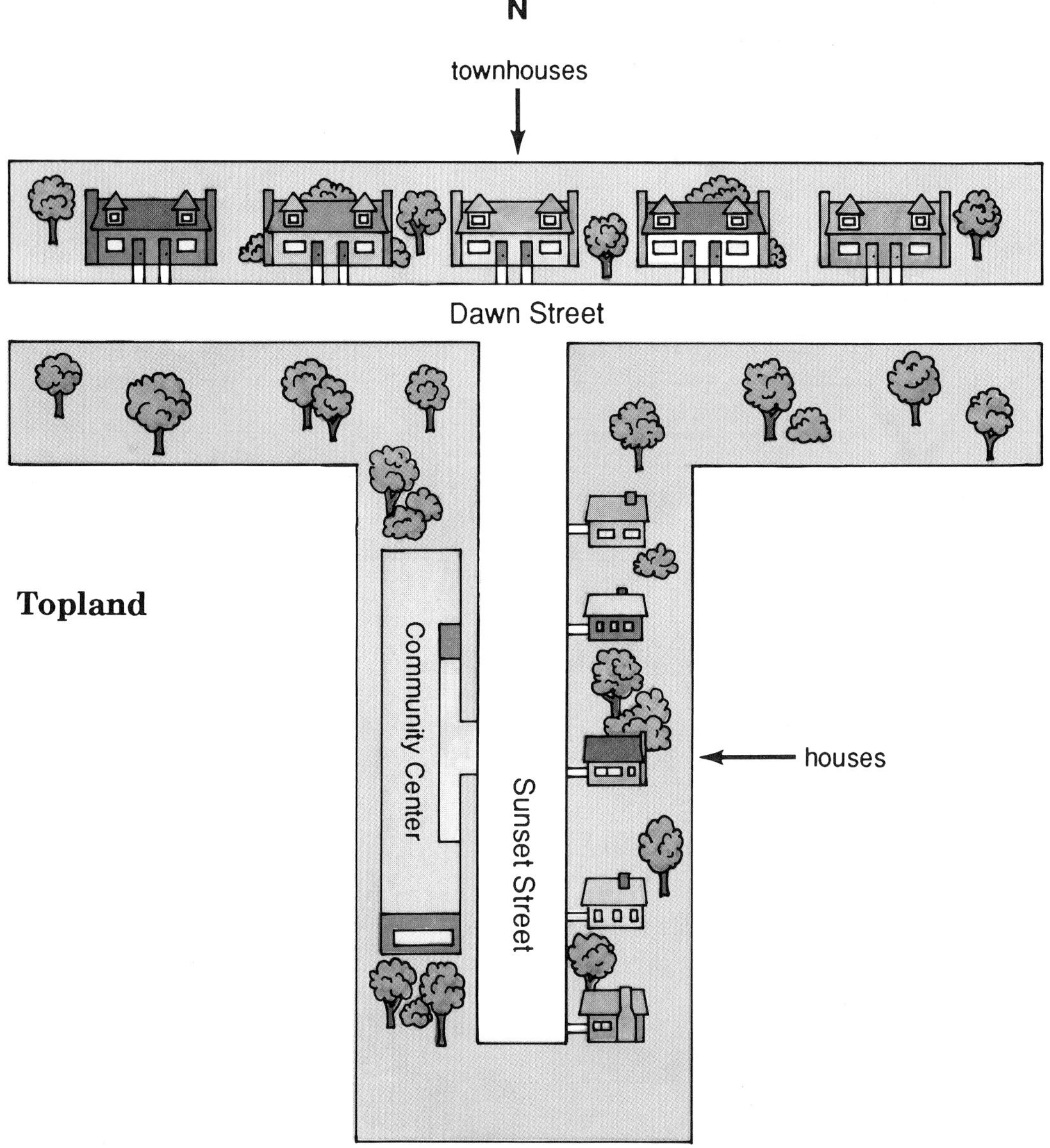

Independent Work Turn to lesson 64, part C. Write a passage that tells about the contradictions.

Lesson 86

Part A

Should School Lunches Be Changed?

Some people have suggested changing school lunches in our schools. Here is my response:

Each school lunch provides students with vitamins. Each lunch also has important minerals. A balanced diet is important. Therefore, each school lunch gives students all the major food groups that they need to grow strong bones, good muscles and a healthy mind. When a school lunch is prepared, we know that everything in it is good for a student's growing body and mind.

Students find it easy to eat all parts of their school lunch. Why wouldn't students eat everything when everything is delicious? How many times have we heard students say, "That meal was just wonderful"? If we listen closely and watch carefully, we'll see why so many students are in the clean-plate club. As little Jenny told me, "The food tastes wonderful!"

And talk about surprises! Students don't know what will be served today or tomorrow, but they do know that there will be delicious choices. There will be variety. And there will be wonderful taste surprises. One day, students will have to make the difficult choice of selecting chicken stew or chipped beef on toast. The next day, there will be other surprises and other difficult choices.

Part B

Copy each sentence. Circle the subject and underline the predicate. Write **A** above each adjective, **N** above each noun and **V** above each verb.

1. The smallest bunny slid down our hill.
2. The morning newspaper had a misleading ad.
3. Did his dog eat your candy?

Part C

Clunkbocker Hotel Ad

Your stay at the Clunkbocker will give you memories that will last a lifetime!

You'll remember your room, the walk to the beach, and that famous Clunkbocker view!

From the Clunkbocker, you follow a lovely curved sidewalk less than 1000 feet from the Clunkbocker to the famous white-sand beach. So you can spend many wonderful hours on the sand or in the warm ocean water.

But possibly you want to stay in your room and enjoy the view from your window. **When you look toward the ocean from your window, you will see nothing but ocean and beach.** It's a view you will remember for a long time.

the CLUNKBOCKER HOTEL

Map D26

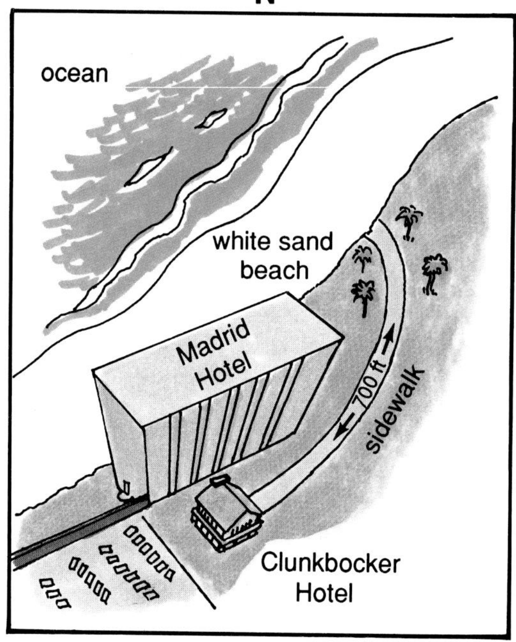
N
ocean
white sand beach
Madrid Hotel
700 ft
sidewalk
Clunkbocker Hotel

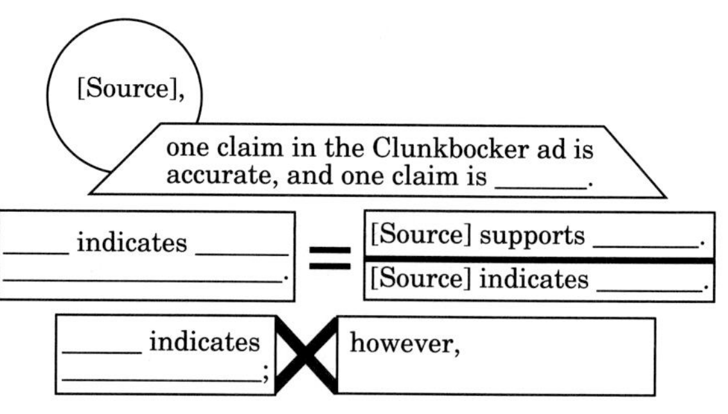
[Source],
one claim in the Clunkbocker ad is accurate, and one claim is ______.
______ indicates ______ ______.
[Source] supports ______.
[Source] indicates ______.
______ indicates ______;
however,

Independent Work

Turn to lesson 34, part F. Make the figure for each set of directions. Then rewrite the second step so it does not have unnecessary words.

Lesson 87

Part A

Lefty's Argument

Bumpos must be the fastest cars there are.

I've never driven a Bumpo, and I haven't read much about cars, but I know that Bumpos must be the best because my brother showed me a window wiper and a door handle from a Bumpo. Wow, were they super. That window wiper was made of the best rubber and best metal you could buy.

And what a door handle! It was really well made, and the metal was very good.

You know that, if Bumpo puts that much care into the window wipers and the door handles, they must make the fastest cars on the road.

Lefty's argument concludes ______________________ ______________________;	however, the evidence is ______________.
	[Tell why.]

Part B

1. A dog was friendly.
   A dog followed that woman.
2. That old man carried boxes.
   The boxes were large and heavy.
3. The passage contained a claim.
   The claim was misleading.

Part C

Account

Mrs. Anderson fired a waiter yesterday. What did he do wrong? He served soup that was not hot. What a shame. Everything else he served was delicious.

Facts

- The restaurant served many types of meals.
- The waiter was named Dave.
- All waiters start work at 5 p.m.
- The soup was cold.
- Dave came to work at 8:30 p.m.

The account gives the impression that _____ ___________________,	but that account is _______ . [Tell why.]

Part D

Write a description of Longview.

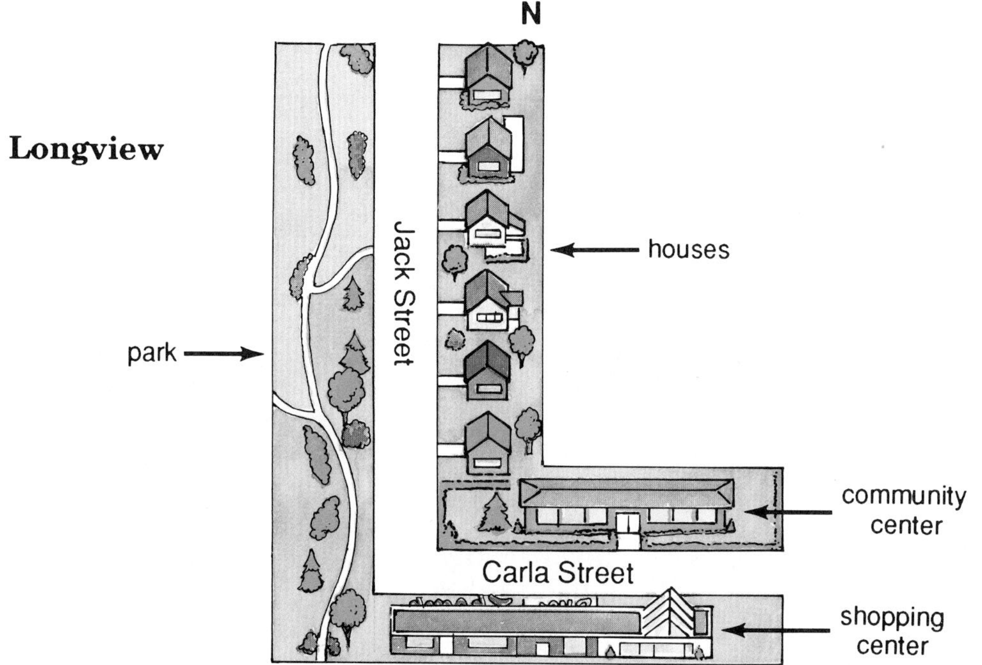

Independent Work

Turn to lesson 35, part C. Make the figure for each set of directions. Then rewrite the second step so it does not have unnecessary words.

Lesson 88

Part A

1. Her argument presented evidence.
   The evidence was irrelevant.
2. That boat won the race.
   That boat was large and blue.
3. The predicate has a verb.
   The verb is unusual.

Part B

Write a description of Hill View.

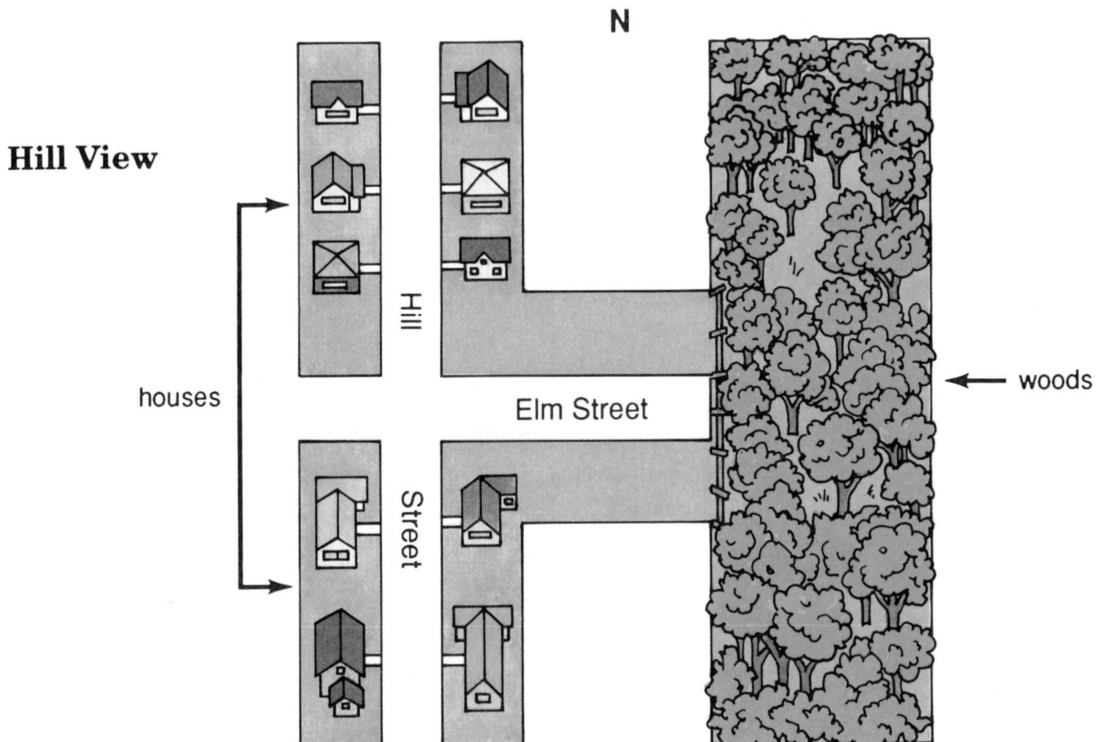

Part C

1. a. His name was Bill.
   b. His name was Bill Watson.
2. a. She lived in Texas exactly 11 years.
   b. She lived in Texas.
3. a. The car stopped on the freeway.
   b. The car stopped.

Part D

Source D29	Source D30
• The Clunkbocker Hotel was built in 1899 by Robert K. Clunkbocker.	• Robert Clunkbocker built the Clunkbocker Hotel in the summer of 1899.
• The original hotel had 86 rooms.	• Before the first addition was built, the Clunkbocker had 86 rooms.
• In 1915, the first addition was built. Forty new rooms were added.	• The first addition was started in 1911 and completed in 1912. That addition added 40 rooms to the hotel.
• The second addition involved 10 large rooms and 30 small rooms. That addition was completed in 1921.	• A second addition was started in 1920 and completed in 1921. That addition involved 40 more rooms.
• Most of the original Clunkbocker burned down in the great fire of 1928. Nobody was injured.	• In 1928, a faulty stove caused a fire in one of the kitchens. The fire burned down everything except 18 rooms and the famous Clunkbocker ballroom.
• In 1930, the Clunkbocker reopened. It had 200 rooms and was called "The most amazing hotel in the world."	• The Clunkbocker was rebuilt and began operating five years after the fire. People came from all over the world for the famous reopening of the Clunkbocker.

Source D30 contradicts ___ details of Source D29.

Source D29 indicates ______________________ ______________________,

but ____________ indicates ______________________ ______________________.

Independent Work

Turn to lesson 46, part D. Follow the X-box rules and tell about description 1 and description 2.

Lesson 89

Part A Write a description of Valley Park.

Valley Park

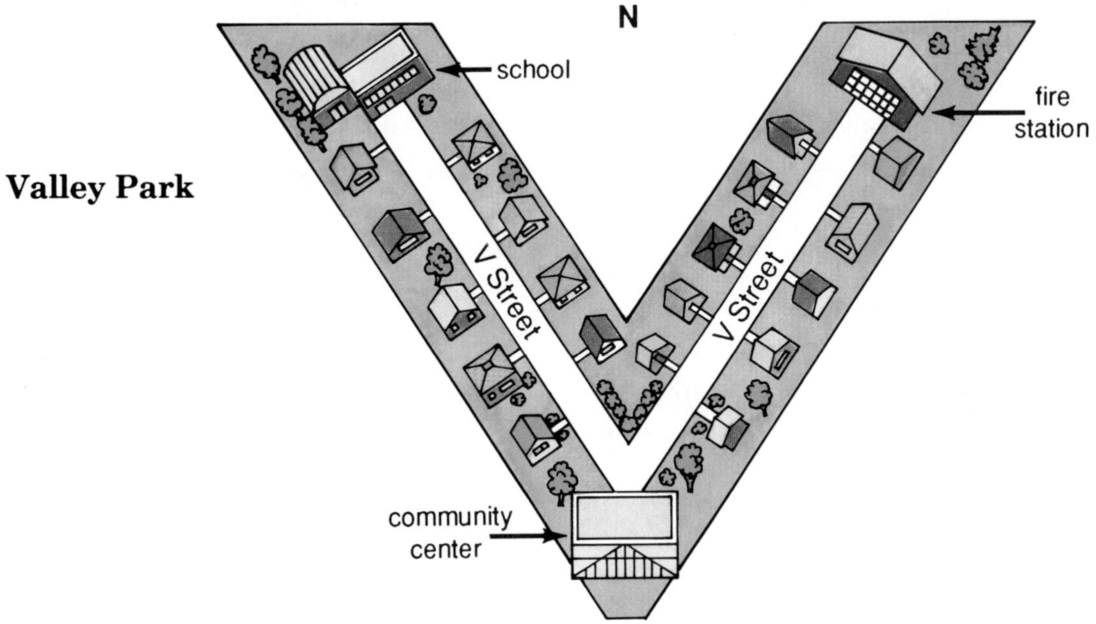

Part B

- Words that tell where something is are not usually adjectives.
- Here's a sentence: **They were in a small room.**
- The word **in** is not an adjective. It doesn't tell about the room. The words **a** and **small** tell about the room:

  a room **small room**

- Here are some words that are not usually adjectives:

  between **over** **beside** **on** **under**

Part C

1. A cloud passed over the city.
   The cloud was enormous and dark.
2. His sister read three books.
   His sister was older than he was.
3. The room had six windows.
   The room was in a hotel.

Part D

Lefty's Account

I was riding my skateboard along the sidewalk through Gilbert Park. I was going pretty fast. All of a sudden, a woman started waving her arms. She hollered, "Go get him," to her dog. And that dog took out after me. It was one big, mean dog. Real big and mean.

I was watching the dog come tearing after me, and the first thing I knew, my skateboard went off the sidewalk. I went flying through the air, and I landed in a ditch. Ouch.

Mrs. Johnson's Account

I was in the park with dear Fluffy. I was throwing sticks for Fluffy to fetch. I threw one stick that landed on the sidewalk and told Fluffy, "Go get it."

Little Fluffy ran as fast as her little legs could move her little body.

Just then a rowdy young man on some sort of platform with wheels came speeding down the sidewalk. He came right up behind Fluffy and frightened her half to death. She scurried off the sidewalk, and that terrible young man steered his platform right after her.

Fortunately, she got out of his way, and he went tumbling into the ditch. Served him right.

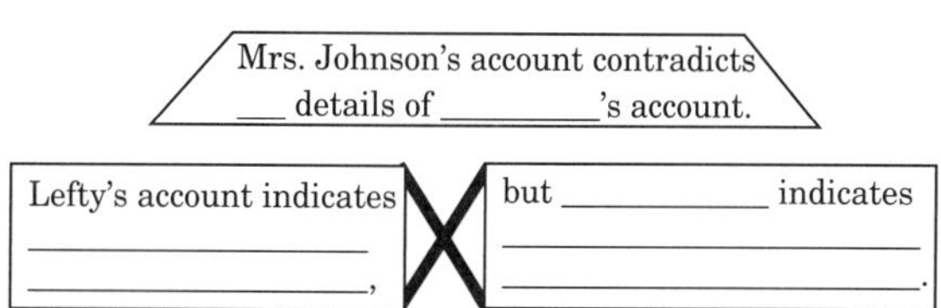

Mrs. Johnson's account contradicts
___ details of ________'s account.
Lefty's account indicates
________,
but ________ indicates
________.

Questions

1. Do the accounts agree on where the accident took place?
2. Do the accounts agree on what Lefty was riding?
3. Do the accounts agree on what Mrs. Johnson said?
4. Do the accounts agree on what Mrs. Johnson was doing?
5. Do the accounts agree on who did the chasing?
6. Do the accounts agree on how the dog looked?

Do the accounts agree on where Lefty ended up?

ɘendent Turn to lesson 65, part B. Write X-box sentences to tell about the problem with each argument.

Lesson 90

Part A

- You've rewritten sentences so they begin with part of the predicate. All the sentences you've worked with begin with a part that tells when.
- Some other sentences work the same way. Those are sentences that have a part that begins with **if, although, unless, because** or **to.**
    - You can take the train **to** get to my house.
      To get to my house, you can take the train.
    - I'll call Mom **unless** you stop.
      Unless you stop, I'll call Mom.
    - I am happy **if** you are happy.
      If you are happy, I am happy.

Part B

1. She worked hard to become a doctor.
2. The car kept moving although the engine blew up.
3. We will never get there if it keeps on raining.
4. That plant will die unless you open the window.

Test 9

Part A

Copy each sentence. Circle the subject and underline the predicate. Write **A** above each adjective, **N** above each noun and **V** above each verb.

1. A newspaper reporter wrote a misleading article.
2. Did her cat drink the milk?

Part B

Combine the sentences.

1. They bought a truck. The truck was large and old.
2. Those horses hid in the trees. The horses were gray.
3. We climbed a trail. The trail was steep and dangerous.

Part C

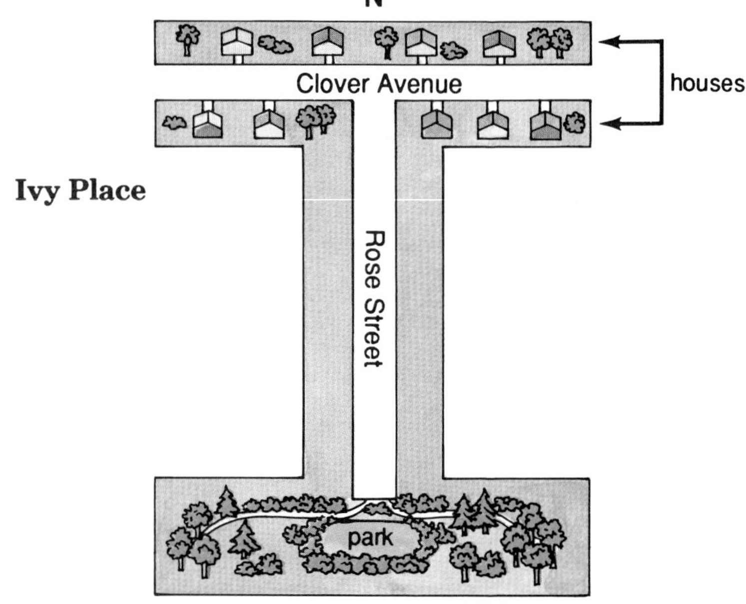
N
Clover Avenue
houses
Ivy Place
Rose Street
park

Part D

Creamo Paint Ad

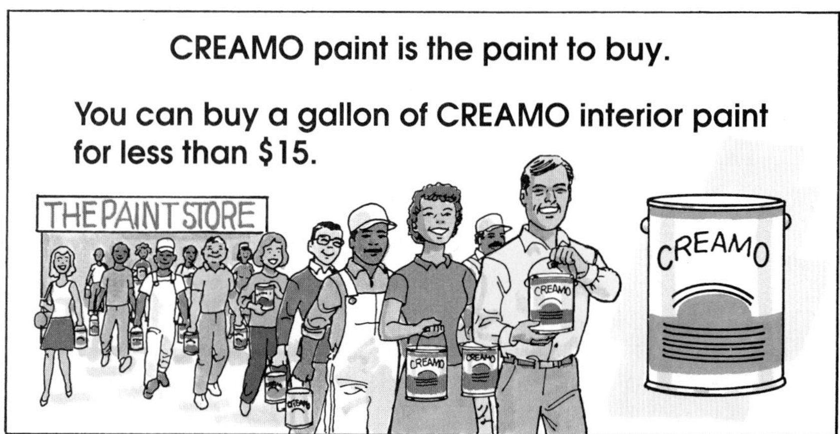
CREAMO paint is the paint to buy.
You can buy a gallon of CREAMO interior paint for less than $15.
THE PAINT STORE
CREAMO

Table D25 Facts about Major Brands of Paint

Brands	How many stores sell the paint	Number of colors	When paint starts fading	Cost of interior paint	Cost of exterior paint
Brighto	5200	165	After 15 months	$21 a gallon	$21 a gallon
Creamo	501	236	After 15 months	$13 a gallon	$15 a gallon
Shino	1426	182	After 15 months	$19 a gallon	$19 a gallon

The ad indicates that ______________________ ______________________.	=	[Source] supports ________. [Source] indicates ________ ______________________.

Lesson 91

Part A Write whether each item is an **argument** or a **claim.**

1. Jane's house is farther from the starting point than Jerry's house is.
2. Jane's house is bigger than Jerry's house. Therefore, Jane's family is richer than Jerry's family.
3. Tim moved last week. Tim now lives next to Jane.
4. Jane's house is bigger than Tim's house. Jane's house has three trees in the front yard.
5. Jane's house is bigger than Tim's house. Therefore, Jane's house must have more windows than Tim's house.
6. You should vote for the best person. Jim Smith is the best person. So, you should vote for Jim Smith.

Part B Rewrite each sentence so it begins with the underlined word.

1. We will get there on time unless the traffic gets bad.
2. He was tired although he didn't admit it.
3. The birds worked hard to build that nest.

Part C

Latest Bumpo Ad

More people are selling their Dancers and buying Bumpos—and for very good reasons.

- Bumpo is known for performance.
- A new Bumpo costs no more than last year's Bumpo.
- And talk about gas mileage! People cannot believe the gas mileage Bumpo delivers.
- If you like attractive colors, you'll have trouble choosing from the dozens of beautiful colors that Bumpo cars come in.
- Remember, you can own a new Bumpo for less than $20,000.

Picture yourself behind the wheel of a Bumpo . . . and then go out and make your dreams come true.

Buy a BUMPO

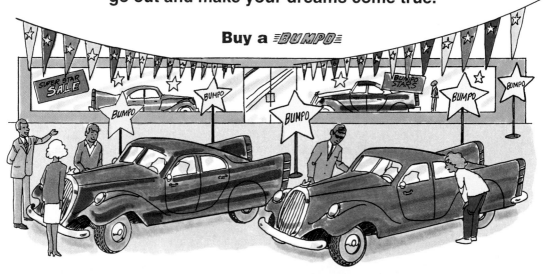

Consumer Fact Chart

	Cost this year	Cost last year	Gas mileage	Colors that are available	Performance
Bumpo	$64,000	$64,000	12 miles a gallon	black or brown	poor
Dancer	$19,000	$19,000	36 miles a gallon	8 different colors	good

Part D

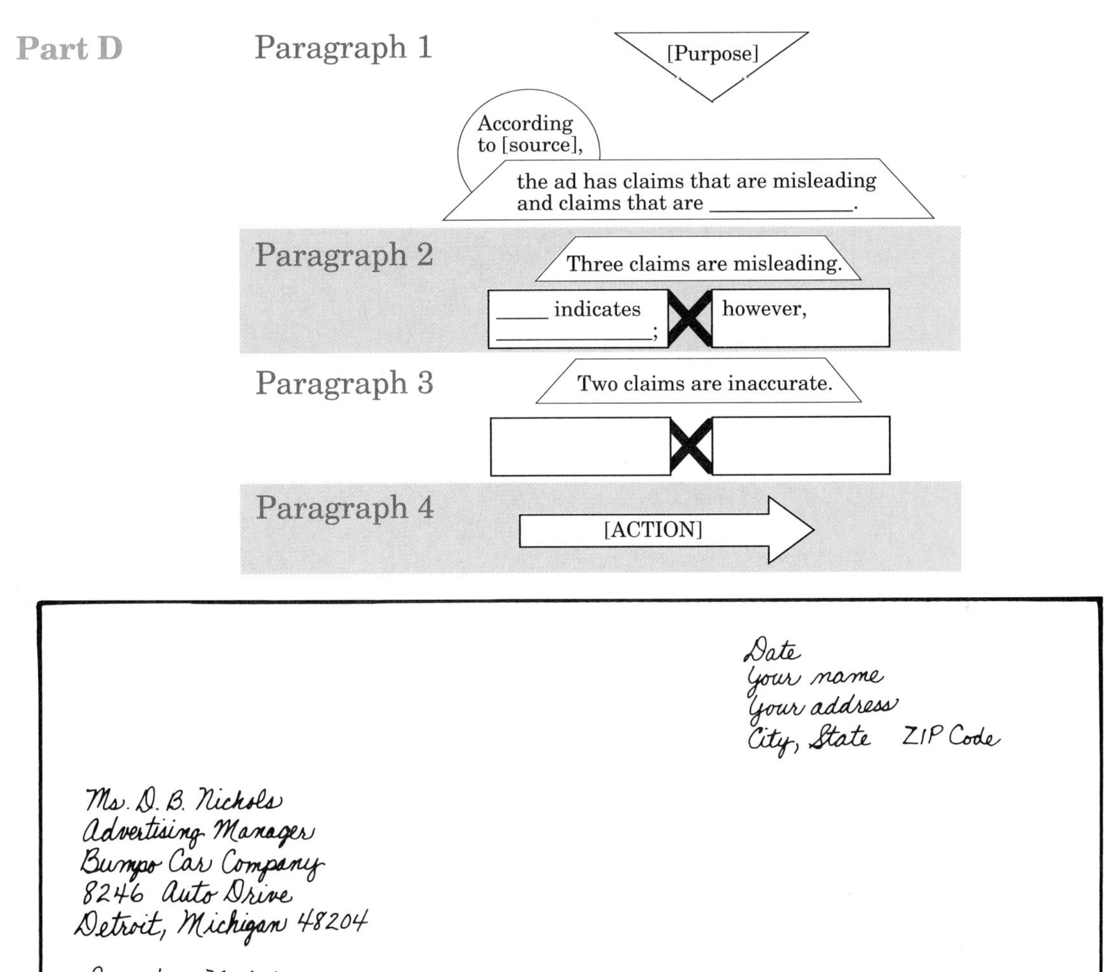
Paragraph 1
[Purpose]
According to [source],
the ad has claims that are misleading and claims that are ____________.
Paragraph 2
Three claims are misleading.
_____ indicates ____________;
however,
Paragraph 3
Two claims are inaccurate.
Paragraph 4
[ACTION]

Date
Your name
Your address
City, State ZIP Code

Ms. D. B. Nichols
Advertising Manager
Bumpo Car Company
8246 Auto Drive
Detroit, Michigan 48204

Dear Ms. Nichols,

(Your letter)

Sincerely,
(Your name)

Independent Work

Turn to lesson 78, part B. Write X-box sentences to tell the problems with the arguments.

Lesson 92

Part A

1. A squirrel was in our front yard.
   The squirrel was frisky.
2. Three crates fell off a speeding truck.
   The crates were wooden.
3. A woman walked along a road.
   The road was winding.

Part B

1. To get to Tina's house, turn left at Fern Street. Go to the second house.
2. Jane Dunkan's house must be the biggest house in the neighborhood. The reason is that Jane is the tallest girl in school.
3. Jane's house needs painting.
4. Two girls named Jane live on Fern Street.

Map D27

N

Fern Street

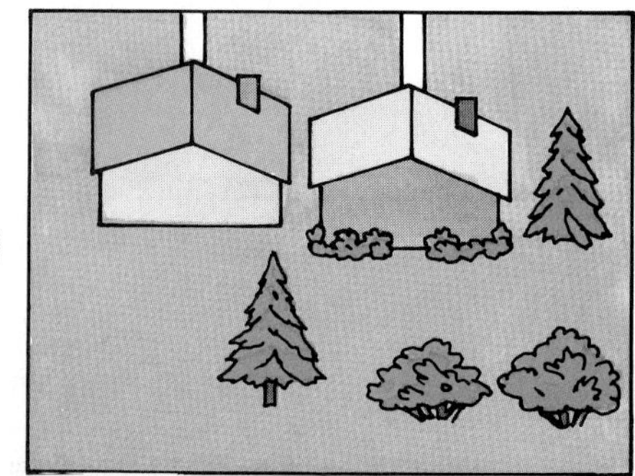

Part C Write a description of Gibson School.

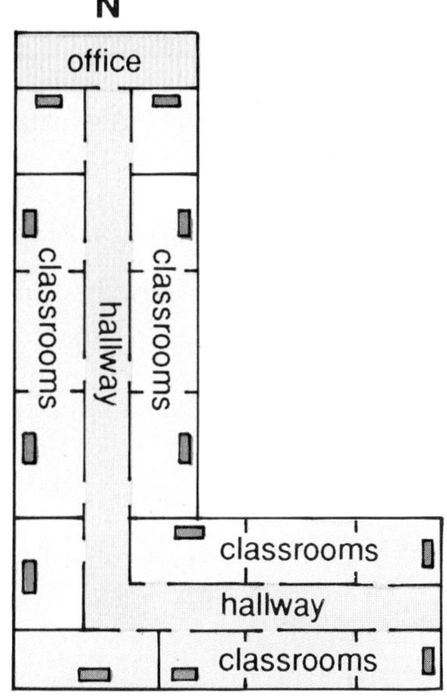

Part D

Argument	Facts
Here's gossip about Mrs. Zee. I happen to know that Mrs. Zee spends a lot more money than she earns. You can find her shopping in stores every day, buying things. On most days, she'll buy more than $1000 worth of products! We all know she doesn't earn that much. Therefore, she must be dishonest.	• Mrs. Zee has a new car. • Mrs. Zee works for Consumer Research Company. • Mrs. Zee's job is to buy products that may be unsafe. • Mrs. Zee is going to law school at night.

Independent Work Turn to lesson 79, part B. Write X-box sentences to tell the problem with the argument. Tell why the evidence is irrelevant.

Lesson 93

Part A Rewrite each sentence so it begins with part of the predicate.

1. Milly found the house although Tim's directions were too general.
2. They worked for hours to remove the fallen tree.
3. Fran was late because the bus broke down.

Part B

1. Bill talked to the girl.
   The girl sat next to him.
2. Bill slept in a bed.
   The bed was falling apart.
3. Fran caught three butterflies.
   The butterflies had golden wings.
4. They sat in a meeting.
   The meeting lasted four hours.
5. They stopped for an old man.
   The old man had been in an accident.

Part C

(Yesterday's date)

Dear (your name),

I have finally decided to buy a new car. I've talked to some people, and I think I'll buy a Springer. I like the way it looks.

The car salesman tells me that the Springer corners better than the BBC. And it accelerates faster than the BBC. Also, the Springer is guaranteed for 5 years.

So the next time you see me, I may be driving a bright red Springer.

Your friend,
James

Consumer Fact Table

	Car Performance (1)	(2)	(3)	(4)	(5)	(6)	(7)
	How it corners	How quickly it accelerates to 60 miles per hour	Cost	Guarantee	Workmanship	Gas mileage	Customer satisfaction
BBC	very well	11 seconds	$15,000	5 years all parts	excellent	28 miles per gallon	highest
Empo	very well	12 seconds	$15,000	3 years all parts	poor	29 miles per gallon	third highest
Speedo	very well	14 seconds	$16,000	1 year all parts	good	28 miles per gallon	second highest
Springer	fairly well	18 seconds	$19,000	2 years all parts	poor	28 miles per gallon	lowest

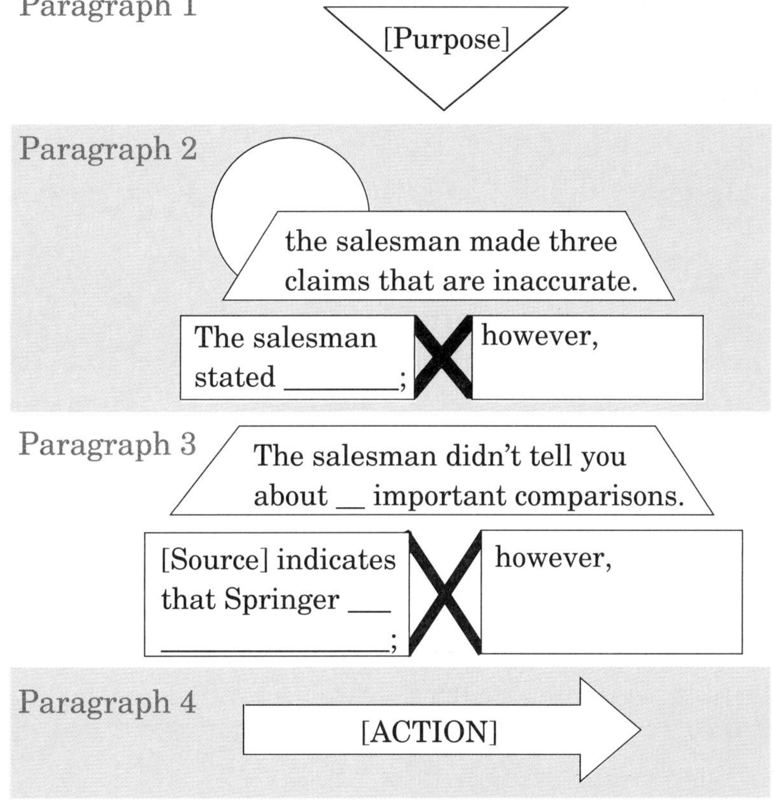

Paragraph 1
[Purpose]
Paragraph 2
the salesman made three claims that are inaccurate.
The salesman stated ________;
however,
Paragraph 3
The salesman didn't tell you about __ important comparisons.
[Source] indicates that Springer ___ ________________;
however,
Paragraph 4
[ACTION]

Independent Work

Turn to lesson 81, part A. Use letters and numbers to tell how to make each figure.

Lesson 94

Part A Use the word **who** or **that** to combine each pair of sentences.

1. We found an old shovel.
   The shovel had a broken handle.
2. We watched the cowboy.
   The cowboy was riding a black horse.
3. We had a Bumpo car.
   The Bumpo car gave us lots of problems.
4. We met a woman.
   The woman had written three books.
5. The room was filled with music.
   The music sounded loud and strange.

Part B

- You've worked with nouns. Nouns are fairly specific names for persons, places or things.
- Words that replace nouns are called **pronouns.**
- Pronouns are not as specific as nouns.
- Here are some nouns that tell about the same person:

  Carla girl female
- Here is a **pronoun** that tells about the same person:

  she
- The pronoun **she** also tells about many other persons: Mrs. Jones, Mrs. Adams, Cindy Ortega and little baby Edna.
- Here is a list of common pronouns:

  he she it they we him her them us

Part C Rewrite the sentences with a pronoun for each underlined part.

1. <u>That truck</u> belongs to <u>Jake</u>.
2. <u>Tina's mother</u> scolded <u>the girls</u>.
3. <u>Terry, Mary and I</u> found <u>the path</u>.
4. <u>Ginger</u> bought ice cream for <u>Terry, Mary and me</u>.
5. <u>Four dogs</u> chased <u>a rabbit</u>.

Part D

(Date)

Dear (your name),

We're making our final plans for our summer vacation. Our whole family is going out West for three weeks. We're going to visit the Grand Canyon, Wally World, and then we're going to spend a week at a wonderful old hotel on the ocean, the Clunkbocker Hotel. It's going to be fun.

According to the brochure, the Clunkbocker is only 200 feet from the beach. It has a fantastic view of the ocean from every window. We'll be able to ride horses free any time of the day. And what's most amazing is that our hotel room costs less than $50 a night.

So we're looking forward to fun in the sun and the water. The next time I write, I'll be in California at the Clunkbocker.

Your friend,
Carla

Map of Donner Beach

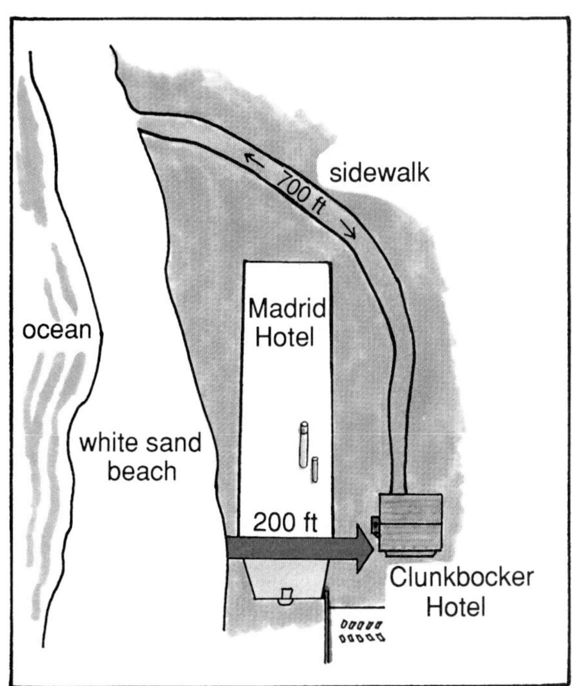

Hotel Fact Guide

Breakfast: Free
Soft drinks: Free
Pool: Free
Horses: Free (between the hours of 4 a.m. and 6:30 a.m.)
Newspaper: Free
Sleeping rooms with kitchens: $45 per night (rooms have dressers, but no beds)
Each bed: $45 extra per night
Bathrooms: $15 extra per night

Independent Work

Turn to lesson 82, part D. Use letters to tell about how to make figures 1, 2, 3 and 4.

Lesson 95

Part A

Rewrite the sentences. Replace each underlined part with the correct pronoun.

1. The water splashed all over Fran and me.
2. Billy and three cats sat on the sidewalk.
3. My uncle found an old coin.
4. Ann looked at Mr. Green.
5. Little Timmy loves Amy, Lisa, Mary and Jimbo.

Part B

For each number, write **N, V, A** or **P.**

They (1) will fish (2) for perch (3).

A (4) little girl caught (5) four large (6) fish (7).

Fran (8) gave (9) the (10) sled (11) to me (12).

Part C

(Date)

Dear (your name),

Thanks for the information about the Springer. I decided not to buy a Springer. Instead, I think I'll buy an Empo. And you can't tell me that an Empo is not the best car.

The Empo salesman showed me some facts right out of the Consumer Fact Table. Empo gets better gas mileage than BBC or any other car in its class. The Empo costs no more than the BBC. And it has a guarantee on all parts, just like the BBC.

The Empo sounds great, so that's the car I think I'll buy.

Your friend,
James

Consumer Fact Table

	Car Performance (1)	(2)	(3)	(4)	(5)	(6)	(7)
	How it corners	How quickly it accelerates to 60 miles per hour	Cost	Guarantee	Workmanship	Gas mileage	Customer satisfaction
BBC	very well	11 seconds	$15,000	5 years all parts	excellent	28 miles per gallon	highest
Empo	very well	12 seconds	$15,000	3 years all parts	poor	29 miles per gallon	third highest
Speedo	very well	14 seconds	$16,000	1 year all parts	good	28 miles per gallon	second highest
Springer	fairly well	18 seconds	$19,000	2 years all parts	poor	28 miles per gallon	lowest

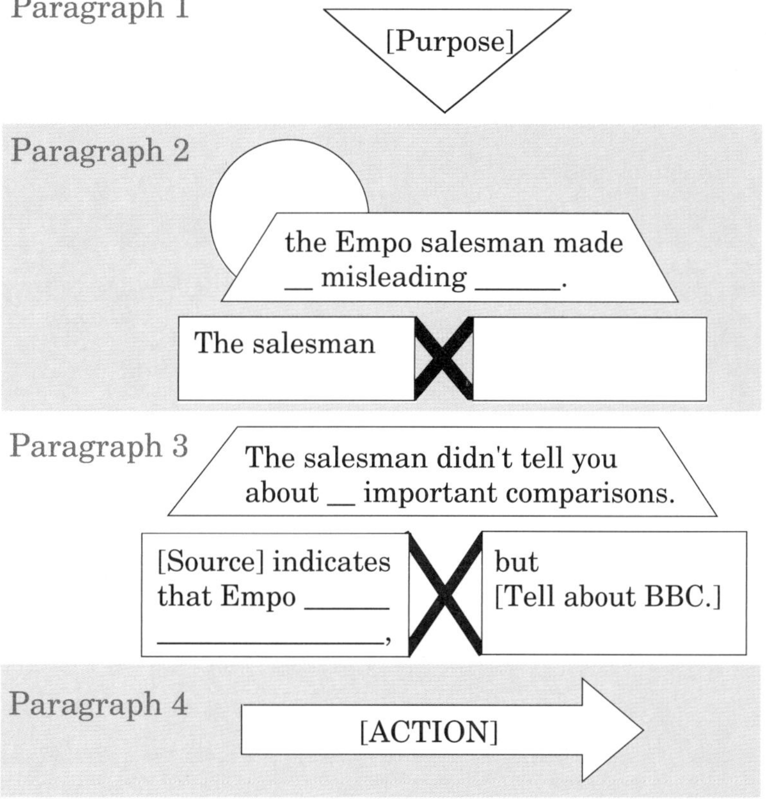

Paragraph 1
[Purpose]
Paragraph 2
the Empo salesman made __ misleading ______.
The salesman
Paragraph 3
The salesman didn't tell you about __ important comparisons.
[Source] indicates that Empo ______ ________________,
but [Tell about BBC.]
Paragraph 4
[ACTION]

Independent Work

Turn to lesson 82, part D. Use letters to tell how to make figures 5, 6, 7, 8 and 9.

Lesson 96

Part A

Copy the number for each word. Write **N** for noun, **V** for verb, **A** for adjective or **P** for pronoun.

1 2 3 4 5
Is she buying another car?

6 7 8 9
Did that man find it?

10 11 12
Are they organizing more meetings?

13 14 15 16
His new clothes make him look handsome.

Part B

Recess
by
Mrs. Johnson

Because of the serious problems with school recesses, I recommend that recess should be eliminated.

In most schools, the morning recess is 30 minutes long. The afternoon recess is just as long. Children spend one full hour every day at morning and afternoon recess. That is too much time to devote to activities that do not help children read better, work better or learn more.

Recess is a very active time for children. They run; they skip rope; they play ball; they shout. Their play leads to accidents every day. Big children run over little children. Balls fly through the air and strike children in the head. Feet accidentally kick. Jump ropes become whips that can hurt children. Other things happen that make the playground a most dangerous place.

When children return from recess, they are still very active. They are screaming and yelling, and running and pushing. Their teachers try to settle them down, but the children find it hard to think about working. Usually the children take 20 minutes or more before they can settle down to start on their arithmetic or reading.

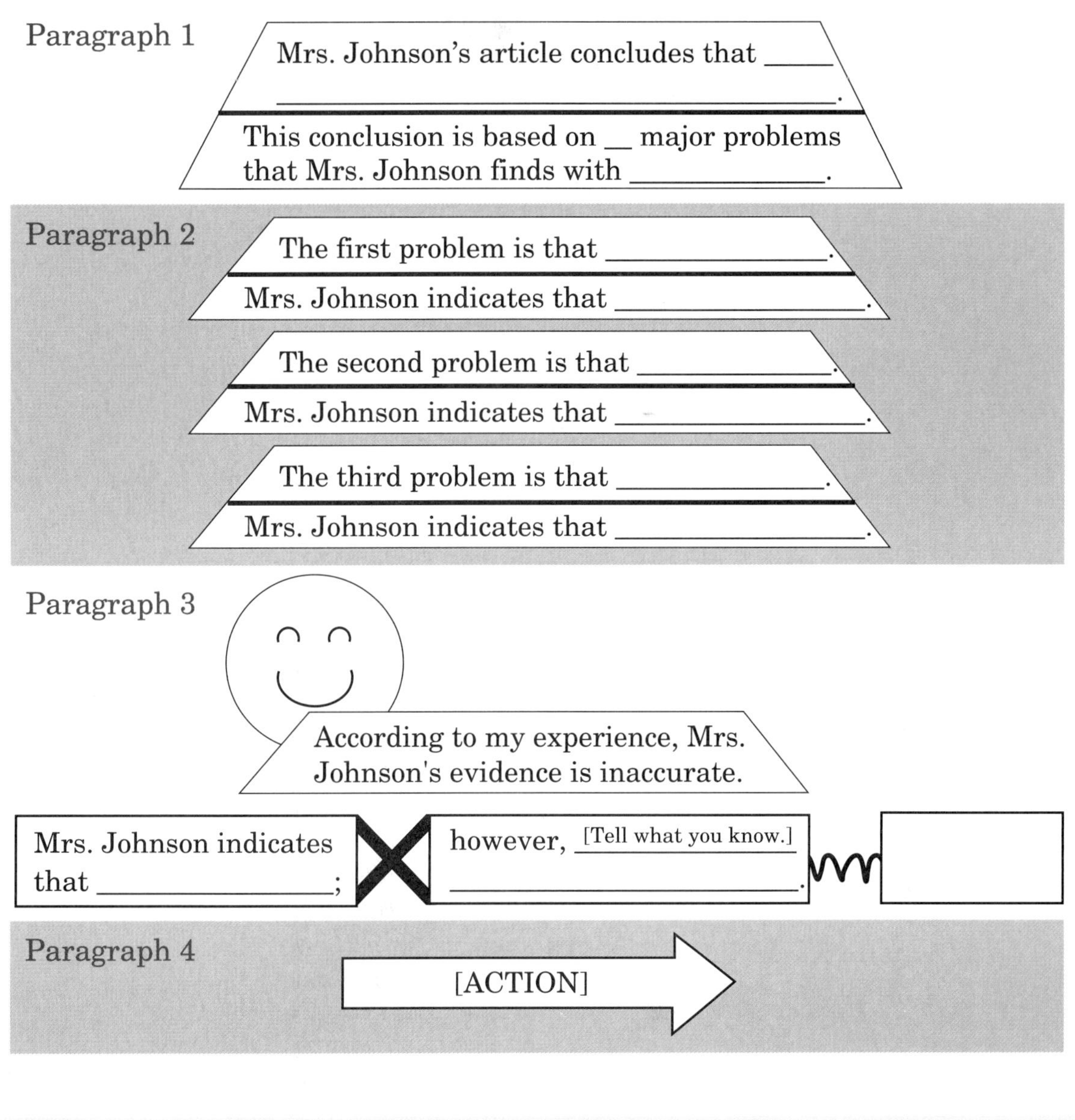

Paragraph 1
Mrs. Johnson's article concludes that ____________.
This conclusion is based on __ major problems that Mrs. Johnson finds with ____________.
Paragraph 2
The first problem is that ____________.
Mrs. Johnson indicates that ____________.
The second problem is that ____________.
Mrs. Johnson indicates that ____________.
The third problem is that ____________.
Mrs. Johnson indicates that ____________.
Paragraph 3
According to my experience, Mrs. Johnson's evidence is inaccurate.
Mrs. Johnson indicates that ____________;
however, [Tell what you know.] ____________.
Paragraph 4
[ACTION]

Independent Work

Turn to lesson 41, part E. Rewrite each step that has a problem.

Lesson 97

Part A

Copy the number for each word. Write **N** for noun, **V** for verb, **A** for adjective or **P** for pronoun.

1 Are 2 they 3 building that 4 strange 5 house?

6 Eric 7 was 8 running after 9 him.

10 Bring 11 your little 12 sister with 13 us.

14 You are a 15 smart 16 person.

Part B

Bicycles

by

Mrs. Johnson

I believe that children under 14 should not be permitted to ride bikes on roads and streets.

The learning process is the first problem we should consider. I know of one youngster who took three years to learn to balance a bicycle. Another little girl took more than four years. Most children require more than one year to learn how to steer and pedal properly.

Another problem has to do with safety rules. Children under 14 do not know how to signal when they turn. They do not know that bikes should not be ridden on sidewalks. They do not know that the rider should watch out for other vehicles on the road. There are many rules. Each one takes time to learn and practice.

Another problem is that younger children ride their bikes when they should be at home washing the dishes or doing homework. The bike makes it easier for them to ride off to a friend's house or to a park. Late at night, parks are filled with youngsters on bicycles who should be at home! Their parents worry about them because they don't know where they are. Children who are over 14 years old do not have these problems.

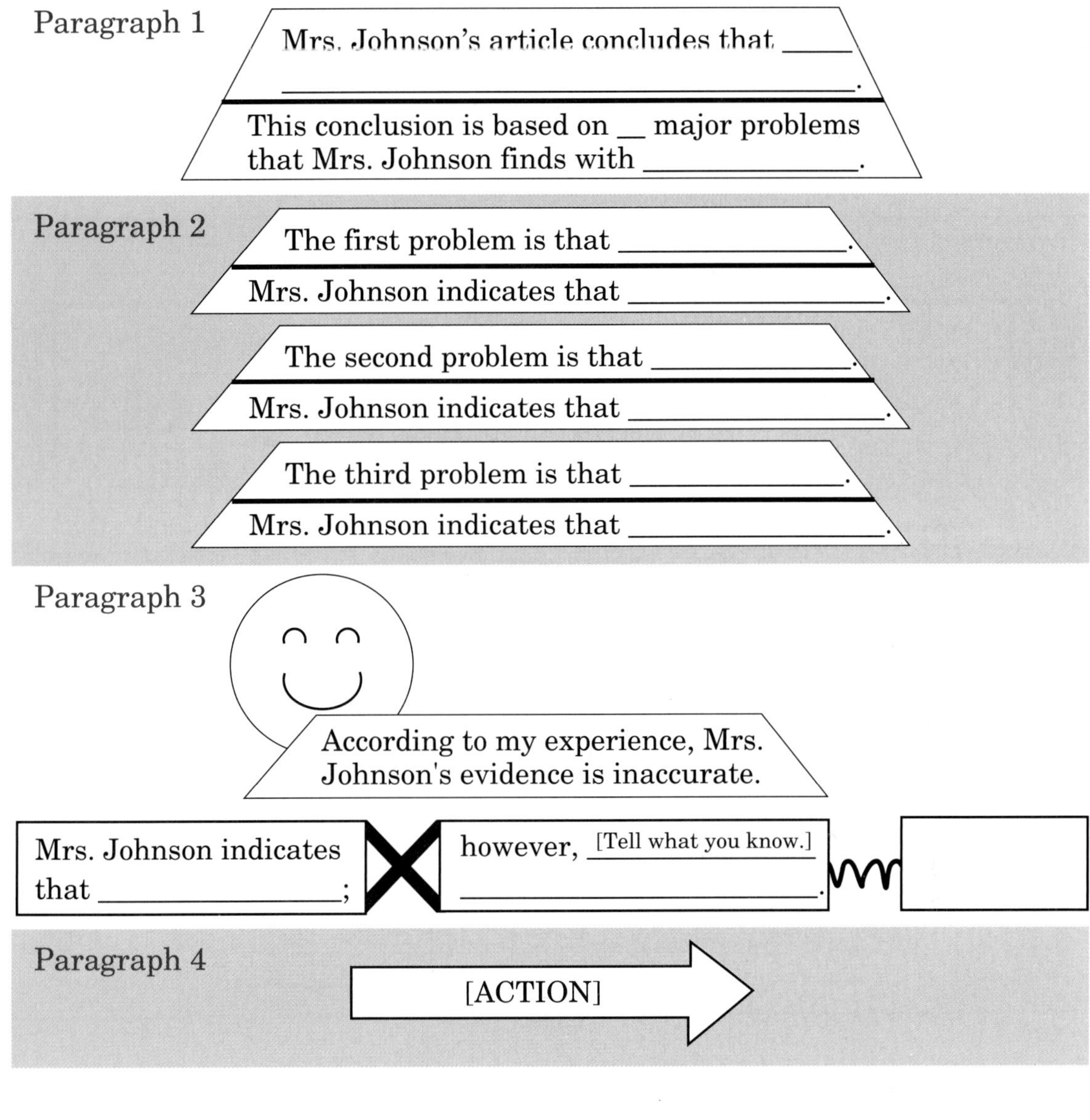
Paragraph 1
Mrs. Johnson's article concludes that ____ ____.
This conclusion is based on __ major problems that Mrs. Johnson finds with ______.
Paragraph 2
The first problem is that ______.
Mrs. Johnson indicates that ______.
The second problem is that ______.
Mrs. Johnson indicates that ______.
The third problem is that ______.
Mrs. Johnson indicates that ______.
Paragraph 3
According to my experience, Mrs. Johnson's evidence is inaccurate.
Mrs. Johnson indicates that ______;
however, [Tell what you know.] ______.
Paragraph 4
[ACTION]

Independent Work

Turn to lesson 46, part E. Write directions for the best way to go from the starting point to Linda's house.

Lesson 98

Part A Come to our __________ store and see the __________ selection of __________ furniture.

Part B Tell about the problem with each argument.

Argument 1: Jim must be one of the top players in the city. After all, Jim plays for the Mob, and the Mob is the best team in the city. Everybody agrees that the Mob is the best team people have seen in ten years.

Argument 2: You should spend more time outdoors. Camping out is a way to spend more time outdoors. Therefore, you should camp out.

Argument 3: The only way to enjoy the outdoors is to own a Big Top tent. People like us want to enjoy the outdoors. Therefore, we should all have Big Top tents.

Part C

Argument

In 1985, the Dino factory started a program to reduce the pollution it put into the Walbash River. The level of pollution in 1990 was half as high as the pollution level in 1985. Therefore, the Dino program for reducing pollution was a complete success!

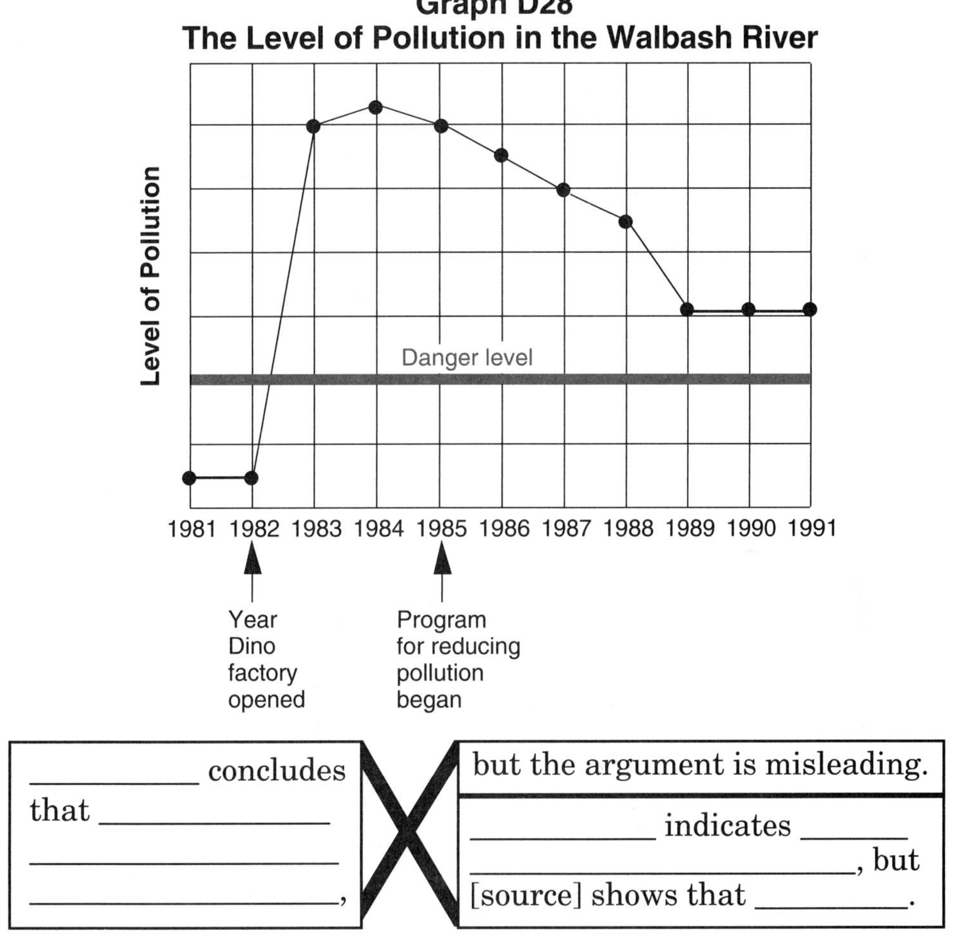

Independent Work Turn to lesson 47, part B. Write directions for the best way to go from the starting point to Ann's house.

Lesson 99

Part A For each item, write two possible meanings for the second sentence.

1. Our hotel rooms come with beds. They are big enough to hold a large family.
2. A gravel walkway leads to the ocean. In the early morning, it sparkles.
3. The soldiers took off their boots. They were covered with mud.

Dr. Bromley's Argument

We all agree that it is important to have a low crime rate. In 1980, the crime rate in our state was very high. There were 20,000 crimes that year. The crime rate didn't drop in the following years. It went up to 30,000 in 1984.

That's when Governor Bill Wise was elected. He promised that he would reduce the crime rate. He said it would take time, and he has had time. In 1990, he had been in office for six years. Yet, in 1990 the number of crimes once more increased in our state. There were 2,000 more crimes in 1990 than there were in 1989.

Part C

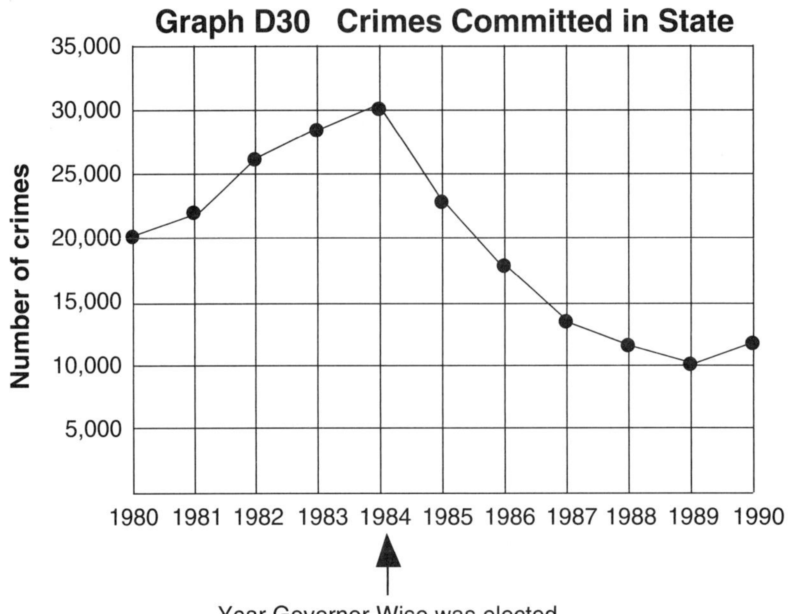

Dr. Bromley's Argument

We all agree that it is important to have a low crime rate. In 1980, the crime rate in our state was very high. There were 20,000 crimes that year. The crime rate didn't drop in the following years. It went up to 30,000 in 1984.

That's when Governor Bill Wise was elected. He promised that he would reduce the crime rate. He said it would take time and he has had time. In 1990, he had been in office for six years. Yet, in 1990 the number of crimes once more increased in our state. There were 2,000 more crimes in 1990 than there were in 1989.

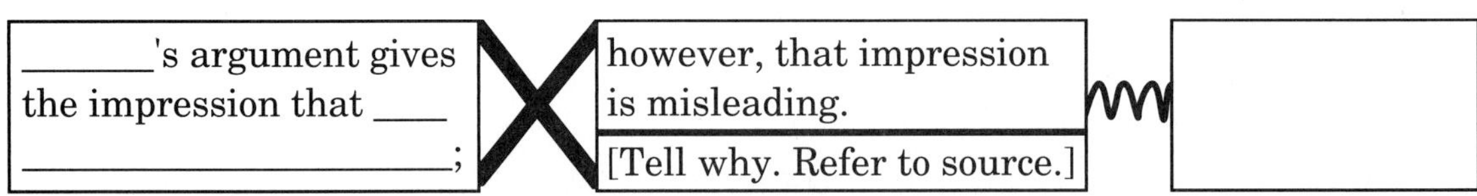

Independent Work

Turn to lesson 48, part A. Tell whether the directions are inaccurate or too general. Then tell what you should do.

Lesson 100

Argument

People say that the Bumpo factory is not fair to all its employees. Nothing could be farther from the truth. Bumpo is well known for its fairness.

At Bumpo, people earn more each year they work. Bumpo has both men and women who earn $35,000 per year.

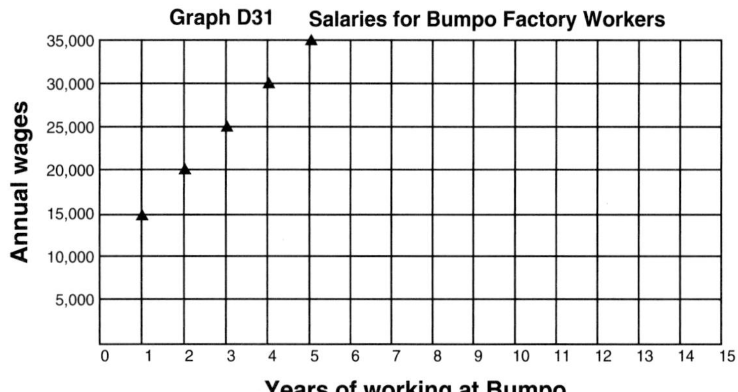

▲ = salaries for people

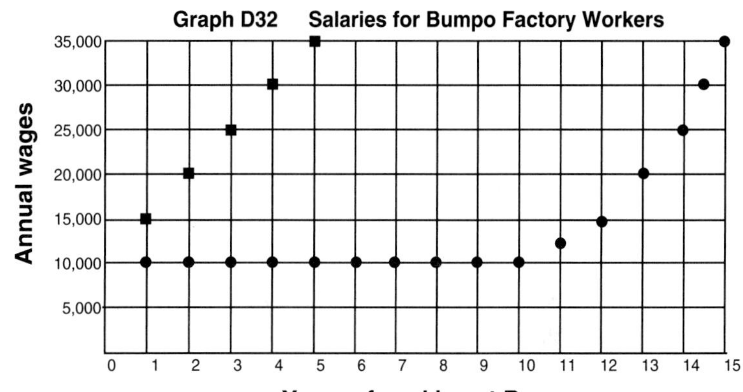

■ = salaries for men

● = salaries for women

The argument gives the impression that _______ ______________________;	however, that impression is misleading. [Tell why. Refer to source.]	

Test 10

Part A Use the word **who** or **that** to combine each pair of sentences.

1. They bought a table. The table was over a hundred years old.
2. We talked to the doctor. The doctor was visiting our school.

Part B Write about each argument. You can refer to the chart at the back of your textbook.

Argument 1: You should learn a foreign language. French is a foreign language. Therefore, you should learn French.

Argument 2: Running is the only way to get strong legs. Everybody wants strong legs. Therefore, everybody should run at least four days a week.

Argument 3: Ted must be very good at math. After all, he is in Mrs. Johnson's class. Everybody knows that her class does very well.

Lesson 101

Part A

I would buy Creamo paint. The reason is that Creamo costs less than Ajax.
Jan

I would buy Ajax paint. The reason is that Ajax lasts longer than Creamo.
Dan

I would buy Creamo paint. The reason is that Creamo is rated excellent in water resistance.
Fran

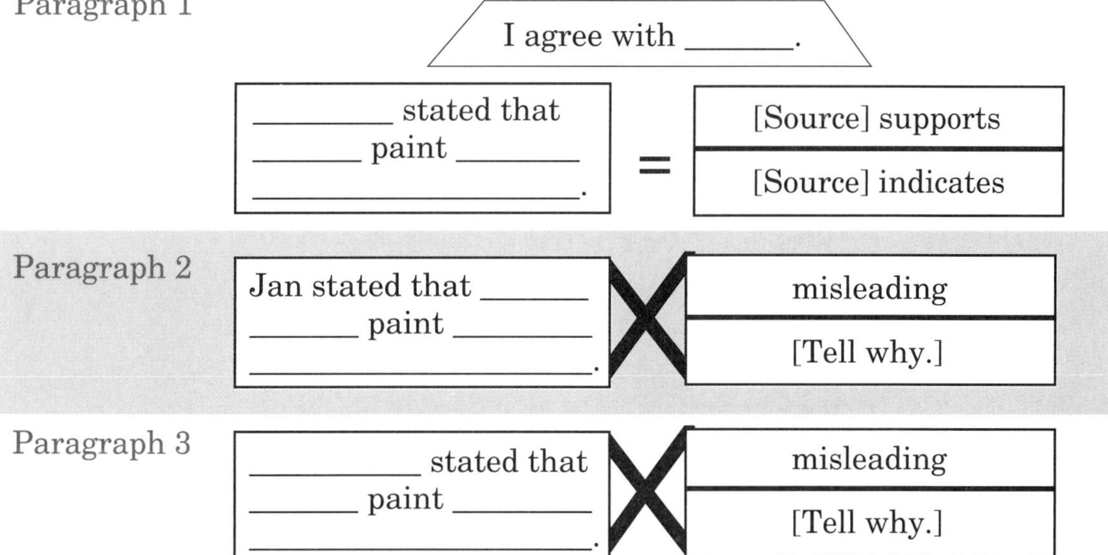
Paragraph 1
I agree with ______.
________ stated that ______ paint ________ ____________________.
=
[Source] supports
[Source] indicates
Paragraph 2
Jan stated that ______ ______ paint ________ ____________________.
misleading
[Tell why.]
Paragraph 3
__________ stated that ______ paint ________ ____________________.
misleading
[Tell why.]

Table D33

Paint	Cost	How long the paint lasts	Water resistance
Ajax	$12.40 per gallon	6 years	best of all brands
Creamo	$12.39 per gallon	3 years	excellent

Part B

1. Write clear directions for going to Fish Lake. Use only paved roads.
2. Write the other clear, short directions for going to Fish Lake. Use paved roads or dirt roads.
3. Write directions for going to Fish Lake. Make the directions so general that a person following them might end up at the jail.
4. Write directions for going to Fish Lake. Make the directions so general that a person following them might end up at the garbage dump.

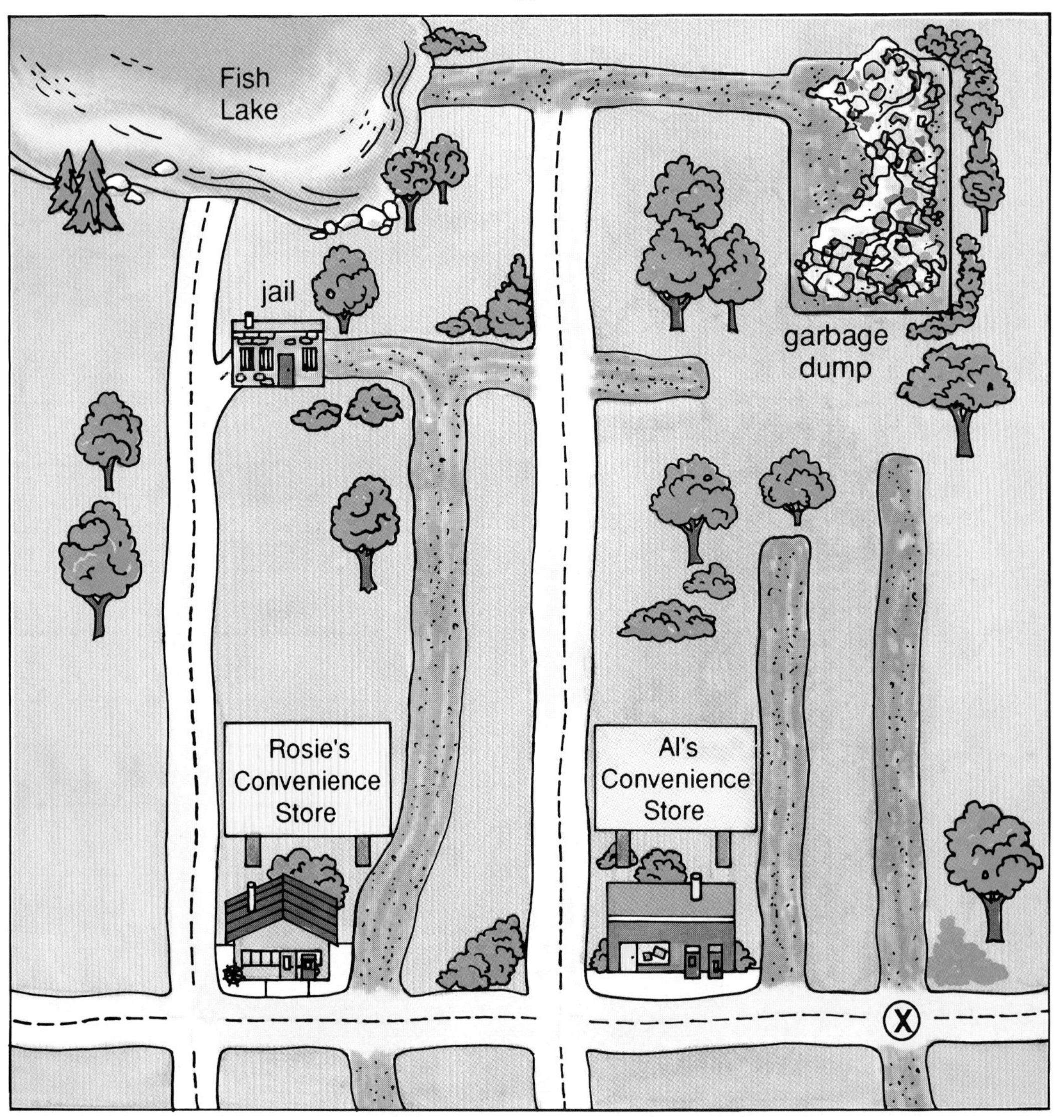

Lesson 102

Part A

- You've learned that you can figure out parts of speech by looking at words in sentences.
- Sometimes you can tell what part of speech a word is when the word is not in a sentence, but sometimes you need to see the word in a sentence.
- Here are two sentences with the word **her:**

  Tim handed the book to **her.**

  She handed Tim **her** book.

  In the first sentence, **her** is a pronoun. In the second sentence, **her** is an adjective.
- Here are two sentences with the word **twisted:**

  He **twisted** his ankle.

  The tree had a **twisted** trunk.

  In the first sentence, **twisted** is a verb. In the second sentence, **twisted** is an adjective.

Part B

For each numbered word, write **N** for noun, **A** for adjective, **V** for verb or **P** for pronoun.

She (1) will land (2) on the floor (3).

They (4) bought (5) more (6) land (7).

She (8) saw (9) an exciting (10) race (11).

Tina (12) will race (13) Fran and John (14).

The bird (15) hopped (16) near an open (17) window (18).

Did (19) little Wilbur open (20) the (21) door (22)?

Part C

Television and Children

by

Dr. H. S. Bromley

Children under 15 years old should never watch TV. There are two reasons for banning TV.

The first reason is that TV makes children lazy. Children who sit and watch TV are not doing other things. They do not do their homework. They do not help around the house. Often, they do not remember to eat dinner.

The second reason for banning TV has to do with the programs. The only programs that children watch on TV contain violence, or they are silly. Cartoons are just silly. They are usually violent. Stories of the police are violent. Comedy shows are silly. Movies are usually violent. That's all there is on TV. Nothing on TV is suitable for children.

Paragraph 1

__________'s article concludes that ____ ________________________________.

This conclusion is based on __ major problems Dr. Bromley finds with ________________.

Paragraph 2

The first problem is that ______________.

Dr. Bromley indicates that ________________.

The second problem is that ____________.

Dr. Bromley indicates that ________________.

Paragraph 3

According to my experience, ____ ________'s evidence is inaccurate.

Dr. Bromley indicates that _______________;	however, [Tell what you know.] ____________________________.

Paragraph 4

[ACTION]

Lesson 103

Part A

- You've worked with sentences like these:

  (She) was tired, but (she) kept working.

  The house was large, and the yard was beautiful.

- These sentences are called **compound sentences.**
- Each sentence is made up of two parts. Each part is a complete sentence with its own subject and predicate.

Part B

1. The meeting was interesting. Half the people fell asleep.
2. The workers painted the garage. They repaired the house.
3. The lights went off. The movie started.

Part C

1. Could we keep that puppy?
2. Will the frost hurt them?
3. Were the dogs chasing butterflies?
4. Is she going on a trip with them?
5. Can he help Sally and me?

Part D

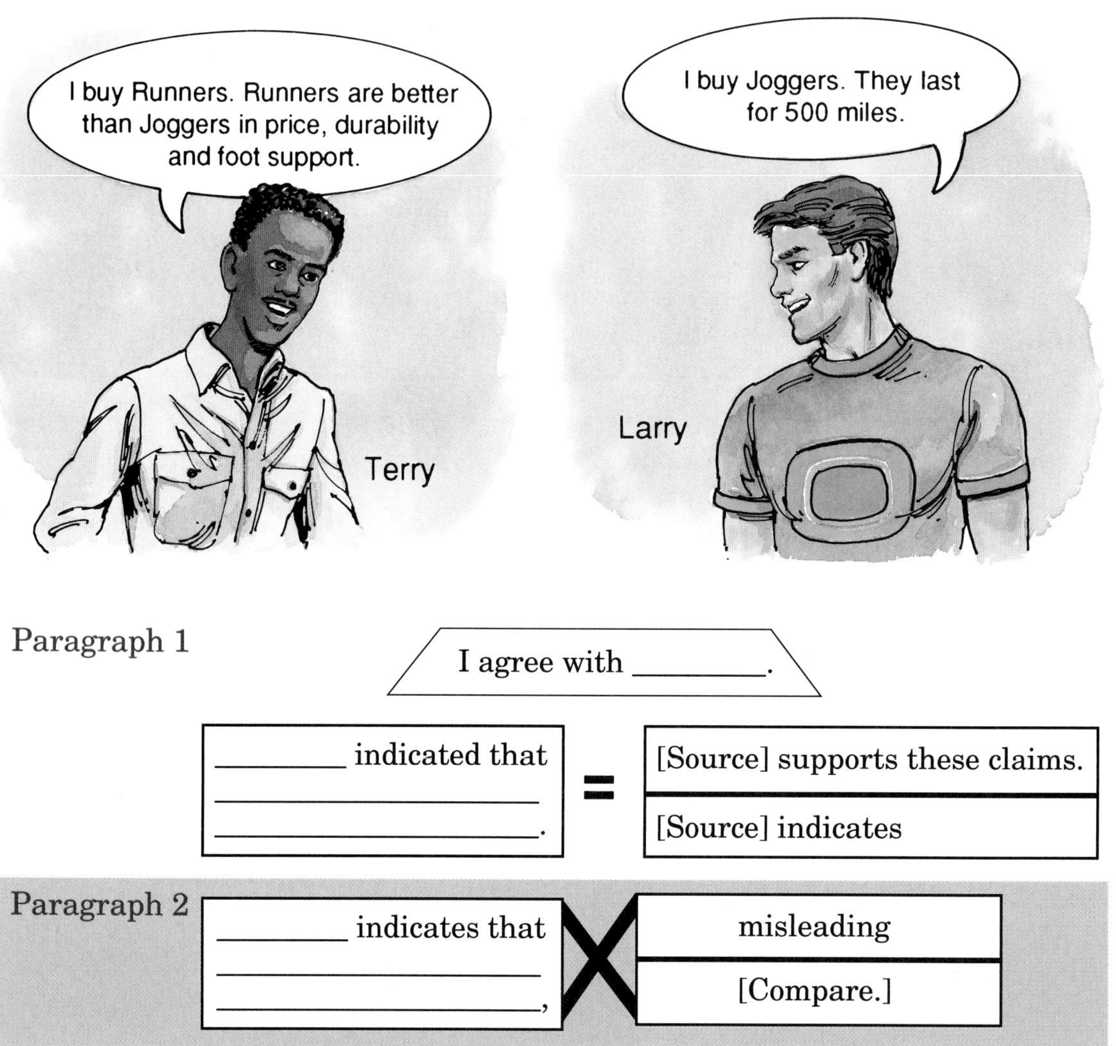

I buy Runners. Runners are better than Joggers in price, durability and foot support.
I buy Joggers. They last for 500 miles.
Terry
Larry
Paragraph 1
I agree with ________.
________ indicated that ________ ________.
[Source] supports these claims.
[Source] indicates
Paragraph 2
________ indicates that ________ ________,
misleading
[Compare.]

Table D34

Shoe	Cost	How many miles the shoe lasts	Foot support	Water resistance
Runners	$40	900 miles	excellent	excellent
Joggers	$70	500 miles	good	good

Lesson 104

Part A

1. It could be sunny tomorrow. Most experts think it will rain tomorrow.
2. Jan's sister is tall. Jan is very short.
3. The H-Mart store is large. It carries thousands of items.
4. The weather was very cold. The workers were sweating.
5. The workers cut down the tree. They trimmed the hedges.
6. The park is a wonderful place. It is only open on Sunday.
7. The birds are hiding in the tall grass. The deer are hiding in the forest.

Part B

School Lunches Are Perfect

by
Mrs. Johnson

A few students complain about school lunches. Anybody who looks at the evidence will see that school lunches are **perfect.**

Each school lunch provides students with vitamins and minerals. A balanced diet is important. School lunches give students all the major food groups that they need to grow strong bones, good muscles and a healthy mind. Every school lunch has a green vegetable. It also has a piece of fruit and a healthy dessert.

Students don't have to worry about not eating every part of their school lunch. Why wouldn't students eat everything when everything is delicious? Every day we hear many students say, "That meal was just wonderful." If we listen closely and watch carefully, we'll see why so many students are in the clean-plate club. The other day I watched students. Every one of them cleaned their plate. Yum! Yum!

And talk about surprises! Students don't know what will be served today or tomorrow, but they do know that there will be delicious choices. There will be variety. And there will be wonderful taste surprises. One day, students will have to make the difficult choice of selecting chicken stew or chipped beef on toast. The next day, there will be other surprises and other difficult choices.

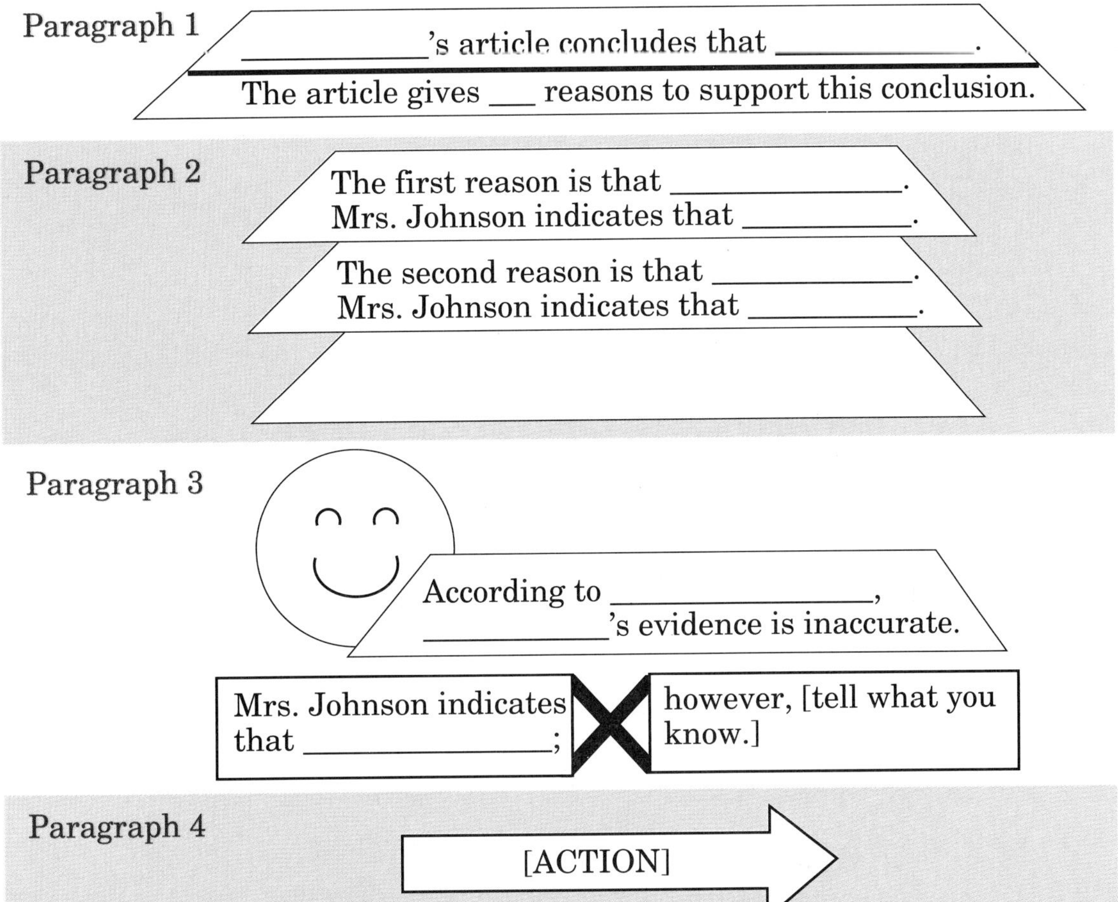
Paragraph 1
_________'s article concludes that _________.
The article gives ___ reasons to support this conclusion.
Paragraph 2
The first reason is that _________.
Mrs. Johnson indicates that _________.
The second reason is that _________.
Mrs. Johnson indicates that _________.
Paragraph 3
According to _________,
_________'s evidence is inaccurate.
Mrs. Johnson indicates that _________;
however, [tell what you know.]
Paragraph 4
[ACTION]

Lesson 105

Part A

1. Will she finish her homework?
2. Are they staining our beautiful, new rug?
3. Is Tommy following the bus?
4. Can that tractor climb steep hills?

Part B

> You do **not** need a comma if the words following **but** are **not** a sentence.

1. The house was expensive but it was very small.
2. The dog was small but dangerous.
3. The meeting was long but seemed very short.
4. The trip was long but it went by quickly.
5. The tree was tall but not very stout.
6. The trees were old but they were not very tall.

Part C

I need a new jacket. I spend a lot of time in cold, wet weather. The jacket should be washable and durable. The jacket should give me good protection against the cold. It must be water resistant.

Rita

Table D35 Characteristics of Jackets

Jacket	Protection against cold	Cleaning	Durability	Cost	Weight	Water resistance
Ranger	very good	washable	lasts 8 years	$75.00	4 pounds	excellent
Trail Blazer	the best	not washable	lasts 8 years	$230.00	2 pounds	the best
Camper	fair	not washable	lasts 2 years	$60.00	6 pounds	excellent
Rover	good	washable	lasts 2 years	$175.00	1 pounds	excellent

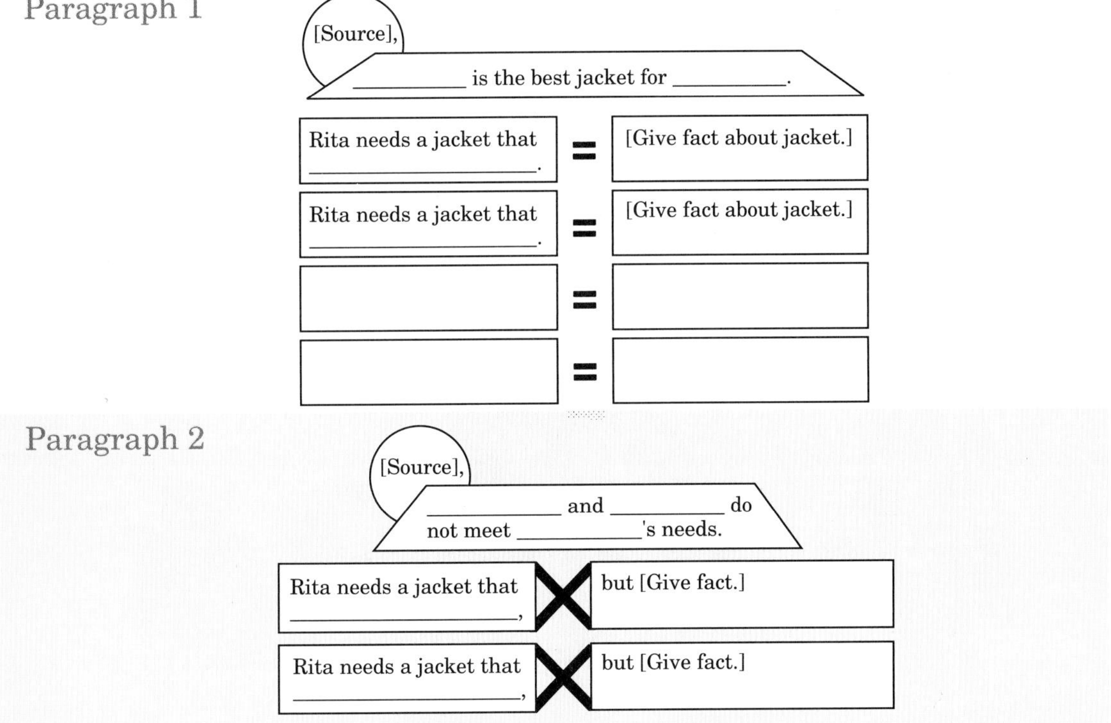

Lesson 106

Part A Use the word **who** or **that** to combine each pair of sentences.

1. She found a pencil. The pencil had a yellow eraser.
2. They met the girl. The girl lived in the house on the corner.
3. My sister started to eat an apple. The apple had a worm in it.

Part B

1. The teachers had a party. These teachers work in our school.
2. A claim was misleading. This claim appeared in our newspaper.
3. Ten farmers had a good crop. All these farmers raised wheat.

Part C Copy each compound sentence and make the comma before the joining word.

1. She was fast and strong.
2. They worked hard and went to a movie later.
3. He may buy a new Bumpo or keep his old one.
4. He bought six hats and he made a dress for his mother.
5. They could not decide whether to buy a hound or a poodle.
6. The rain will stop or our basement will flood.
7. They started out fast but slowed down very soon.
8. The road was slippery but we kept moving.

Part D

I need a new jacket. I'm going to be in places that are extremely cold, so I need the best protection against the cold. I also need a jacket that weighs no more than 3 pounds. This jacket must also have good water resistance.
Dan

Table D35 Characteristics of Jackets

Jacket	Protection against cold	Cleaning	Durability	Cost	Weight	Water resistance
Ranger	very good	washable	lasts 8 years	$75.00	4 pounds	excellent
Trail Blazer	the best	not washable	lasts 8 years	$230.00	2 pounds	the best
Camper	fair	not washable	lasts 2 years	$60.00	6 pounds	excellent
Rover	good	washable	lasts 2 years	$175.00	1 pounds	excellent

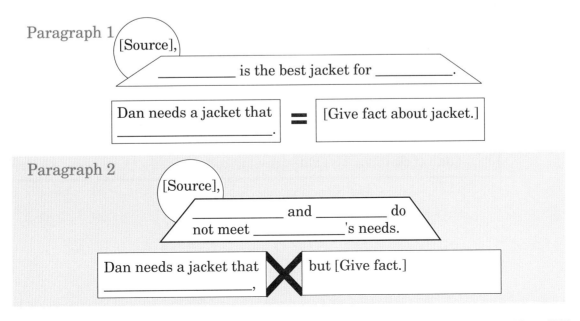

Paragraph 1

[Source],

__________ is the best jacket for __________.

Dan needs a jacket that __________________. = [Give fact about jacket.]

Paragraph 2

[Source],

__________ and __________ do not meet __________'s needs.

Dan needs a jacket that __________________, ✕ but [Give fact.]

Lesson 107

Part A

Use the word **who** or **that** to combine each pair of sentences.

1. They flew a kite. That kite had red stripes and a long, blue tail.
2. A woman won the race. That woman was almost 60 years old.
3. A bowl fell from the table. The bowl was worth $200.
4. Tina was in love with a man. That man was very handsome.

Part B

Table D36 Characteristics of Popular Running Shoes

Shoes	Weight of pair	Price	Durability	Foot support	Appearance	Water resistance	Popularity
Swiftos	2 pounds	$48.00	900 miles	good	good	fair	fourth most popular
Rangers	2 pounds	$47.00	1010 miles	fair	good	good	third most popular
Runners	$1\frac{3}{4}$ pounds	$45.00	1100 miles	excellent	good	excellent	second most popular
Joggers	2 pounds	$75.00	800 miles	good	good	good	most popular

Questions

1. Did you make Rangers seem inexpensive?
2. Did you make Rangers seem very durable?
3. Did you make Rangers seem very attractive?
4. Did you make Rangers seem superior in water resistance?

Part C

Make an ad for Ranger shoes. Include a headline and several misleading claims. You can draw pictures.

Lesson 108

Part A Use the word **who** or **that** to combine each pair of sentences.

1. The girl lives in Westville. The girl found our puppy.
2. Brittany worked in a store. The store sold clothing and appliances.
3. Lou just missed the bus. That bus went to Cleveland.
4. The bus almost hit a boy. The boy ran into the street.

Part B Copy each number. Write **N** for each noun, **P** for each pronoun, **A** for each adjective and **V** for each verb.

Her (1) mother (2) followed (3) us (4) to the park (5).

A misleading (6) article (7) told (8) about homeless (9) people (10).

Part C Write an ad for the best shoe.

Table D36 Characteristics of Popular Running Shoes

Shoes	Weight of pair	Price	Durability	Foot support	Appearance	Water resistance	Popularity
Swiftos	2 pounds	$48.00	900 miles	good	good	fair	fourth most popular
Rangers	2 pounds	$47.00	1010 miles	fair	good	good	third most popular
Runners	$1\frac{3}{4}$ pounds	$45.00	1100 miles	excellent	good	excellent	second most popular
Joggers	2 pounds	$75.00	800 miles	good	good	good	most popular

Lesson 109

Part A

Our ___________ hotel is close to a ___________ beach.

Our ___________ rooms have ___________ windows and a ___________ bed.

Our menu offers a ___________ variety of ___________ dinners.

Hotel A

Menu
1. Chicken in a basket with soup, salad and dessert $4.50
2. Broiled fish with french fries and a vegetable $3.85
3. Spaghetti and meatballs with bread, butter and a special sauce $4.15
4. Hamburger, fries and salad $2.80

Hotel B

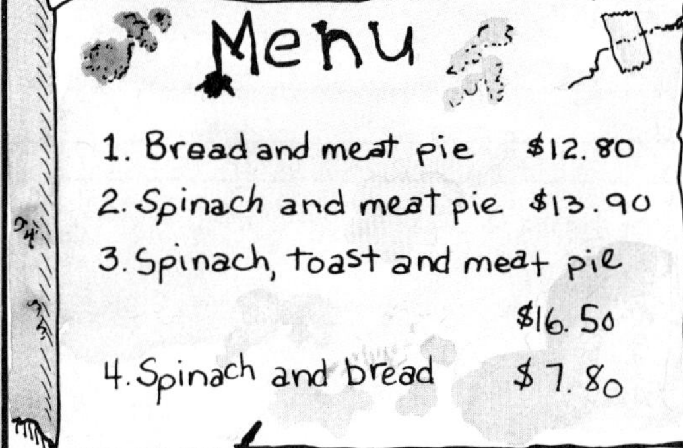

Menu
1. Bread and meat pie $12.80
2. Spinach and meat pie $13.90
3. Spinach, toast and meat pie $16.50
4. Spinach and bread $7.80

Part B

Clunkbocker Hotel
3247 Donner Beach Road
Astoria, Oregon 97103

A Very Special Offer from the Clunkbocker Hotel

Dear Friend,

For years, people have heard about the Clunkbocker's value.

Now, you can stay at the Clunkbocker for even less than ever!

Normally, you would pay $45 a night for a room at the Clunkbocker. For a limited time, you can stay at the Clunkbocker for only $38 per night.

You'll still get all the benefits that Clunkbocker guests normally enjoy. You'll experience the same incredible view from your room.

You'll enjoy free soft drinks and free breakfasts.

As a bonus, you'll sleep in a king-sized waterbed, and you'll pay no more than you would for a regular bed!

Act now. Remember, the Clunkbocker is an experience you will never forget.

Sincerely,

Mark Barker

Mark Barker
Manager

Part C

Make an outline diagram. Then write a letter to Mark Barker. Use the Map of Donner Beach and the Hotel Fact Guide in lesson 94.

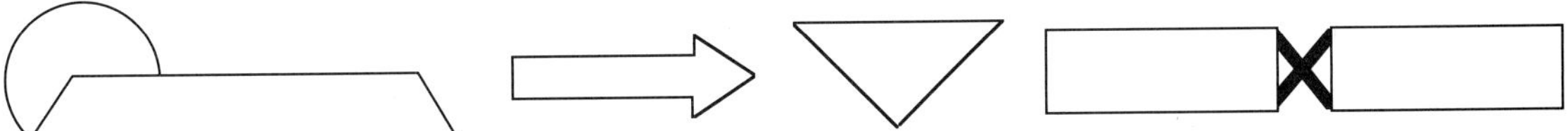

Test 11

Part A Use the word **who** or **that** to combine each pair of sentences.

1. A woman spoke to our class. The woman had traveled around the world.
2. An article was inaccurate. That article appeared in our newspaper.

Part B Copy the sentences that are compound sentences and make the comma before the joining word.

1. They worked hour after hour but didn't finish the job in time.
2. The office had two computers but nobody knew how to use them.
3. Lefty wrote directions and drew a map.
4. We have to study for three hours or we may fail the test.
5. We could make the ad more specific by adding an adjective or adding another sentence.

Part C Copy the numbers. Write **N** for each noun, **V** for each verb, **P** for each pronoun and **A** for each adjective.

Her(1) uncle(2) will(3) send(4) her a new(5) computer(6).

They(7) had a(8) wonderful(9) experience(10).

That(11) dog(12) may(13) follow the children to a rocky(14) beach(15).

Write about the jacket that you think is the best value.

Table D35 Characteristics of Jackets

Jacket	Protection against cold	Cleaning	Durability	Cost	Weight	Water resistance
Ranger	very good	washable	lasts 8 years	$75.00	4 pounds	excellent
Trail Blazer	the best	not washable	lasts 8 years	$230.00	2 pounds	the best
Camper	fair	not washable	lasts 2 years	$60.00	6 pounds	excellent
Rover	good	washable	lasts 2 years	$175.00	1 pounds	excellent

I believe that __________ is the best jacket.

[Tell why.]

Dear Student,

You have learned some very important things about writing.

You've learned about parts of speech and punctuation.

You've learned how to give clear directions.

You've learned how to write different types of sentences that give specific information, and you've learned how to combine sentences.

Most of all, you've learned to tell about problems with claims, statements and directions. You've learned how to **find** these problems. Finding problems with what others say and write helps you learn to be a clear thinker. You just look for problems with the things that **you** say and write.

Examining your own writing is one of the hardest things to do, but it's one of the things that helps you get very smart. Get good at critiquing **your** plans and beliefs. Fix up your writing so it does not have parts that are too general or conclusions that are not supported by evidence. You'll become very smart.

Sincerely,

Zig Engelmann

Jerry Silbert

CLAIMS
or
DIRECTIONS

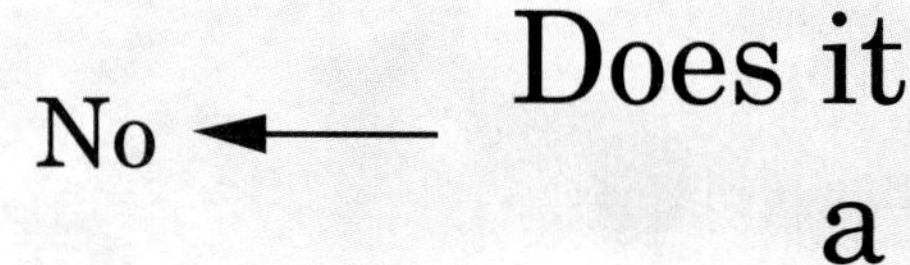

- **Is the (claim / direction) accurate?**

Yes

No

The (claim / direction) states that ______________, ✕ but that statement is inaccurate. [Tell why.]

- **Does the claim give the correct impression?**

Yes

No

The claim states that ______________, ✕ but that statement is misleading. [Tell why.]

- **Is the (claim / direction) specific enough?**

Yes

No

The (claim / direction) indicates that ______________ ______________, ✕ but that statement is too general. [Give fact.]

- **Is the (claim / direction) consistent with other sources?**

Yes

No

The (claim / direction) indicates that ______________ ______________, ✕ but [source] contradicts that statement. [Source] indicates that ______________.

The claim indicates that ______________. = [Source] supports this claim. [Source] indicates ______________.

have conclusion? → Yes

ARGUMENTS

- **Is the rule acceptable?**

Yes

No

The rule is faulty.

______ is not the only ______________________.

___ could __________ ________ by ________ ______________________.

- **Is the evidence relevant?**

Yes

No

The argument concludes that __________________ ______________________;

however, the evidence is irrelevant.

That evidence shows only that ____ ______________________________.

- **Does the argument present all the important facts?**

Yes

No

The argument concludes that __________________ ______________________,

but the argument is misleading.

[Tell why.]

- **Is the conclusion the only possible conclusion?**

Yes

No

The argument concludes that __________________ ______________________,

OC

Other conclusions are possible because ____ ________________.

______ is ____________. Therefore, ______________ ______________________.

- **The argument does not have a problem.**